WITHDRAWN

GREENLAND

By

VILHJALMUR STEFANSSON

My Life with the Eskimo, 1913
Anthropological Papers (American Museum
of Natural History), 1914
The Friendly Arctic, 1921
Hunters of the Great North, 1922
The Northward Course of Empire, 1922
The Adventure of Wrangel Island, 1925
My Life with the Eskimos (abridged), *1927*
The Standardization of Error, 1927
Adventures in Error, 1936
  (In collaboration with ELOISE MCCASKILL)
The Three Voyages of Martin Frobisher, 1938
Unsolved Mysteries of the Arctic, 1938
Iceland: The First American Republic, 1939
Greenland

BOOKS FOR YOUNGER READERS

  (In collaboration with VIOLET IRWIN)
Kak, the Copper Eskimo, 1924
The Shaman's Revenge, 1925
The Mountain of Jade, 1926

  (In collaboration with JULIA SCHWARTZ)
Northward Ho! 1925

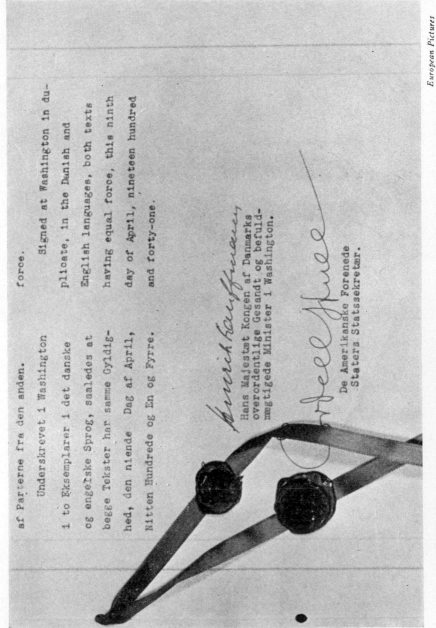

America's answer to the Axis; the pact with Denmark which put strategic Greenland under United States' protection for the duration.

GREENLAND

Vilhjalmur Stefansson

Doubleday, Doran & Company, Inc.

GARDEN CITY   1942   NEW YORK

PRINTED AT THE *Country Life Press*, GARDEN CITY, N. Y., U. S. A.

Contents

CHAPTER   PAGE

I   GEOGRAPHIC PRELIMINARIES   1

II   PREHISTORIC DISCOVERIES OF GREENLAND .   10

III DISCOVERY BY THE GREEKS 325 B.C. . . .   28

IV THE IRISH DISCOVER GREENLAND   42

V   THE ICELANDERS DISCOVER GREENLAND . .   61

VI THE GREENLANDERS DISCOVER AMERICA . .   73

VII GREENLAND BECOMES A CHRISTIAN REPUBLIC .   85

VIII LIFE AND LETTERS IN GREENLAND . . .   101

IX SAGAS OF ERIK THE RED AND EINAR SOKKASON   120

X   THE DECLINE AND DISAPPEARANCE OF THE COLONY   160

XI WHAT EUROPE KNEW ABOUT GREENLAND IN THE MIDDLE AGES   198

XII THE REVIVAL OF GREENLAND SAILINGS . .   220

XIII RESETTLEMENT OF GREENLAND AND EXPLORATION OF THE EAST COAST   235

XIV EXPLORATION OF THE NORTH AND WEST COASTS   265

CHAPTER   PAGE

XV   ADMINISTRATION AND DEVELOPMENT OF GREEN-
LAND 275

XVI STRATEGIC IMPORTANCE IN A WORLD AT WAR   294

ACKNOWLEDGMENTS 317

BIBLIOGRAPHY 319

INDEX 329

Illustrations

HALFTONES

America's answer to the Axis . . . . . . Frontispiece

FACING PAGE

The umiak of the Eskimo resembles the Irish curragh ⎱
A kayak somersault ⎰ . 24

Fifteenth-century robes found at Herjolfsnes ⎱
Hoods found at Herjolfsnes ⎰ . . . 104

A fleet of Eskimo kayaks 136

Farm similar to those of early Norse settlers ⎱
in Greenland ⎰ . . 212
Ancient Norse church ruins near Kakortok ⎰

The young: mother and child ⎱
The old: two old women of Greenland sit smoking ⎰ . 244
their pipes ⎰

Port of the cryolite mining village of Ivigtut ⎱
Greenlandic miners at work ⎰ . . 284

The settlement of Marmorilik ⎱
Slabs of marble from Marmorilik quarry ⎰ . . . 288

vii

ILLUSTRATIONS
LINE CUTS

PAGE

Map of Greenland 2

Runic Stone Found at Kingiktorsuak, Lat. 72° 55" . . 184

Cairns on Washington Irving Island 187

Eider Duck Shelter 188

GREENLAND

CHAPTER I

Geographic Preliminaries

GREENLAND was named Green Land by Erik the Red in 984; it was called Land of Desolation by John Davis in 1586 but the Land of Comfort by James Hall in 1606. Rockwell Kent, after visits to Greenland and a winter there far north of the Arctic Circle, said in 1941: "But that Greenland is not my native land I would choose to live there always."

The largest of islands or smallest of continents, Greenland is nearly as big as the combined twenty-six states that are east of the Mississippi River. It is so long from north to south that if one tip were in Canada, near Winnipeg, the other would be far out in the Gulf of Mexico, farther south than the most southerly spot in Texas. In statute miles, its greatest north-south length is about 1670; its greatest width about 810. The area is near 736,000 square miles. Its northern cape, Morris Jesup, is some 1200 miles north of the Arctic Circle; its southern tip, Cape Farewell, 500 miles south of it—as far south as Oslo or Leningrad. Its Cape Alexander is a little farther west than Boston, Massachusetts; its Northeast Foreland is a little farther east than Dakar, West Africa. Greenland is the most eastern of all lands that are west of the Atlantic.

Although Greenland is west of the main stream of the Atlantic that runs between it and Norway, a line drawn south from its northeast corner runs forty miles east of Iceland, skirts the west shores of Ireland and of Spain, and slices through Africa to leave more than a thousand miles of African coast line west of it. Greenland's Northeast Foreland is about straight north from Monrovia, the capital of that Negro commonwealth, Liberia, which was established by the United States in connection with our freeing of the slaves.

The nearest countries to Greenland are Ellesmere and Ice-land. In late winter you can walk across to Ellesmere in three brisk hours, for the distance is but twelve miles. You cannot walk from Greenland to Iceland, but you can see across if you

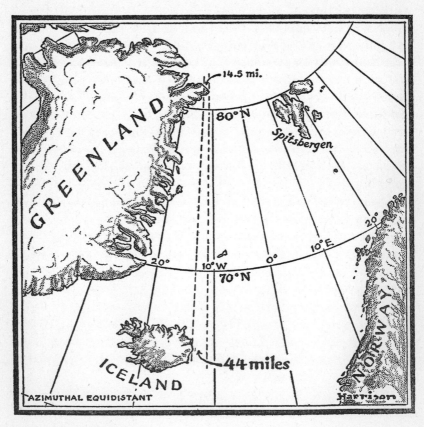

climb the mountains of the Blosseville coast. The distance is about one hundred eighty miles.

Probably Europeans discovered Greenland by looking west from Iceland, which they had discovered first, or else they saw it from vessels that were rounding Iceland; for both countries are frequently seen nowadays, and have always been, from ships rightly placed between them.

Probably Americans discovered Greenland by seeing it from the west. Those Americans may have been pre-Eskimo, but they were likely Eskimos, and they saw it first when its mountains rose above the horizon while the migrating hunters were working northward along that east shore of Ellesmere Island which was doubtless then, as it has been in our time, one of the rich game districts of the New World.

It is anybody's guess whether Americans or Europeans were first to discover Greenland. It is not a guess, but a practical certainty, that when they found this land it was in climate and condition just about the same as today. But there was a much earlier time, or at least we think so, when the coldest winter did not freeze Smith Sound to permit a walk from Ellesmere and when all the snows of Greenland winters disappeared in summer.

Anyway, we speculate upon how things may have been in that very remote age. There are two main theories:

By one theory, our land without ice had the contours which it now has beneath the ice. There was a high mountain range along the west coast; another, higher, range followed the east coast; between stretched a low interior. On these mountains, either because they were slowly rising to greater heights or because precipitation was being increased, the snows of winter ceased disappearing during summer. Perennial snowdrifts formed in high valleys and grew in size until they became large enough to be called glaciers.

With sluggish flow the ice moved farther and farther down the valleys and began to cover the rest of the slopes. On the west side of the western range the glaciers slid into the sea, broke off, and drifted away as icebergs; along the eastern slopes of the eastern range the same thing happened. But from the eastern slope of the western range, and the western slope of the eastern, the ice plowed and ground its way across prairie or through forest, whichever it was, until finally the east-moving western glaciers and the west-moving easterners met somewhere near the central belt of the lowland.

Because the sun delivers no heat to the earth, but only light which may be changed to heat on striking a dark object, and because everything now was white, little heat was generated and most of the snow which fell stayed there or was drifted back and forth by the wind. So the bowl of Greenland filled rapidly—rapidly in the geological sense—and the country became what we have now, an elongated dome, like the back of a turtle. In time even the mountains were covered, except a few peaks of the coast ranges. Through the valleys of these coastal mountains the glaciers flowed with increasing rate and volume to the eastern and western sea, to form icebergs. These drifted south then, as now, for the ocean currents were doubtless the same.

Probably, then as now, an exception was the northernmost part of Greenland; for it seems a rule that the most northerly lands are not, and never were, glaciated. For instance, that prairie of Alaska which is north of the most northerly mountains has no permanent snow upon it now, and seemingly did not have in any of the recent ice ages—if, indeed, in any ice period.

There are some who believe that northernmost Greenland has been ice-capped once or oftener. It is not snow-covered today; it resembles northernmost Alaska and northernmost Siberia in that the snowfall of each winter disappears the next summer, except where the land is high and the valleys deep.

Such is the first view. The second theory of the Greenlandic Inland Ice is that "originally" the country was sporadically mountainous throughout, or even that it had a central range of mountains. In the central range, or in the scattered ranges, glaciers developed somewhat as we have been telling, with the difference that they became tremendous in the center while as yet the coasts were reasonably free. Mile after mile, by this theory, the snow heaped itself up toward the sky near central Greenland until the weight of ice became so great that it squashed down the interior highland into a lowland, reciprocally elevating the coast lines into what are now the shore mountain ranges.

Many have a rule of life that "the truth is somewhere in between." If you belong to that school you will think that the correct story of the Greenland ice is to be found about halfway between the theories just presented.

It has seemed probable to some that the development of the Inland Ice, or its last rebirth, coincided with that glacial period which was last on the mainland of North America. Greenland may have been nearly or quite ice-covered (except probably for its most northern parts) at the time when the mainland ice was upon southern New York State and central Iowa.

This is debated with particular heat by the botanists, pro and con. Some of them maintain that all the hundreds of species of plants now found anywhere in Greenland have come in since a time when all vegetation was plowed out and crushed out by glaciers that mantled the coasts along with the interior. Another school contends we have no proof there was ever a much more extensive ice sheet in Greenland than there is now and feel they have a good many reasons to believe the plants we find today should be looked upon as aborigines—at the very least, that they came over in some botanical *Mayflower* of a geologic time exceedingly remote in terms of the history of vegetation upon the earth.

Fifty years ago and even more recently we had, at least in the English-speaking countries, the curious situation that the church appeared to know more than the school about the true nature of the ice in this northern country. For the church was singing hymns about Greenland's icy *mountains,* conceding at least the possibility of verdure in the lowlands; but the schools were telling us that everything there was always snow-covered. True, the church was committed to its view by only a passing reference—"From Greenland's icy mountains to India's coral strand." The schools were explicit and detailed, all the way from the "dear little Eskimo in his house of ice and snow" to the last line of the kindergarten classic, "For in Greenland there is nothing green to grow."

While the debate was still on between church and school the scientists of fifty years ago had come to the view that Greenland was about 90% permanently snow-covered and that most of the snow-free land was along the southern half of the west coast. They thought the greatest distance from promontory to Inland Ice would be around 150 miles, and that this would be found on the west coast in the Holsteinsborg District, right near the Arctic Circle.

But Peary discovered great stretches of snow-free land at the north end of Greenland in 1892. There has been a lot of exploring in the world's most northerly country since then; and the more we explore the more we infringe upon the supposed domain of the ice. We believe now that the largest snow-free districts are either on the northern east coast, well north of the Arctic Circle, or else on the north coast in Peary Land.

During the last fifty years, then, the estimates of Greenland's permanent snow cover have been decreasing steadily. First they came down from 90% to the 86% estimate that was common twenty years ago and then to the 82% estimate you frequently hear now. Some would bring it down to 80%.

If you take the estimate that the snow covers 85% of Greenland, it may seem to you that the remaining 15% is little; and it is little in proportion to Greenland as a whole. But the country is so large that a snow-free 15% is 110,000 square miles, and that is more than the whole of Great Britain, from Wales to northern Scotland. If but 80% of Greenland is snow-covered, then you have in Greenland toward the end of every summer more snow-free land than in Great Britain and Ireland combined; as much as in ten eastern seaboard American states, beginning at the northeast with Maine and running through Virginia.

But snow-free Greenland is not a forest like Maine or parts of Britain. Except for being so rugged, we would think of it as prairie; actually it resembles more our treeless mountain country, like sections of Wyoming or Utah. The proportion of grass found on the coastal belt by the Norse settlers of 985 was not so high as it would have been in Montana, but higher than what the Mormons of 1847 found in Utah.

It is not a blanket truth, as commonly believed, that the absence of a forest in a sufficiently rainy land must be due to absence of warmth; or at least the belief requires interpretation. We can see that best, as in a laboratory demonstration, by making our study in Greenland's neighbor, Iceland.

The south coast of Iceland has during its coldest months, January and February, average temperatures like those of eastern Pennsylvania or northern Italy. Reykjavik, the capital, has a January mean which differs by only about a degree from those of Milan and Philadelphia. Yet there are no trees, as we think of them, in southern Iceland; nor has it been possible, with all the resources of modern science, to develop a variety of any tree which will grow there.

The last suspicion that our trouble is with intensity of cold as such will disappear when we find that trees which cannot grow at Reykjavik, on the south coast, grow moderately well at or inland from Akureyri, on the north coast of Iceland.

We are told, and clearly with at least approximate truth, that it is easier to raise trees at Akureyri *because* the winters there are longer and colder. For it is reasonably clear that what prevents the development of trees near Reykjavik is that most years, or once every few years, there comes in winter a spell of weather that is like May in New England. Day after day the trees, or the saplings which the horticulturists are trying to develop into trees, become greener and greener. The sap flows; the leaves come out, not merely as buds but sometimes in considerable spread. Then will follow one or several nights that are cold enough to freeze every plant to its core. The death of most trees and the stunting of the rest is said to be the result of cells bursting as the liquid in them freezes.

It is, then, true for parts of Greenland, as, for instance, the Julianehaab and Godthaab districts of the southwest coasts, that the winters resemble in chill those of the coast of Maine; but they have other features of climate so different from those of New England that the final horticultural result is not a Maine forest but a treeless country of grasses, sedges, and small bushes.

In spite of the grasses and bushes, the fact remains that Greenland is, north of the equator, a peculiar country. It resembles appreciably, and no other Arctic land does, that concept of the Arctic which we borrow from Greek philosophy—a land capped with ice.

With its hundreds of species of flowering plants, and its more than a hundred thousand square miles of snow-free coastal belt, Greenland does not quite fit the Greek picture of northern desolation. But it has had to serve, and has served, those who clung to the doctrines of medieval cosmogony. The disciples of the cosmographers have been able to use Greenland with reasonable effectiveness by claiming or implying that what little there was of grass and warmth was confined to the south. Even after this claim had been made difficult by Peary's discovery of flowers and bees in Peary Land, there were writers who found ways and means. For instance, J. Gordon Hayes, author of two books on the Antarctic and one on the Arctic, has said within the last ten years that Greenland fulfills the concept sufficiently; it has enough permanent snow to get under the wire. To him there are no other genuine Arctic lands, no matter how northerly. All the rest are changelings; Greenland is the one lawful child of cosmogony.

So we are trying in this book to sketch the portrait, and to outline the story, of a land which has at least a family resemblance to the old concepts of the Frozen North.

CHAPTER II

Prehistoric Discoveries of Greenland

WE HAVE BEEN ABLE to touch the written history of Greenland at no point more remote than the fourth century B.C. But through converging the light from a number of sciences, chief among them archaeology, paleontology, and geography, we can arrive at certain speculations on its prehistory that are dependable within the limits of reasonable ifs and buts.

If the first men who ever saw Greenland came from the west, our timing for the discovery depends on when it was that mankind invaded North America from Asia.

By the varying judgments of archaeologists and paleontologists, Bering Strait was first crossed by the eastward-moving people of Siberia between 10,000 and 20,000 years ago; for after the crossing it surely must have taken Folsom man 2000 years to reach the Texas Panhandle and leave behind him there the relics that are now being dated at from 8000 to 18,000 years.

But in order to be in a position to cross from northeastern Siberia to Alaska, man of that remote time must have been already a successful prairie hunter; he must have possessed the technique of comfortable or at least safe existence in a land which had the climate, the vegetation, and the animals of the high north.

If you are a prairie hunter you do not like a forest; you do not know how to live in it. This we have learned by watching the Eskimos. For they were, when Europeans first explored North America, a much more successful and aggressive people than the Athapaska Indians to the south of them; yet they declined to leave their sealing coasts and their caribou grasslands for the river and lake fishing, the rabbit and moose hunting, which would have been theirs had they occupied the forest. At times they made long journeys south beyond the tree line, for instance, on the Mackenzie; for Sir John Richardson tells us they used to follow the river several hundred miles into the wooded land, to where is now Fort Good Hope. But they always returned in the fall to the coastal prairie—indeed as soon as they had acquired on each trip enough of the stone they wanted for knives and missile points. The Athapaskans, Richardson says, were so frightened of them that each summer they abandoned the locality of the river and did not return until the season was so far advanced that they knew the Eskimos would be gone. They were cowed, and the Eskimos could have taken their land without a battle. But there is no sign they ever wanted to.

Since we cannot judge Arctic man of the past except by what we know of him in recent times, we must conclude that the pioneers who crossed from Siberia to Alaska were at first more inclined to follow the prairie coastlands east toward Greenland than the forest coastlands southerly toward Montana and Texas.

It may have been that the pioneer crossing from Siberia to Alaska was during an age warmer than ours; likely it was under a climate such as we have today. True, it used to be contended that of necessity the first Asiatics came to America on a footbridge of glacier ice during the last or the second last of the periods called ice ages; but that view rested upon the belief that man of 20,000 years ago had not yet invented boats, or at least not vessels good enough for crossing anything like fifty miles of salt water. But, as we shall see later, man probably in-

vented boats earlier than he did such weapons as we know
Folsom man possessed; so that if the first settlers of our
country really did walk in, it was probably for some reason
other than the want of adequate shipping.

The geologists tell us that if the possible crossing afoot was
during, say, the last ice age, or, indeed, during any ice age of
which we know, there were not only glaciers in the mountains
of Alaska but the Yukon Basin was also probably so full of ice
that a southeast or southward passage of the migrating tribes
was not possible; that there was almost certainly no ice on
Alaska's northern prairie and northern coast line; that the
country north of the Brooks Range was grasslands then as it is
now, with similar prairies in northernmost Siberia whence the
immigrants would have come. It seems, therefore, that even
had they preferred to move east or southeast they may have
been compelled to move northeast from Bering Strait so as to
keep on land that was free of snow every summer, a pasture
for reindeer and musk oxen. Northeast and east is the direction
toward Greenland.

The chief demurrer against the theory that this migration
reached and occupied Greenland is from the geologists who
believe that at the time when it may have been more difficult
for Asiatic man to move southeast from western Alaska than
northeast, Greenland was all, or practically all, covered with
an ice sheet. However, even these geologists will admit that
what snow-free land there may have been in Greenland at that
time was probably in the north. And it is at the northwest
corner of Greenland that the ancestors or cousins of Folsom
man would have crossed from Ellesmere Island.

If the geologist demurs further that Ellesmere itself was
then under ice, and therefore not a thoroughfare to hunters,
the halfhearted rejoinder is that possibly Ellesmere was so far
north as not to be glaciated—that the winter cold was as dry
there as in northern Alaska and that snow did not accumulate
sufficiently to last through the warm summers.

It is agreed on all hands that, since we know the prairie of Alaska north of the Brooks Range was not glaciated, we know also that the summers must have been hot. They run above 90° in the shade now, with rare extremes above 95°; they would have run within ten degrees of that heat then.

But if we suppose that the first eastward migration to reach Greenland was the true Eskimos, and not Folsom people with an Arctic culture, we shall have to say that Asiatic man has not been in Greenland much more than twenty-five hundred years; for it appears certain that the forefathers of the Eskimo did not reach America longer ago than around 1000 B.C.

We feel we know that the Eskimo came to America from Asia so well clad and housed, and so much master of an Arctic prairie way of life, that he was then, as he has been in our time, more comfortable and in less danger from his environment than the forest Athapaskans who now occupy, and probably did then, the Yukon Basin and the lower Mackenzie Valley. It is because an Arctic people will have had to learn new ways of life (necessarily slow, for changing his mind is hard for primitive man) that we think it must have taken the Folsom migration 2000 or 3000 years to reach Texas. It should not in comparison take more than 200 or 300 years for people with an Arctic way of life to move east along the mainland coasts of Alaska and Canada and northeast through the Canadian archipelago until the mountains of Greenland rise above the horizon. For an eastward movement does not compel you to change your way of life as a southward movement does.

If Folsom man reached Greenland, he will not have required for the trek more than the two or three centuries we grant the Eskimos. However, it is the Eskimos we specifically discuss, for we know they did get all the way.

We learn from digging up and studying the earliest ruins of northwestern Greenland, where the Eskimos are known to have entered our continental island, that the first of them were hunters of the whale, walrus, and seal, as well as of the polar bear, musk ox, and caribou. But we think it probably was the musk ox which tended most to speed up their eastward movement. For this animal has a trait that draws a hunting people on and on, to new and ever-new pastures.

The whale, seal, and walrus tend rather to keep hunters stationary. For, if you have once found a good locality for any of these, then you catch them there every year, or at least during every season that is favorable, which naturally inclines you to stay. The caribou is in this respect similar. Not until they received breech-loading firearms during the nineteenth century have a caribou-hunting people, so far as we know, ever killed enough of these animals in any good caribou section so that moving on in search of a better hunting ground would seem particularly desirable. True, caribou are not always in great numbers here this year just because they were numerous here a year ago; but all hunters consider them at least a little more likely to come again to places where they have been numerous before than to others where they have been scarce.

The situation is the reverse with musk oxen. They can run faster than you would think from their clumsy build, but they cannot run as fast as the chief enemy of all northern grazing animals, the wolf. Since there was no point in fleeing, they did not flee; they stood their ground for defense in their equivalent of the British square, the strong and shaggy in an outer circle, the calves and youngsters within. Or else they would back against a cliff, the big ones in the front line, the smaller behind.

The defense of the musk ox was impregnable to the wolf. Those travelers who have been thoughtful students of animal behavior have reported again and again, from every part of the Arctic, the full and mutual realization of the musk ox and the wolf that there is nothing to fear and no use to attack. Sverdrup, for instance, tells from Ellesmere Island that a cow, with a newborn calf close by her in the grass, merely gave a casual glance now and then to a wolf that was passing near.

The wolf, with corresponding disinterest, looked now and then toward the cow and calf, without any sign that he even thought of trying to sneak up. Members of our third expedition reported like cases from Melville Island; and they gathered information to the same effect from the Eskimos of Victoria Island and those of the musk-ox district east of the Coppermine.

The British square had proved its worth in European warfare; it was suicidal when Braddock tried it in Pennsylvania against the Indians and the French who had learned Indian methods. Even more so, what had been an impregnable defense against the wolf proved suicidal to the musk ox when hunting man came along with his bow and arrow, with his dog and spear. Upon the approach of the dogs, or of shouting men running toward them from several directions, musk oxen form their defensive ring and stand there uncomprehending beneath the shower of arrows or bullets till just possibly the last two or three do run when they find themselves no longer protected by comrades on flank and rear.

And the musk ox is no more a migrating animal than a fleeing animal. Hanbury has said for the mainland between Hudson Bay and the Coppermine that if you find a group of them this year you can come back next year reasonably certain that they will be within ten or fifteen miles. Our third expedition reported from Melville Island that the herds would feed along, moving no faster than they ate up nearly all the vegetation, the rate being from 100 to 500 yards a day—of course not always in the same direction.

Primitive man usually kills all the game he can. Therefore he exterminates the non-fleeing musk ox as he goes along. New herds do not come in by migration to replace those that have been killed off. So the group of hunters moves forward to new village sites and pastures.

But when a hunting people discover a good locality for other game, as for whales and seals at Point Barrow, they have a tendency to make a permanent settlement—migratory by the season, but permanent in the sense that at a given time of year they would be back where they were last year. When all musk oxen have been killed that are within a practical radius from a place like Barrow there would be a tendency for the people to sort of forget about the musk ox and to depend on the beasts that come to that locality regularly or at least recurrently. These are the sea mammals, the fish, the birds, and the caribou —in fact, all the beasts upon which northerners depend, except the musk ox.

But some groups who had passed east of Barrow, and who found themselves in a locality not particularly good for whales or the other recurrent game, would find themselves also too far off for returning. To these herd after herd of musk oxen would be one magnet after the other pulling them forward throughout all the natural country of this animal, which is the prairie north of the tree line, going into the sparse forest to a certain extent.

There is, of course, the tendency of man to rove in search of better hunting. We think of the musk ox, then, as merely an additional pulling force, one that tends to control the direction of movement from Bering Strait, making it first northeastward, where the prairie is narrow between the forest and the sea, then letting it spread into a Y, or a delta, when you get east beyond the Mackenzie. Some of the migration streams are then directed southeastward toward Hudson Bay and Labrador, some eastward toward Baffin Island, some northeastward toward Ellesmere.

It is the view of geologists that 2000 or 3000 years ago the relation of permanent ice and of snow-free land was about the same as now in Ellesmere and in Greenland. Then, even more than now, Ellesmere was surely a good musk-ox and a fair caribou land, for man had not been there destroying. Also the waters furnish increasingly, as you move northeast from Melville Island, the mainstays of northern hunters, the seal, the walrus, and the white and other whales.

With the hunt improving, it would be natural for a migration to be fairly rapid north along the east coast of Ellesmere Island until Greenland was visible, and finally Smith Sound, where in a few hours of travel with dog sledges or afoot they could cross to Greenland.

Once in Greenland the Eskimos would find themselves in a novel situation. No longer was most of the country open to their migration; they had not the usual choice between following a shore and going inland, for ice covered most of the country and the free land was but a ribbon along the shore.

In modern times the glaciers of Melville Bay have been enough of a barrier so that it was sometimes generations at a stretch that little or no intercourse took place between Eskimos living south and north of the Melville glaciers. Therefore some have believed that the first migration for the occupation of Greenland was by the easier route northeastward from Smith Sound, around through the musk-ox pastures of Peary Land, and down along the east coast where musk oxen were then no doubt even more abundant than they are today.

To account for the facts of today we have to assume that the migrating Eskimos did not stay long enough on the north coast, or on the northern east coast, to exterminate the musk ox; for the animals are on these stretches by the thousand now, grazing over ruins of Eskimo habitations that have not been occupied for centuries, perhaps some of them not for two millenniums.

If the glaciers of Melville Bay were really a barrier to the first immigrants, then Greenland was occupied, as we said, by following the shore northeast, then southeast, and finally southwest around Cape Farewell, and so up the west coast to the southern part of Melville Bay. More likely, however, the occupying migration was bifurcated at Smith Sound, one stream going northeast, the other southeast, the two finally meeting—likeliest, many think, on the southern east coast.

As we keep digging into the kitchen middens and house ruins of the Greenland Eskimos, we find evidence that they were much the same kind of people 1000 or 2000 years ago as they have been these last 200 or 300 years and were until they began to be "civilized." Except for the early period, when they no doubt lived mainly on the readiest of all their kills, the musk ox, they have depended, according to locality, on animals of the sea and land. In a few places, particularly the northwest, eggs and seabirds have been a considerable part of their food. Where the snow-free land is widest, whether on the east coast or the west coast, the caribou has been important. In the Smith Sound region and southward the walrus is of great consequence, but it is secondary in much of Greenland. The white whale is important here and there, and so have been the larger whales. Fish are of local significance. The great mainstay has been the seal.

We cannot tell whether the first inhabitants of Greenland were possessed of what is perhaps the most unique and most interesting of all Eskimo inventions, the snowhouse. Likely they were not and this was a later discovery of their cousins whom they had left behind in the region between the Mackenzie and Hudson Bay; for the only Greenland district known ever to have used snowhouses at any time is also known to have received, as Knud Rasmussen tells us, a migration from Baffin Island within the last 200 years. Greenland snowhouses are known today only from the 200 or 300 people who dwell between the Melville glaciers and Peary Land and who are, in part at least, descended from these newcomers.

By archaeology, then, we can follow the story of Greenland Eskimos through perhaps two millenniums; it is less than one millennium since we got our first historical glimpse.

When the Icelanders began to settle Greenland, in what are now the Julianehaab and Godthaab districts of the southwest coast, they found on the shore skin boats and stone utensils. This was in the years immediately following 982. During the first decade of the eleventh century, about 1004, the Norse (Icelandic) settlers of Greenland, now on a voyage to Labrador and southward, met people using the same kind of skin boats and gear they had found abandoned in Greenland. From this they inferred, as we believe correctly, that the same kind of people they now saw on the mainland had been in the Julianehaab and Godthaab sections of Greenland at some time before the European colonization.

It has seemed strange to those unfamiliar with northern countries that Eskimos who once had been in the Julianehaab district, "the best part of Greenland," should have moved out again, and "to less desirable sections." The point is, of course, that a section desirable to a farmer and husbandman is not necessarily desirable to a hunter and fisher. This is particularly so with northern hunters, for the animals upon which they depend are many of them in their turn dependent on sea ice. A year of much ice seemed an obviously bad one to the Icelanders, who were unfamiliar with sea ice and did not understand the hunting technique of Greenland. To Eskimos the same year would have been a good season.

Later in this book we shall have occasion to mention settlements north of the middle of the western coast of Greenland which have been moving still farther north in recent years. This has been because the near extermination of the caribou has made the people more and more dependent on the walrus and other sea animals, which they have been pursuing through a gradual northward movement of the hunting villages. For these animals come with the ice and go with the ice.

If Eskimos of less than 2000 years ago were the first people from the west to reach Greenland, it appears probable that they were not its discoverers. The discoverers in that case were from Europe.

It cannot be contended, if you follow the thought of the

archaeologist and ethnologist, that man of far antiquity was unable to reach Greenland from Europe because the ocean between is wide. For if you once adhere to that school you must believe also in the high antiquity of navigation. It is only those who get their controlling ideas from written history and tradition who consider that seafaring is merely of the last few thousand years and that it reached its first high development in the countries around the Old World Mediterranean.

Anthropologists do not usually make even a guess at where navigation started, if in any one place. They admit it is impossible to demonstrate the great antiquity of navigation; but they commonly believe that the invention of boats that would carry a number of passengers goes back, at a minimum, twenty thousand years.

There are not many anthropologists on printed record for the antiquity of boats as an invention. Accordingly, a few years ago a questionnaire was sent to a number of prominent anthropologists asking them for a maximum estimate on the antiquity of the bow and arrow and for an opinion as to which was the older invention, the bow or the canoe. The general reply was that arrows were probably shot from bows more than thirty thousand years ago, and that the probability seemed to be that the canoe was older than the bow.

Unless you are a devotee of the Elliot Smith school and have it for a dogma that all real inventions are each made only once, spreading from a center to whatever remote parts it now occupies—unless you are fanatically of that school, you will likely agree that boats were invented in various climates, under various conditions, in a number of different parts of the world.

Be that as it may, you will agree upon study that two of the most primitive forms of the boat are each about the most seaworthy craft ever devised by man; and you will think it probable that these two between them have to their credit the discovery of every land in the world which had to be reached by water and which was inhabited, or which contained signs of former habitation, when known Europeans came there first. These boat forms are the wooden outrigger canoes of the South Seas and those skin boats which we know best from the Irish and the Eskimos.

In this book we are speculating on the discovery of Greenland and not on the entire development of prehistoric navigation. So we do no more with the outrigger canoe than to remark that little dots of land in a thousand miles of bare ocean, as, for instance, Easter Island, were inhabited when known Europeans first saw them, and that almost certainly they were discovered and colonized by the navigators of outrigger canoes.

We shall find when we come to the historical account of northern Atlantic discovery that Greek navigators of twenty-two hundred years ago were told when they reached the north of Scotland that there was an island in the sea farther north. The Greeks sailed northward six days and found it—their Thule, now called Iceland.

So far as written records go, it was these Greeks who were the first Europeans to sail beyond Iceland in the direction of Greenland, till they were stopped by the ice of the Greenland Current. It is part of our job to discuss how it was the Scots of 325 B.C. were able to furnish the Greeks with sailing directions to the New World.

There are many ways in which this could have happened. One of them, and sufficient by itself, is the development of boats made from hide stretched over a wicker frame. We know these as curraghs from the Irish and as umiaks from the Eskimos.

To historians and other speculators who knew the curragh chiefly from the coracle of Julius Caesar, and to whom the umiak was a museum specimen from a benighted people who use skins because their land is woodless, it seemed folklore bred of a childish imagination when the Irish told of curraghs with threescore men aboard that made deep-sea voyages in stormy weather to remote countries. Most critics felt that either the journeys had never happened or that the vessels must have been of timber and of something like the Greek or Viking type. They were correct on the basis of their premises, if they drew them from Caesar and his coracles. But were they not probably wrong in assuming that Europeans could not have done with cowhide and wood from their native forests, or driftwood from their shores, what Eskimos have done with the skins of the bearded seal, the walrus, and the white whale stretched over frames of driftwood?

Lisiansky tells us that in 1805 he saw Eskimos, seventy in a boat, making long journeys around Bering Sea and the Aleutian Islands. From much nearer Ireland, from Greenland, witnesses of several nationalities have reported skin boats even larger than those found by the early Russians around the North Pacific and in Bering Sea. Nor can it be assumed that the storms are worse in the North Atlantic than in the North Pacific and Bering Sea, nor worse in the Atlantic between Greenland and Ireland than around Greenland itself. The contrary is the verdict of those of our sailors who know the Alaskan and Greenland waters best.

The Eskimo skin boat, the umiak, is a dory.

It is a commonplace among those who know dories to say that, apart from certain "patent" boats invented for lifesaving and similar purposes, there is probably no craft ever devised in which you are safer in a storm at sea. It happens now and then with the fishers of New England and eastern Canada who work the Newfoundland Banks that a dory with one or two men in it disappears in a sudden storm. If the boat is found in time the men in it are safe; if they are lost it is seldom by drowning, more often through exposure or starvation. That kind of boat just naturally stays right side up and will ship the waves only under the most adverse circumstances.

The dory-shaped umiak is made of skins instead of boards. It is lighter and therefore floats more easily—rides higher in the sea with a given load. It is slightly flexible, which does not detract from its seaworthiness. Because of its shallower draft it can run inshore over a bar that has less water on it and it is so tough that striking a rock it is less likely than even the heaviest wooden dory to be injured in a way to let the water in. Being much lighter, it is far easier for the crew when making land in a surf to leap overboard at a safe stage and drag their craft ashore. Being tougher as well as lighter, it can be dragged over a rocky beach more easily and with less injury.

With testimony in hand from officers of the United States Coast Guard, who have seen skin boats heavily laden and with crews of thirty to forty weathering stiff gales in Bering Sea; with witnesses agreeing to this all around the north coast of Alaska and all around southern Greenland, we are in a position to say that, but for one thing, the skin boat is as capable of long sea voyages as the outrigger canoe that discovered the remotest islands of the Pacific or the Viking ships of a thousand years ago that crossed the North Atlantic freely between Europe and America. The one doubt is on whether sufficient bacterial decay would take place before the end of a long voyage so that the seams would let go.

There is testimony that when an Eskimo uses his umiak on the lakes and rivers of Alaska he must dry it thoroughly enough to kill the decay bacteria at least once every four days—or that this is the standard practice. However, Eskimos who follow a coast do not dry out their boats nearly that often and, so far as the literature goes, we apparently have no testimony on how long a boat can go in salt water and not spring a seam.

The emphasis is on *salt* water. We salt our beef and it remains in its brine for years without decay. Is there perhaps enough salt in sea water so that decay of the seams of a skin boat is prevented indefinitely?

When seams go on a fresh-water journey, it is not the rawhide that decays materially but the sinew which is thread used for the seams. This sinew is not greased to protect it from water because it is the desire of the Eskimo that it shall swell by absorbing moisture, thus filling the holes made by the needle and making the seams waterproof. They understand, however, that a seam not otherwise waterproof can be made so by the application of grease. The North American forest Indians secured a like result by the use of pitch.

Eskimos who fear that they may not be able to dry out their boats often enough when traveling along a river will grease the seams to keep the water out and thus prevent decay. If a boat were being prepared specially for a long salt-water journey it might very well be greased the same way. It seems likely enough that if we, who now grasp all the principles, were to fortify an ordinary skin boat against a long voyage by special care of the seams, and by tar, oil, or tallow on the skins generally, we would be able to travel an indefinite distance over salt water.

The curragh in which, by Irish tradition, the people of old made their deep-sea journeys, was not ever, so far as we know, a boat of the dory type. By combining what we learn from a curragh model of the second century B.C., found in an Irish hoard, with what we know from drawings of curraghs that were in Irish use during the seventeenth century, we conclude that the shape of this craft during at least two thousand years has been approximately that of the Algonquin bark canoe; or, speaking more familiarly, that of the modern Peterborough or other similar canoe that you can buy from a sportsmen's outfitter.

A Peterborough does not have quite the marvelous safety features of the dory and umiak, but it is a mighty good craft, capable of what are to the uninitiated breath-taking feats. Even in our day we can still see canoemen, whether Indians, frontiersmen, or city dwellers of the sportsman type, shooting in the Algonquin type of canoe rapids that are white with foam

The umiak of the Eskimo resembles the curragh, the skin-and-frame boat in which the Irish probably discovered Greenland; either can carry fifty to seventy-five people in a rough sea.

A kayak somersault; watertight boat and suit are lashed into one piece.

and where both canoe and canoeman are frequently out of sight from the riverbank, hidden by the waves. With such pictures in your mental eye it is hard to deny the possibility that the Irish, and their neighbors of Britain two thousand years ago, may have made in their overgrown Peterboroughs just such voyages as their traditions describe.

A fact demands an explanation. No facts are more insistent on being explained than those of man's spread over the earth during prehistoric times; so that when the first historically recorded visitors came along they found other people ahead of them on most of the islands of the Pacific, Atlantic, and Indian oceans, some of these much farther from any inhabited land than Greenland is from Europe. Even those islands which had no people were in some cases known. For instance, the Azores seemingly had no people when the Portuguese visited them in 1432, but the balance of evidence probably is for the authenticity of a find there of a hoard of Carthaginian coins dating from a number of centuries before Christ. Iceland may not have been inhabited in the fourth century B.C., but the Scots were able to tell the Greeks about it.

There are two groups of islands north of Europe where the balance of probability is that they had never been inhabited prior to the first European visit of historic time—the Spitsbergen and Franz Josef groups. These are the exceptions to our rule.

And who is there to say that even these islands may not have been seen frequently? After all, we have not during modern times colonized every land we discovered, nor is there reason to think that primitive man differed from us in that respect.

To those of us brought up in the pedagogic tradition of forty and more years ago, where navigation of the high seas was supposed to have started with the Phoenicians, it is more than a little against the grain to believe that man swarmed over at least three of the oceans, the Atlantic, Indian, and Pacific, during remote periods. In fact, about the only group of scholars to whom that type of thinking appears to be natural or ingrained is the archaeologists, particularly those who devote themselves to the late Stone and various Bronze ages.

A man like H. O'Neill Hencken, professor of archaeology at Harvard, takes it in his stride to consider reasonable and probable that man of the Bronze Age used to do what we would now call great circle sailing between Spain and Ireland and between northwestern Spain and southwestern England. Professor A. W. Brögger created no great stir, or at least aroused no storm of protest, when at an international congress of archaeologists at Oslo in 1936 he lectured, as president of the congress, about a golden age of deep-sea navigation which he thinks may have been at its height as much as three thousand years before Christ and which was on the decline after 1500 B.C., so that the very period which we used to select as the beginning of real seamanship, the Phoenician, is shown as having been (by that theory) at the bottom of a curve, which thereafter rose slowly until it attained a new high in the navigational cycle of the Viking Age which started less than fifteen hundred years ago.

That man of the Old World discovered the Americas, from Brazil to Greenland, during Brögger's golden age of navigation five thousand years ago, and perhaps earlier, rests merely on possibilities and probabilities. As yet we cannot prove it certain, though we can prove it likely.

But nobody can prove it did not happen. There is not merely the well-known difficulty in proving a negative; we can really cite nothing much against the proposal beyond reluctance born of traditional thinking. That is, however, a difficulty only to those of us whose school days were passed among historical writings that gave no weight to archaeology, or none that was derived from other than Mediterranean countries. During the last twenty or thirty years the archaeology of northwestern Europe has been crowding its way toward the attention of historians, and more recently the Americas and the Pacific islands are beginning to have their day. Perhaps it will be as congenial to the next generation as it has been uncongenial till recently to assume that there probably were a great many crossings of every ocean and a great many discoveries of nearly or quite every land before the earliest that can be found in those histories which depend solely on books, on monuments with written inscriptions, and on "dependable tradition."

CHAPTER III

Discovery by the Greeks around 325 B.C.

WRITTEN HISTORY of voyages from the Old World to the New, from the eastern side of the Atlantic to the western, begins with Pytheas of Massilia, now Marseilles, who was a contemporary of Alexander the Great. Pytheas made his journey by sea northward and westward about the time his Macedonian countryman was campaigning southward and eastward from Greece. He wrote a book concerning the voyage, which may have been called *On the Ocean* or *Description of the Earth*. This book is lost, and so are all the works of those who read the original and were able to quote it direct. However, the writings of these firsthand quoters, though now lost, were extant during the lifetime of a number of scholars whose works we do still have.

But the secondhand quotes which we possess are many of them under suspicion for a special reason. Our conception of Darwin and his teachings would be inadequate, to say the least, if we knew of him and them only the things quoted by churchmen and those generally who were attacking Darwin as a heretic. Pytheas was the most startling and most complete heretic of his day—recalcitrant against a doctrine of Greek philosophy which was at least as firm in the minds of the learned of the centuries just before Christ as the Genesis story

of creation was in our culture when Darwin published his
Origin of Species.

We are perhaps oversimplifying, but we do not vary from
the essential truth when we say that there were in Greece and
Italy during the centuries following Pytheas two main sets of
views about the earth, those of the unlearned and those of the
learned or philosophers. The folklore conception was pictur-
esque and without consistency; it was built up from many
sources, "real" and imagined. The philosophical view had
consistency and logic. Pytheas was to an extent in conflict with
both views; he was in fundamental conflict with the doctrines
of the philosophers.

From the time of Pythagoras in the sixth century B.C. the
earth had been spherical to the philosophers. Along with this
idea they worked out a Doctrine of the Five Zones and a
theoretical explanation for the distribution of heat and cold.
The orthodox view in the time of Pytheas, or more properly
in the centuries which immediately followed, was simple and
rigorous.

The tropics of the earth were too near the sun; the rocks
were red hot, and the water, if any, was boiling, or at any rate
too hot for man, beast, or plant. The polar regions were too
far from the sun; they were always cold; land and sea were
covered with snow; the earth was lifeless and so was the ocean,
which was frozen to its bottom. Greek lands and those east
and west of them were at about the right distance from the
sun. It might be too hot or too cold on any given day; the
average was pretty good. But if you traveled south from
Greece you would enter gradually a realm of heat that grew
more and more intense, until finally you came to the limits of
human endurance. Beyond that you would die; beyond that
were the Burning Tropics which no man would ever cross, by
sea or land. And if you went north from Greece the cold became more and more intense gradually, until you finally reached
the limits of bodily endurance; beyond was the Frozen North,

without plant or animal life, a still and white realm of death, unknowable except by theory.

Pytheas became the Ananias and Münchausen of Greek history because he claimed to have sailed north far beyond what the philosophers "knew" were the utmost bounds of human and animal life and said he had found conditions there to differ comparatively little, and only in degree, from what was familiar in Greece and in France inward from his home town of Massilia.

What made Pytheas the supreme heretic of Greek philosophy was that he could not be dismissed; for when he started telling these things, which obviously could not be true, he was an elderly man who had established himself through the career of his early and middle years as one of the greatest of mathematicians and cosmographers. During his lifetime, and even after his death, he was known throughout the Greek world as a keen and skeptical thinker, as ingenious and practical in his construction of scientific apparatus, as an inventor of scientific instruments of precision, as one of the most reliable and respected men of his aggressive and prosperous city. It runs through many of the comments upon him during many centuries how strange it was that a man so able and so long honorable should have turned into the worst of liars just by making a sea voyage.

However, it does not appear the Greeks found Pytheas a liar immediately upon his return. To us there seems no doubt that the sailors who had been with him told the same stories as he did when they came ashore in Massilia. Besides, the Massilians were great traders and were receiving goods from the remote North that came by river and overland across what is modern France. Neither does the theory which Pytheas flouted, about the impenetrable and frozen North, seem to have had so firm a hold in his day as it did upon later generations. Perhaps he had been dead as much as a hundred years before the doctrine of the five zones, two habitable and three uninhabitable, had clamped itself so firmly upon the thought of Mediterranean Europe that the smallest skepticism about it had become the greatest heresy.

This has not been a digression, for it is necessary to explain why Pytheas, the first European known to have reached the Greenland region, was so little quoted by writers who were in a position to quote him, and why we have reason to be so dubious about the accuracy of those who did quote him. A few of the writers whose books have been preserved cite Pytheas because he was well known to be a liar; those who cite him do so frequently, if not usually, to prove him such—to poke fun at him or denounce him and those who perchance might believe in him.

The learned of the centuries just before and after Christ were unable to believe Pytheas because he said that as he went north along the west coasts of Europe he found the summer days getting longer and longer, exactly according to one firmly held tenet of Greek philosophy, *but did not find the weather getting correspondingly chillier.* He had gone to where he had seen the sun at midnight in midsummer, which was far within the dead and solidly frozen world of the learned, and had perceived there no ice or snow in the water; instead he claimed to have viewed the sun over a liquid ocean as it dipped down until it nearly touched the sea and then rose slowly again. What was worse, Pytheas had thereafter sailed the equivalent of one hundred of our miles north beyond the point whence he had seen the midnight sun, and therefore beyond the Arctic Circle, and still without finding the conditions that the philosophers demanded. True, he had run at last into a very dense fog and some slush ice; but this was no more than a crumb of comfort to those who required the ocean to freeze solid only a little north of Scotland, as Strabo, the famous geographer, did, for instance.

But now that we know that in July there is reasonable warmth northward along the coast of Spain and the coast of

France and the coast of England, now that we know that
ice has never been seen on the direct run from Scotland to
Iceland, now that we know that a hundred miles north from
Iceland in midsummer you would be likely to meet just such
dense fog and such broken ice—now that we know, in short,
that Pytheas told the literal truth about what he had seen,
we have begun to search through all of the literature, culling
from the unlikeliest places fragmentary references to Pytheas,
to what he said, to what he may have said, and to what was
said about him. Gathering these fragments together and inter-
preting them in the light of our modern knowledge, we can
follow the Greek voyage of 325 B.C. almost step by step from
the Pillars of Hercules to the edge of the Greenland Current
at the Scoresby Sound region, a hundred miles north of western
Iceland.

We know that Pytheas saw the Greenland ice, if only the
mashed fringes. We do not know whether the fog he describes
so vividly was always dense; if it lifted while he was still a
hundred miles north of western Iceland he must have seen
Greenland. His book may have contained, for all we know, a
detailed description of what he saw as he looked across the
drifting floes. That is speculation. We now present what we
do know and what has been reasonably conjectured by scholars
who have studied the pieced-together account of this earliest
chronicled voyage to Iceland and beyond it, to where Greenland either was seen or would have been seen had the fog lifted.

From our general knowledge of Massilian shipping in the
fourth century B.C., we feel sure that the vessel of Pytheas
was either a bireme or a trireme. The reasons for thinking it
may have been a trireme seem the least convincing. They are
that the Greeks might have felt the need of impressing the
natives of the lands to be visited with their power and mag-
nificence, and that with three banks of rowers instead of two
you could make greater speed. But there are many reasons to
believe that trading voyages northward along the coast, al-

though never before performed by Greeks, were frequent around 330 B.C. by the inhabitants of North Africa and by those of the Atlantic coast of Spain; and that, being trading voyages, they were peaceful. The reasons which favor the use of a bireme by Pytheas are that they were customarily used on trading voyages, that they were more seaworthy, and that there are no speeds mentioned in the Pytheas narrative which are greater than might be expected from a bireme.

Some students of naval architecture have considered that the bireme of Massilia, while not as maneuverable or quite as seaworthy as the Viking ship of the tenth century, was more seaworthy and more maneuverable than any of the three vessels Columbus had with him on his 1492 voyage. We give a characterization of them by Sir Clements Markham, president of the Royal Geographical Society of London, himself both a sailor and a polar explorer. In his article "Pytheas, the Discoverer of Britain," *Geographical Journal,* June 1893, Markham is discussing the voyage from Scotland to and beyond Iceland and says:

"A large Massilian ship was a good sea-boat, and well able to make a voyage into the northern ocean. She would be from 150 to 170 feet long—the beam of a merchant ship being a quarter, and of a war-ship one-eighth the length—a depth of hold of 25 or 26 feet, and a draught of 10 to 12. Her tonnage would be 400 to 500, so that the ship of Pytheas was larger and more seaworthy than the crazy little *Santa Maria* with which, eighteen hundred years afterwards, Columbus discovered the New World."

Such ships were equipped with square sails. Through the auxiliary power of their oars they escaped complete dependence on the wind. In the same discussion Markham tells us that "The rowing power of ancient galleys, supplementary to the sails, has been looked upon as the equivalent to the [auxiliary] steam-power of modern times." (Markham was writing in 1893.)

The voyage along the mainland coast of western Europe is spaced in its northward progress by references to the length of the day—that the sun was in the sky for sixteen hours in one place, seventeen in another, eighteen in a third. This would not refer to how many hours the sun was above the horizon, as actually viewed by Pytheas, but would be the result of his calculation of the maximum length of the day at a given place. Be it remembered, the commander of this voyage was no amateur like Columbus but a mathematician who had himself invented the instrument by which he measured the latitude of Massilia and who had either thought out or correctly applied the astronomical knowledge which made this possible. His determination of the latitude of the Greek colony was said in antiquity to have been, and was so far as we know, the first latitude determination anywhere on the earth.

After reaching Britain, Pytheas mentions three lengths of day—seventeen hours, eighteen hours, and nineteen hours, which will have been at the northern parts of England, Scotland, and the Shetlands.

At the north of Scotland we come to a vagueness in the quotations which has made the students divide about evenly on whether Pytheas meant to say that he left there, sailed north and found Thule in six days, or whether he meant to say that the people told him that if he sailed north he would find Thule in six days. Textual criticism does not help us much here—great masters have pondered on the meanings and have remained doubtful, or at any rate have failed to agree.

After the writings of Pytheas which were lost had been quoted by a few of his contemporaries whose works are also lost, and when these had been quoted, usually for purposes of ridicule, by a dozen or so writers that have been preserved to us, it is reasonable that there would be a good deal of confusion, and practically on every point. Then there was the added difficulty that writers of the ancient time did not use quotation marks and did not have the feeling we moderns do that one should quote with scrupulous exactness. They had the contrary feeling, indeed, that it was their duty to improve the quotation according to their superior knowledge, modestly refraining from making a claim that they were responsible for the improvement. So it is not strange that writers like Strabo would mix up with their statement of what Pytheas had said he had seen other statements of what they felt sure he must have seen or what they "knew" in any case was true.

We have elsewhere written a critical discussion of the voyage of Pytheas (*Ultima Thule,* New York, 1940), citing nearly every scrap of quotation, paraphrase, or reference to the man and his work that we have been able to find in the ancient writers. Here we merely summarize.

What we think of the probability as to whether Pytheas himself sailed north and found Thule in six days or whether the people of Scotland told him it lay six days' sail to the northward will depend on our belonging to one or the other of the schools of thought we have described with regard to navigation. If we think the great pioneers were likely the Egyptians, Cretans, Phoenicians, or some other Mediterranean people, we are inclined to believe that the Greek astronomer, impelled by curiosity to learn what he could, sailed north and happened upon Iceland. But if we belong to what we have called the archaeologist school, we are more inclined to believe that the Scots had been there first, that they told the Greeks where to find Iceland, and even that one or more of them went along as guides.

Some students of the quotations that refer to Thule have considered that Norway was meant, not Iceland, because there is reference to honey and to corn being made into beer. However, even those who favor Norway as Thule, as, for instance, Fridtjof Nansen, admit it is very unlikely that there was honey in a part of Norway so far north that the midnight sun was visible. Almost certainly those are right who believe that the reference to beer and honey is neither to Norway nor to

Iceland but to Britain. Nansen himself concedes this as a probability, and the view is generally taken by students of English history. For they commonly cite as the earliest literary reference to the food habits of Britain the statement of Pytheas that they had corn and honey and that they made beer.

In the discussions of the identification of Thule, particularly in the dispute on whether the identification should be with Iceland or with Norway, it has been said by critics that Pytheas may have thought he was sailing north when actually he was sailing east (from the north tip of Scotland in either case). Pertinent, then, is the known fact of his quarrel with Eudoxus —known in the sense that the ancient writers did not dispute it, not even those who thought Pytheas unreliable in his travel tales.

Eudoxus, a philosopher of standing who wrote some decades before Pytheas, said that the pole of the heavens was marked by a star, the one which we still speak of as the Pole Star. It was, he said, straight north—as we say by implication when we speak of it as the North Star. But it was the intellectual bent of Pytheas to check any statement, no matter how famous and revered its author, no matter how seemingly obvious its truth.

So Pytheas decided, even in the face of the high reputation of Eudoxus, to check whether the star really was at the pole— whether the true pole marked by the circles described by the rest of the northern stars was really designated in the heavens by one of the stars. To do this he constructed, and perhaps invented, the necessary instrument. He was able to make this so accurate, and his observations with it were so precise, that he was able to announce (what we believe to have been the fact at the time of his observation) that there was no star at the true pole. But he found two stars so located that if you imagined a third to complete an equilateral triangle, then that imaginary star would be at the true pole of the heavens—true north from the observer.

So Pytheas is the one of all known figures of antiquity about whom it is most difficult to believe that he traveled east for six days when he thought he was going north. The difficulty, in fact, is much greater than that; for Pytheas did not merely go from Scotland to Thule; he also returned from Thule to Scotland. We are, therefore, asked to believe not merely that he thought he was sailing north during a week when he was sailing east but also that he thought he was sailing south during another week when he was sailing west.

Nearly or quite every reference in the Pytheas quotations to Thule (if we credit to England the one on the food and drink) applies better to Iceland than to Norway; some which cannot be applied to Norway at all apply to Iceland, one of them with precision. For we are told that, looking north at midnight in midsummer, the sun just skims the horizon and does so for only a few days. If you are at the north of Norway in midsummer you will find both that the sun is fairly high in the sky at midnight and that it is continuously visible not for a mere few days but for several weeks.

A passage correct for the north coast of Iceland, if by length of continuous day you mean that summer period when you can do such things as reading, writing, or sewing at midnight even with a cloudy sky, we choose from Cleomedes of the second century A.D.:

"In reference to the island called Thule, where rumors say that the philosopher, Pytheas of Massilia, went, it is said that the entire circle described by the sun at the summer solstice is above the horizon, so that it coincides in these places with the Arctic Circle. In these regions, when the sun is in Cancer, the day lasts one month, if at least all the parts of that sign are visible."

For a passage which is as correct as if you had written it home from the north coast of Iceland when you were there last summer, we cite Mela:

"Thule . . . on that island . . . the nights in summer are

light, because at that time of the year, the sun, mounting higher, without being itself visible, nevertheless illuminates with its neighboring splendor the places which are nearest to it. But during the solstice there are no nights because then the sun shows not only its radiance but also the greater part of itself."

We have seen that northern Iceland fits the report of Pytheas, that from its north coast you see the midnight sun just skimming the northern oceanic horizon for a few days; even more convincing is the reference to the midsummer sun as showing at midnight most but not all of itself—which would mean that the observer was in one of the north coast fjords, as, for instance, Eyjafjordur, near the present location of Iceland's second largest city, Akureyri.

Evidently, then, since he brought home the two reports, Pytheas made his observations both from the most northerly promontories (or from a vessel rounding them) and from fjord heads. This shows a leisurely voyage; and, since we know the temperament of the man, the procedure of a genuine scientific expedition.

There is still another way of locating Iceland from the descriptions of Pytheas, and more pertinent to us, since our chief concern is with Greenland. For he gives us also the north-south distance of Thule from the margin of the ice. This distance will have to be measured from the northwestern corner of Iceland; for it is called a day's sail and is therefore, by Greek practice of the time, in the vicinity of a hundred of our miles. You may well find ice at that distance in midsummer if you sail straight north from Iceland's northwestern peninsula; you would, of course, have to go several hundred miles north if the journey were from the northeastern corner.

Whether or not Pytheas was the first European to reach the margin of the drift ice, he gave us what is almost certainly the first written description. We have of this a paraphrase which we take from Strabo:

"He had also undertaken investigations concerning Thule and those regions in which there was no longer any distinction of land or sea or air but a mixture of the three like sea-lung, in which he says that land and sea and everything floats, and this [i.e., the mixture] binds all together, and can neither be traversed on foot nor by boat. The substance resembling lung he had seen himself, as he says; the rest he relates according to what he has heard. This is Pytheas' tale . . . "

During the time when it was a commonplace to speak of Pytheas as the biggest of known liars it was, of course, easy to make fun of this passage, and Strabo was not the only one who did so. Now we consider that Pytheas was as meticulous in his report of the Thule voyage as in his application of astronomy and mathematics to the determination of latitude, and the scholars have found numerous ways to interpret the passage that are not alone charitable but even creditable to Pytheas as an observer.

The expression "sea-lung" may have been a figure of speech, perhaps a Massilian term not known, or at least not properly interpreted, by the Athenian Greeks or by Greek scholars resident in Italy like Strabo. Or it may have been a term that he picked up on his voyage, from the Carthaginians, from the Spaniards, the French, or the British.

Few things used to be more common with the Yankee sailors of the Bering Sea and western Arctic whaling fleet than saying that a dense fog was like soup—unless it may have been more common to say that the fog was soupy or merely that everything was soup outside. From this it was but a step, frequently taken by the whalers, to explain that the soup was so thick you could cut it in chunks and pile it up like bricks.

Imagine a Chinese scholar, completely unfamiliar with the idiom of Yankee sailors, trying to determine with the aid of a dictionary what a sailor meant by saying the vessel found itself in a soup so thick that you could pile it up like bricks!

Certainly a reference to the sea being like a lung would not puzzle him more.

Few commentators on Pytheas are better grounded than Fridtjof Nansen. Examine his two-volume *In Northern Mists* and you will find that he was a scholar who had assembled pertinent information with regard to the northward trend of geographic discovery not merely from Greek, Roman, and medieval sources but also from the Arabs, the Phoenicians, and many another people of North Africa, the Middle East, and Europe. He was a marine biologist and oceanographer as well as an explorer. We give his comment on this passage, quoting it from Vol. I, pp. 66–67:

" . . . As it has come down to us the passage is extremely obscure, and it does not even appear clearly how much Pytheas asserted that he had himself seen, and how much he had heard; whether he had only heard of the stiffened and congealed sea (the Polar Sea), while he had really seen the condition that he compared to a lung. . . . What Pytheas himself saw may have been the ice sludge in the sea which is formed over a great extent along the edge of the drift ice, when this has been ground to a pulp by the action of waves. The expression 'can neither be traversed on foot nor by boat' is exactly applicable to this ice sludge. If we add to this the thick fog, which is often found near drift ice, then the description that the air is also involved in the mixture, and that land and sea and everything is merged in it, will appear very graphic."

It is, then, among the firsts of Pytheas that he gave us the initial European description of that almost preternaturally dense fog which you find where warm and cold waters sort of brush against each other, particularly if the cold waters contain fragments of ice. Specifically, he described to us the meeting of the icy Greenland Current with the comparatively warm sea north of western Iceland that derives its temperature from the Gulf Stream.

The fog that Pytheas describes will lie for days and even weeks so dense that the horizon of visibility is in dozens, scores, or hundreds of yards. But a shift in the wind may bring clear weather any time and a sky of greater clarity and farther vision than any with which Pytheas can have been familiar in southern latitudes. With such a clearing Pytheas would have seen the noble cliffs and the towering peaks of the Scoresby region or of the Blosseville coast.

Pytheas may have seen them. We think he did not, for there is nothing so frequently emphasized by Greek and Roman commentators as the distinction of Thule in being the farthest land beyond Britain, the most remote of lands. In saying this we refer, of course, only to those writers who either took Pytheas seriously or who discussed him in a hypothetical sense—that if his yarns were fact (which the writer usually disclaimed believing), then Thule would be the last land on earth, the land beyond all others, the land nearest the slushy and stiffened waters of the northern sea.

CHAPTER IV

The Irish Discover Greenland

WE FEEL REASONABLY SURE that Pytheas did not discover Greenland proper, but only its fringing stream of southbound ice with its cloak of fog; for apparently he was in a position to see the land during but one day and the quotations that have been preserved from him tell only about the slush and the fog. But we feel we know that people from Ireland, and perhaps others from Scotland and from Norway, were in a position to see Greenland upon innumerable days in the course of a number of centuries that preceded the Norse colonization.

To begin with, there is the interpretation of many scholars that the people of northernmost Scotland told Pytheas about Iceland and how to reach it. But if the Scots were in the habit of sailing to Iceland they were certainly in the habit also of moving back and forth across the North Sea to the Bergen region of the Scandinavian coast. A. W. Brögger is among the more recent of many writers who have argued that Norwegian seafaring is of ancient date. Nor can we see any logic in thinking that there was such a difference in ability or enterprise between the Scots and the Norwegians that the islanders could visit the mainland without the mainlanders learning how to return the visit.

True, Scotland is a bit nearer to Iceland than is Norway— it is 500 miles from Scotland, 600 miles from Norway. But the Faeroes are so located that they are almost as logical a halfway station when you come from Norway as if you were coming from Scotland. Then there cannot have been much traffic between the Scots and Norwegians without a deal of conversation, and the Scots would have told the Norse what they had told the Greeks. It seems probable, then, that sailors from the Scandinavian countries, from Britain, and from Ireland were all of them in the habit of visiting Thule from time immemorial.

But if you have the enterprise to visit an island you are sure to have the curiosity to circumnavigate and explore it. And as we have said before, you cannot go far offshore from northwestern Iceland without being in a position to see both countries, Greenland looking ahead to the northwest, Iceland looking back southeast. You cannot climb the mountains of northwestern Iceland on many different days without some-time catching a glimpse of the Blosseville coast. Mirages are frequent, but you do not need a mirage. The mountains of the two countries are of such height that the tops are inter-visible whenever the skies are clear.

We shall deal later with the first recorded Norwegian who saw Greenland, which was about the year 900; here we merely remark that he was apparently on his way to take up a homestead in the northwest of Iceland and was, therefore, on an ordinary coasting voyage such as anyone would make who for any reason was following the west shore north.

Now there happens to have been just the difference between the vessels of the Irish and those of the Vikings that, while both were seaworthy, the Norse were a great deal better for keeping up into the wind. This meant that an offshore breeze was much more likely to carry an Irish ship than a Norwegian one into sight of the Blosseville coast.

It is because the Irish may have had chances to see Green-land during their voyages that we must scan every possibly significant thing they have to say in their folklore, their traditional literature, and in their sober chronicles about their seafaring, particularly to the northwest and north of Ireland.

We consider first, then, what they and others who knew believed about their ships and what could be done with them. This resolves itself into gathering their views on curraghs and curragh voyages, for the proof is ample that vessels of hides stretched upon a wicker frame, with oars, sails, and steering gear, were standard in their voyaging.

When first we know of them the Irish were a seafaring people and believed themselves long to have been so. By their oldest traditions, they derived their culture from settlers who came in ships from the eastern Mediterranean. They had the belief, too, that there had been a Danish immigration before the Christian era.

In the first century A.D. Tacitus said of Ireland that although the people and climate were similar to those of England, the navigation and harbors of Ireland were better known, through merchants and commerce. A century later Ptolemy was able to give a list of sixteen communities in eastern and southern Ireland. He speaks of the Hebrides as belonging to Ireland and not to Britain—a further indication of Irish cultivation of the sea.

O'Kelly finds cumulative evidence that in this period, when Ireland was both culturally more advanced than Britain and farther developed in seamanship, the curragh was the mainstay of her navigators, although they had wooden ships also. At least into the sixth century the curragh, to judge by Irish lore, maintained itself in the confidence of the people as the right craft for long journeys. This is substantiated by the Brendan legend where we learn that for his projected voyages St. Brendan built a curragh with mast, sail, and steering equipment. He took in it provisions for forty days and butter to dress the hide as needed.

Estimates vary on the number of men per curragh. "In the Life of the Book of Lismore," says Hornell, "three curraghs are mentioned, each carrying twenty persons; in the Metrical Life the number is raised to thirty in each." This curragh was made of cowhide, tanned in bark.

On his first voyage to Iona, 563 A.D., St. Columba had twelve companions. Logan says that the length of Columba's skin boat is usually given at forty feet but that "from its dimensions preserved in an earthen mound at Iona it appears to have been sixty-four feet long"—thus about the size of the longest skin boats reported from the Eskimos.

Cormac, one of Columba's disciples, used a curragh in his three voyages in search of an uninhabited island. On the third journey a wind drove the boat steadily northward, where he and his companions "found themselves beset by unfamiliar dangers." After fourteen days the wind changed and they returned home.

That the Irish believed the skin boat as suitable for voyages to the Mediterranean as to Iceland, we learn from "The Overflowing of Lough Neagh, and the Story of Liban the Mermaid," where it is told that St. Comgall sent Beoc from Bangor to Rome in a curragh to discuss church matters with Pope Gregory.

Bran, of seventh-century Irish lore, was a great voyager and is said to have traveled with a fleet of three skin boats, each having a crew of nine. Another figure of the seventh century, or the beginning of the eighth, Maeldun is, according to Joyce, more certainly historical than Bran. He made a curragh journey with sixty-three people.

It is, then, in accord with the uniform tradition of the Irish that sea voyages of from one to six weeks in length were numerous, and that although wooden boats were known the curragh was the ordinary and seemingly the preferred vehicle. Thus it was in ships which the Irish people trusted that their heroes—imaginary, real, usually a little of both—voyaged the high seas in quest of the things they most desired. Cormac and many another were seeking an island without people; the desire to find solitude in which to worship God better is a usual motive given by the tales. Brendan, Bran, and many in their class journeyed so they might view in distant places the greater glories of God and the strange miracles of His handiwork.

Whatever the motives, the Irish believed their heroes to have reached lands beyond the western sea.

The Irish saint Brendan, called also Brandon or Brandan, is said to have been born 484 A.D. in Tralee, Kerry, and to have died in 578 as abbot of a Benedictine monastery which he had founded twenty years earlier at Clonfert in eastern Galway. The traditional date for his celebrated voyage across the Atlantic is 565–573, and the earliest extant account of the journey is from the eleventh century.

The tales of Brendan's voyages and discoveries, with many variations, are among the most widespread of western European folk literature; they occur in prose or verse in Latin, French, English, Saxon, Flemish, Irish, Welsh, Breton, and Scottish Gaelic. Although there is no Arabic variation of the voyage, several of its incidents appear to have been incorporated into Arabic legends, among them landing on a whale mistaken for an island. It is generally considered that many of the adventures later attributed to Brendan were borrowed from the legend of the seventh- or eighth-century Maeldun.

Solambier, in a critique of Roman Catholic historians whom he upbraids in connection with the relation between the Vatican and Greenland, points out that in the fourteenth and fifteenth centuries the Brendan narrative was generally believed, by Church and laity. But during the century or two that followed the voyages of Columbus and Cabot, faith in the Brendan accounts dwindled, for no one discovered lands that could be identified readily with his descriptions. More recently historians of geographic discovery and students of folklore have applied to the narratives a sober criticism analogous to that by which we differentiate between factual and imaginative elements of the Bible, and a rehabilitation of Brendan has tended to be the result.

Use, for instance, the device to separate from the Brendan narratives what sounds miraculous, the things which are in accord with the now discarded "superstitions" of the Middle Ages. Place in another grouping the things which could readily be true according to our standards, and you will find in this second lot the framework of a voyage narrative both credible and with places and conditions reasonably identifiable—the directions of travel are approximately correct; the descriptions seize upon striking features of places with which we are now familiar; even the distances between, as measured in sailing days, seem reasonable.

Still, the method is chiefly applicable to the earlier voyages —the tales about journeys to the places identified as the Hebrides, the Faeroes, the Shetlands, Iceland (and, as we think, Jan Mayen). These accounts are comparatively simple; on that it is difficult not to agree with the Reverend Denis O'Donohue, whose *St. Brendan the Voyager in Story and Legend* we shall therefore parallel and paraphrase.

Except by mere passing inference, we shall pay no attention to the journeys which criticism has related to the Hebrides, Shetlands, and Faeroes, beginning our detailed consideration with what has been interpreted as a description of an iceberg, or, more reasonably, of a glacier front. It is our bent to feel it unlikely that Brendan was the first European, or even the first Irishman, to see these things; but he seems to be the first whose account has survived in a recognizable form.

We feel somewhat more strongly than O'Donohue that it is hard to winnow much wheat from the chaff of the later Brendan voyages, those of forty days and a tangle of miracle and didacticism; they are not represented as being in the direction of Greenland, anyway, so they fall beyond our limits. We agree with O'Donohue that the early voyages, those of eight, seven, or fewer days, are reasonable in the distances that are given in days of sailing. The descriptions themselves, making allowance for intentional "improvement" and for perversions due to misunderstanding by narrators who memorized them and passed them on, are identifiable with known conditions and places; the religious teaching and preaching are within bounds.

If we take in the usual order the descriptions which have been identified with those of a glacier front, of Iceland, and of Jan Mayen, it will appear that the saint and his companions first sailed northwest from Ireland to southern east Greenland, from there to Iceland where they followed the south coast east and the east coast north, and finally to Jan Mayen.

We dip into the narrative where Brendan approaches Greenland, where his "column in the sea" may have been an iceberg. This is the usual identification; we, as intimated, feel the description more nearly corresponds to that of a glacier front. Such a front might be a good many hundred feet sheer from the water; there would be caverns hollowed out by the waves through which a boat could enter, and there could be galleries such that you might row out from them through a different archway; from a distance the cliff of the glacier front would blend with the inland ice and the slope could rise toward 9000 feet, nearly two miles into the sky; with the coast clear on a summer's day it is not unusual for the tops of the mountains to be hidden by cloud. Many writers have testified that nothing they ever saw is so romantic, that nothing so combines the awe inspiring and majestic with the fairylike as does a glacier front when you are near or beneath it in a small boat. Even so, there is imagination and a deal of embroidery in what, as we suggested above, may be the first preserved description by a European of a glacier that meets the sea and rises to the clouds:

"One day," says a version of the Brendan narrative, "they saw a column in the sea, which seemed not far off, yet they could not reach it for three days. When they drew near, St.

Brendan looked towards its summit, but could not see it, because of its great height, which seemed to pierce the skies. It was covered over with a rare canopy, the material of which they knew not; but it had the colour of silver, and was hard as marble, while the column itself was of the clearest crystal.

"St. Brendan ordered the brethren to take in their oars, and to lower the sails and mast, and directed some of them to hold on by the fringes of the canopy, which extended about a mile from the column, and about the same depth into the sea. When this had been done, St. Brendan said: 'Run in the boat now through an opening, that we may get a closer view of the wonderful works of God.' And when they had passed through the opening, and looked around them, the sea seemed to them transparent like glass, so that they could plainly see everything beneath them, even the base of the column, and the skirts or fringes of the canopy, lying on the ground, for the sun shone as brightly within as without.

"St. Brendan then measured an opening between four pavilions, which he found to be four cubits on every side. While they sailed along for a day by one side of the column, they could always feel the shade as well as the heat of the sun, beyond the ninth hour; and after thus sailing about the column for four days, they found the measurement of each side to be four hundred cubits. On the fourth day, they discovered on the south side a chalice of the same material as the canopy, and a patena like that of the column. . . . Next day they rowed towards the north, and having passed out through an opening, they set up the mast, and unfurled the sails again, while some of them held on by the fringes or skirts of the canopy, until all was right in the boat. When they had set sail, a favourable wind came on in the rear, so that they had no occasion to use the oars, but only to hold the ropes and the tiller. And thus for eight days were they borne along towards the north."

Actually the direction would be northeast, if Brendan stood

parallel to the Greenland coast until he could see Iceland.
But in those days, as in ours, it was common to speak of as
north or northerly any direction between northwest and northeast.

In preparation for the Brendan account of what has been
identified as Iceland, we review those qualities of the island
which are suggested by the description.

Iceland is perhaps the most volcanic of all countries. Much
of it is today covered with lava so recent that we think a good
deal of it may be only one or two thousand years old, so that
Brendan may well have come at a period more actively volcanic
than any since the history of the land became continuous (following 870 A.D.). Still we have reports from the last thousand
years of the earth shaking, the rocks being cleft, fire, smoke,
ash, and lava belching forth. There have been vile fumes and
clouds of steam from rents in the crust, rivers of boiling water,
and gushing springs—one of which, named by the Icelanders
Geysir, has conferred its name on springs of that sort wherever
we now find them.

This volcanic land has coasts more rugged than any in Europe, more spectacular to the view of those who approach from
the sea. There are no trees, and even bushes are not likely to
be found unless you go some way inland. There is a great deal
of bare rock, although stretches of lowland may be fertile and
the slopes may be green and lush.

It is a commonplace of vulcanism that during an eruption
clouds of ash and smoke may darken the sky and pillars of
them may be seen from afar. The evil smells may be carried
scores if not hundreds of miles to seaward. When streams of
molten rock flow down the slopes into the ocean there is a
mighty fuming and sputtering; the sea boils like a furious
caldron, and there are clouds of steam. The hiss of water
against the lava stream may be heard a mile or two away; the
reverberation of a volcanic outburst can be heard still farther,
of course.

So much for the pertinent facts of nature. We must keep in mind, too, as we read the Brendan account, some of the applicable beliefs that were common in the Middle Ages.

Hell was under the earth and was manifest through such things as earthquakes, volcanic eruptions, hot springs, and fumes. Since it was beneath the earth, and roomy enough to accommodate the multitude of the wicked, Hell was extensive and had many gates. The chief portals were two: in the south, Vesuvius of Italy (or Aetna of Sicily); in the north, Hekla of Iceland. (A modern version of the belief in these northern and southern gates of Hell is the Jules Verne story of an underground journey between Snaefellsjokul in Iceland and Stromboli in the Lipari Islands.)

The strictly Christian belief was that the devil ruled in Hell, but Vulcan and other heathen gods had ruled beneath the earth previously. There was a mixture of the Christian with the heathen views, and sometimes it was considered that dwarfs and partly transfigured heathen gods were smiths down in the ground and that the smoke and flames came from their furnaces, the noises from their hammer blows and from their wheezy and resonant bellows. One of the satisfying variants of this belief was that if you found a crack in the earth, through which smoke and heat were arising, you could drop into it a hunk of iron with an appropriate number of silver coins and come back later to find a sword or ax fashioned from your iron—always a good weapon and sometimes with magic qualities.

With such facts as these in memory, and these beliefs, we turn to the part of the Brendan narrative which some consider to have been originally a description of Iceland, upon which were later hung festoons of medieval embroidery.

"When those [eight] days had passed, they came within view of an island, which was very rugged and rocky, covered over with slag, without trees or herbage, but full of smith's forges. . . . they heard the noise of bellows' blowing like

thunder, and the beating of sledges on the anvils and iron . . .
Soon after one of the inhabitants came forth to do some
work; he was all hairy and hideous, begrimed with fire and
smoke. When he saw the servants of Christ near the island,
he withdrew into his forge, crying aloud: 'Woe! Woe! Woe!'

"St. Brendan again armed himself with the sign of the
Cross, and said to the brethren: 'Put on more sail, and ply
your oars more briskly, that we may get away from this island.'
Hearing this, the savage man . . . rushed down to the shore,
bearing in his hand a tongs with a burning mass of the slag,
of great size and intense heat, which he flung at once after
the servants of Christ . . . It passed them at a furlong's
distance, and where it fell into the sea, it fumed up like a
heap of burning coals, and a great smoke arose as if from
a fiery furnace. When they had passed on about a mile beyond
the spot where this burning mass had fallen, all the dwellers
on the island crowded down to the shore, bearing, each one
of them, a large mass of burning slag, which they flung, every
one in turn, after the servants of God; and then they returned
to their forges, which they blew up into mighty flames, so
that the whole island seemed one globe of fire, and the sea
on every side boiled up and foamed, like a caldron set on a
fire well supplied with fuel. All the day the brethren, even
when they were no longer within view of the island, heard a
loud wailing from the inhabitants thereof, and a noisome
stench was perceptible at a great distance. Then St. Brendan
sought to animate the courage of the brethren, saying: 'Soldiers
of Christ, be strong in faith unfeigned and in the armour of
the Spirit, for we are now on the confines of hell; watch,
therefore, and act manfully.' "

Jean Charcot has identified Brendan's next point of call as
Jan Mayen Island. Charcot was more famous as an Antarctic
explorer but is recognized also as an authority on the Green-
land-Iceland-Jan Mayen district, and as a historian and medie-
valist, particularly a student of voyages—see, for instance,

his book *Christophe Colomb vu par un Marin*, Paris, 1928. It appeared to him that Brendan had sailed 300 miles north from northeastern Iceland and had given us the first known description of Jan Mayen.

The island is tiny, only thirty-four miles long, generally narrow, and so particularly narrow in the middle that it has nearly a dumbbell shape. There is nothing remarkable about it except a mountain that is perhaps the most remarkable in the world, rising as it does from the shore steeply to greater heights than any other mountain that stands right by the sea.

Iceland is frequently described as having the most spectacular of coast lines, but none of its mountains by the sea attain more than 4000 or 5000 feet. Beerenberg's volcano towers 7680 feet. The crater is resting now; in Brendan's time it may have held aloft a torch flaming into and above the clouds.

The Brendan account says:

"On another day there came into view a large and high mountain in the ocean, not far off, towards the north, with misty clouds about it, and a great smoke issuing from its summit, when suddenly the wind drove the boat rapidly towards the island until it almost touched the shore. The cliffs were so high they could scarce see the top, were black as coal, and upright like a wall. . . .

"Afterwards a favourable breeze caught the boat, and drove them southwards; and as they looked back, they saw the peak of the mountain unclouded, and shooting up flames into the sky, which it drew back again to itself so that the mountain seemed a burning pyre. After this dreadful sight, they sailed for seven days towards the south. On a rock washed by the sea they found and talked with Judas Iscariot who, on certain Lord's Days, was allowed to leave the island of demons and cool off.

"St. Brendan afterwards made sail for some time towards the south," and passed from the sphere of our immediate concern, the region of Greenland's ice cliffs, Iceland's heat and fumes, the towering peak of Jan Mayen.

These, then, are the sections of one version of the Brendan legend that may refer to Greenland, and to those way stations from Europe to Greenland, Jan Mayen and Iceland.

Most students seem to feel that probably before and certainly after Christ the Irish prowled the sea to their northwest enough so they had many chances to see Greenland. Perhaps Brendan had one of these. With a few of the trimmings removed, his is a good description of such ice fronts as are common on the southern east coast. If it was near Cape Farewell the given sailing distance north to Iceland, eight days (seven in other manuscripts), is not badly out—many a sailing vessel has taken more time than that in recent centuries though others have made it in less.

We feel that Brendan probably saw Greenland; probably also Iceland and possibly Jan Mayen.

It may be that the first little disputed and fairly datable reference to Iceland in the literature of Ireland is by Adamnan, Abbot of Iona (679–704), where in his life of Columba (521–597) he refers to three ocean voyages which were made by Cormac in search of an uninhabited island in the ocean. This reference does not sound as if Cormac were an explorer in the modern sense, just looking to see if there might be an island; rather it appears he was searching for an island about which he had information and of which he had been told that it was uninhabited—in other words, a land that had been visited but not colonized.

It is a trait of the early references to Iceland by the Irish that they speak as if it were well known, which implies that it had long been known. There is never any suggestion of who first discovered it nor any indication that there was a still-surviving interest in who had been the discoverer. Thule was more remote than Scotland and thereby stranger; apart from this, they took Scotland and Thule equally for granted.

In his *De Ratione Temporum* the Venerable Bede, who lived from 674 to 735, speaks of some contemporaries of his who had been in Thule and who reported that in midsummer the sun was there continuously visible for several days—showing that they had been on the north coast, which implies that they, or others of their time, had circumnavigated the island. But this means passing between Iceland and Greenland, thus with a chance of seeing the Blosseville coast.

Apart from tales like Brendan's, vague, full of irrelevancies and needing much interpretation, the first thing concerning Iceland that is more than a passing reference is a discussion of astronomical and other natural phenomena in Thule contained in the work *De Mensura Orbis Terrae,* of which there are several manuscripts in various European libraries and of which we have three printed editions.

The author of the *De Mensura* was an Irish monk resident in a Continental university at the time he finished this work, A.D. 825. We know of him little except what we gather from his own writings: As a teacher he resided in the Frankish Kingdom during the "Carolingian Renaissance," probably at the court of Charlemagne and of Louis the Pious. Between 814 and 816 he compiled installments of an astronomical treatise as a series of yearly gifts to Louis the Pious.

From Dicuil's own statements, and from the implications of his writings, we think of him as grammarian, astronomer, and geographer. He was a wide reader, for he no doubt read more authorities than he cites, and he cites at least thirty.

The *De Mensura Orbis Terrae* is a work on geography. *Britannica* gives as Dicuil's chief distinction that this work " . . . contains the earliest notice of European discovery of and settlement in Iceland and the most definite western reference to the old fresh-water canal between the Nile and the Red Sea,

blocked up in 767." There is plenty of evidence from other
sources that what Dicuil tells about the Nile canal is substan-
tially correct; the sufficient confirmation of his report that
the Irish were cultivating Iceland around 795 is that the
Norsemen who began to visit Iceland around 850 tell us that
when they arrived they found Christian Irish people there
before them.

The mentioned three editions of the *De Mensura* are all in
Latin: the Walckenaer, Paris, 1807; the Letronne, Paris,
1814; and the Parthey, Berlin, 1870. The first two are printed
from a tenth-century manuscript in Paris (Biblioth. Nat.
4806), and the last from a tenth-century manuscript in Dres-
den (Regius D. 182). Later manuscripts are to be found at
Cambridge, Munich, Oxford, Rome, Venice, and Vienna.

The steps in the discovery of Iceland are necessarily steps
in the discovery of Greenland. We quote, therefore, what
Dicuil has to say about the Faeroe Islands:

"The Faeroes: There are a great many other islands in the
ocean to the north of Britain which may be reached in two
days' and nights' straight sailing, with a favorable wind, from
those islands which are north of Britain. A holy man worthy of
belief related to me that in two summer days and one night
between, in a little boat of two thwarts, he landed upon one of
them. These islands are for the most part very small. They
are nearly all separated from each other by narrow straits,
and upon them, for almost a hundred years, hermits sailing
from our Scotia (i.e., Ireland) lived. But just as they have
been deserted from the beginning of the world, so, now, because of the Norse pirates, they are empty of the anchorites
but full of a vast horde of sheep and many different kinds of
sea fowl. We have never found these islands mentioned by
any authors."

The Faeroes, a cluster of islets and rocks, are visible from
afar, since they are of mountain contour, the highest of them
about 2900 feet.

It is nearly or quite inevitable that the Faeroes would be discovered from Scotland. The passage between Scotland and the first of the Orkneys is scarcely wider than the Mississippi, and you can see from island to island in that group. The farthest of the Orkneys could not be long inhabited by people who had come by water from Scotland before somebody was caught by a southeasterly or easterly wind so that he drifted in sight of the Faeroes.

The Faeroes discovered, people would every now and then head for them from the Orkneys, from the Shetlands, or from Norway. Do this several times; on one occasion you will miss them in thick weather, and then it is not far until you will see Iceland ahead of you when the fog lifts. This, as we shall see a little farther on in discussing Naddodd, was exactly how the Norwegians, around 850, are said to have rediscovered Iceland.

Perhaps the discoverers of Iceland did find the country in just that way—by striking toward the Faeroes and missing them. The discovery may not have been earlier than Pytheas, although we think it probably was. At any rate, it was so long before Dicuil's time that he had either no knowledge of or no interest in the discoverer; voyages between Thule and Ireland were such a commonplace by his day that it did not occur to him to describe them, even though the one he mentions was made at the very worst time of year—when the weather is coldest, about the most stormy, and with days as yet very short. For the men he tells about left Ireland in January. The year was 795—if it was, as Dicuil says, thirty years before he wrote about it in his book.

We give in full what Dicuil tells about Iceland, translating his Latin from the Parthcy cdition, Berlin, 1870:

"Ever since I got together a pamphlet about ten questions involved in the art of grammar, I have thought a book ought to follow about the extent of the earth's regions, according to the authority of those whom the holy Emperor Theodosius sent to measure those regions; and I wish to show, with some supplementary material, following the distinguished authority of Pliny the Younger, what the extent of these lands is."

From page 1 of the Parthey edition, where the above is found, the matter is irrelevant and we skip. Pages 41 to 44 are the ones that take us island by island from Europe to Iceland and therefore within possible sight of Greenland:

"We do not read of any islands being in the sea west or north of Spain. Around our own island of Hibernia [Ireland] there are islands, but some are small and others are infinitesimal. Near the island of Britain there are many islands, some large, some small, and some middle-sized; some are in the sea to the south and others to the west, but islands are found more abundantly in the region of the Arctic Circle and the north. Upon some of these I have dwelt, others I have landed upon, others I have just seen, and others read about.

"Pliny the Younger in his Book IV informs us that Pytheas of Marseilles relates that Thule is six days' sailing distant from Britain. In Book XIV he speaks of it as always deserted. Isidore in his *Etymologiae* writes as follows: 'Thule; the remotest island of the ocean between the northern and western zones beyond Britain, taking its name from the sun because the sun makes there its summer solstice.'

"Priscian in his *Periegesis* speaks of it more clearly than Isidore:

"He skims with his ships the open plain of Ocean,
Coming to Thule which gleams both day and night
With Titan's rays, he ascends with his car to the poles
Of Heaven, kindling the boreal realms with his torch.

"Julius Solinus, in that portion of his selections dealing with Britain, writes more clearly and fully than Priscian about this same island, thus: 'Thule, the remotest isle, where during the summer solstice when the sun crosses the constellation of Cancer, there is no night, during the winter no day.'

"It is now the thirtieth year since some monks who dwelt upon that island from the Calends of February [February 1] to the Calends of August [August 1] told me that not only during the summer solstice but also during the days near that time, towards evening, the setting sun hides itself as if behind a small hill, so that there is no darkness for even the shortest time; but a man may do whatever he wishes, actually pick the lice from his shirt just as if it were by the light of the sun; and if they [the monks] had been on top of the mountains the sun probably never would have been hidden from their eyes. In the middle of that short period of time it is midnight in the middle of the earth; and so I believe that, on the other hand, during the winter solstice, and during a few days around that time, dawn occurs for only a brief time in Thule, that is to say, when it is mid-day in the middle of the earth. Therefore [it is evident that] those are lying who have written that the sea around Thule is frozen and that there is continuous day without night from the vernal to the autumnal equinox; and that, *vice versa*, from the autumnal to the vernal equinox there is perpetual night; those monks who sailed there during a time of year when naturally it would be at the coldest and landed on this island and dwelt there always had alternate day and night after the solstice; but they found that one day's sail from it towards the north the sea was frozen."

Since Dicuil, like Pytheas, gives six days of sailing as the distance from the British Isles to Iceland, it seems likely his "day of sailing" was about equal to our "100 miles." Like Pytheas he gives, then, 100 miles as the northward distance from Iceland to the ice of the Greenland Current.

It is about 180 statute miles to Greenland from northwestern Iceland, and the ice stream of the Greenland Current normally fills less than half the width of the strait, so the estimates of our two authorities are about right, if one is steering the nearest way, which is northwest. Nor is the distance necessarily wrong if you go straight north, for on that course you might easily meet floes of the same Greenland Current inside a hundred miles.

Scholars who feel ungenerous toward the claims of the Irish are wont to concede first that there is no doubt in their minds that Dicuil conversed with people who had been in Iceland, then to say it is suspicious to find our author quoting Pytheas about it being six days northward from the British Isles to Iceland, and finally to say, as if not quoting him but some priests who had been in Thule, the very same thing that Pytheas says about how far it is from Thule to the edge of the ice. These critics make two suggestions: that certainly Dicuil, and likely enough the priests, knew the Pytheas estimate; and that the priests did not *find* the ice a day's sail north of Iceland, as Dicuil makes them say they did, but merely believed it was there because they believed Pytheas.

But what else than a day's sail (100 miles) could these wretched victims of the critics have reported? A hundred miles is what you and I would probably have to report if we tried it out; that is what the priests discovered if they did make the voyage. Is it not too much to demand that a traveler disagree with a previous traveler on a correct distance estimate just to show he is not a plagiarist?

CHAPTER V

The Icelanders Discover Greenland

AN EXACT DATE cannot be assigned to the first Scandinavian voyages to Iceland, but they must have been around the year 850. For us the significant thing about them is that the Norse literary sources agree with those of Ireland on the main point: The Irish say they were in Thule before the Norse; the Norse say they found the Irish there upon arrival.

It is disputed whether the first recorded Scandinavian to visit Iceland was a Swede or a Norwegian. We give first the earliest reference to the Swede, translating it from the Hauksbok version of *Landnama* as used by Thorvaldur Thoroddsen in *Landfraedissaga Islands,* published at Reykjavik, 1892: "Concerning Gardar: A man was named Gardarr, the son of Svavar the Swede. He owned land in Sealand but had been born in Sweden. He went to the Hebrides to collect his wife's inheritance from her father. When he sailed through the Pentland Firth he got into bad weather and his ship was driven out into the western sea. He struck land east of Horn where there was a harbor. Gardarr sailed around the country and determined that it was an island. He entered a fjord which he named Skjalfandi. They put out a boat manned by Nattfari and by a slave that belonged to him. The rope (by which they were being towed) broke and the boat went ashore in Nattfaravik beyond Skuggabjörg. Gardarr landed on the other side of the fjord and spent the winter. That is why he called the place Husavik (Bay of Houses). Nattfari stayed behind with a man slave and a woman slave; that is why the place is called Nattfaravik. Gardarr sailed back east and praised the land greatly, naming it Gardarsholm (Gardar's Island)."

We translate from the same work the account of the Norwegian who was there just before or just after Gardar:

"Concerning Naddodd: A man was named Naddodd, the brother of Öxna-Thorir, brother-in-law of Ölvir Barnakarl. He was a great Viking. He settled in the Faeroe Islands, for elsewhere he was unwelcome. He sailed from Norway towards those islands but went astray at sea, struck Gardarsholm, reaching Reydarfjord in the Austfjord district. They climbed the highest mountains to see if they could discern any dwellings of people or smokes but they saw none. As they were sailing away from the country, a heavy snow fell on the land; therefore they named it Snowland."

The third of the recorded Norse explorers was Floki, who put out from the Shetlands to look for Gardarsholm. Like their two predecessors his party struck the east coast. They sailed westward along the south coast. Their account of the various fjords and of the qualities of land and sea are more circumstantial than those of the earlier visitors; no doubt they took more interest because they came with definite purpose to settle. After a winter on the west coast they climbed one of the high mountains and saw, for the first time in their lives, ice floating about in the sea. Apparently this was one of the exceptional years when strong northwesterlies bring the Greenland pack to Iceland.

From this view of pack ice by a tenderfoot, a place whose coldest winters are less cold than those of New York State received the name Iceland. That name will probably rest through all the millenniums of history upon a land whose capital city in midwinter has about the temperature of Milan, a land from which half its present inhabitants have never seen a cake of sea ice, a land where children have difficulty in learning to skate because the ice on the ponds is seldom strong enough.

There were three chief men on this first Norse colonizing expedition, Floki and his colleagues Herjolf and Thorolf. The sagas relate that when, after two winters spent in Iceland, the party returned to Europe they told three stories. According to Floki the land had no merits; according to Herjolf there were good and bad points; according to Thorolf there was scarcely a drawback.

It was a joke on Floki that Iceland some years later became so fashionable that he felt he had to join the crowd and move there—when the best parts had been homesteaded, so that he, who once could pick, now must be content with land which others had rejected.

Floki's colonization attempt had failed because he got discouraged. The first permanent Norse settlement was made by the second to attempt it, Ingolf, in 874. He colonized the district where has grown up, through ten and a half centuries, the largest city in Iceland and it present capital, Reykjavik, with about 40,000 inhabitants in 1942.

None of the accounts of Gardar, Naddodd, and Floki say anything about any of them finding Irish people in Iceland; there are even specific denials that human signs were discovered. Historians do not, however, consider this to place the three saga narratives in real opposition to Dicuil, since the fourth and best account of Iceland's first period does tell that the Irish were there ahead of the Norse.

Iceland is, after all, a big country, about one fifth larger than Ireland, with many bays and fjords; and the sagas claim for the first three voyagers only that they touched at a few places and climbed a few mountains for lookout purposes. Still the Irish cannot have been numerous or they would have been found.

It is consonant with all we know from Norse and Irish

sources to suppose that there were only a few score or a few hundred Irish in Iceland when the Norse colonization began —about seventy-five years after the voyage of Dicuil's anchorites.

The *Islendingabok* (Book of the Icelanders) is considered to have been written about 1122 and was composed by the famous historian Ari Thorgilsson. We translate from the Reykjavik, 1891, edition of that work the passage about the Norsemen finding the Irish ahead of them:

"Iceland was settled originally from Norway in the days of Harald the Fair Haired, son of Halfdan the Black. . . . The man is named Ingolf, a Norwegian, about whom it is truly said that he was the first to go thence (from Norway) to Iceland when Harald the Fair Haired was 16 years old, that he went a second time some winters later. . . . At that time Iceland was forested from shore to mountains. There were already in the country Christian people whom the Norsemen called Papar, but they went away later for they did not want to dwell here in association with heathen. They left behind them Irish books, bells, and croziers, from which it may be seen that they were Irish."

The other great source on the colonization of Iceland by the Norsemen is the *Landnamabok* of Sturla Thordarson (1214–84). We translate from the Reykjavik, 1891, edition, pp. 25–26:

"Before Iceland was settled from Norway, there were here people whom the Norse called Papar. They were Christians . . . there have been found as remains of them Irish books, bells, croziers, and other articles which show that they were Westmen. These were found to the east in Papey and in Papili. Moreover it is stated in English books that at this time there were sailings between the countries."

Westmen had been for a century or more the regular Norwegian designation for the Irish, and was logical since the Irish were not only west of Norway but also west of England

and Scotland, countries with which the Norwegians were also thoroughly familiar. The word had become so germane to the language that by the time of the Icelandic colonization it was just a name and its use was continued by the Icelanders, although Ireland was now to the southeast. (Occasionally the word was so used that it would include any inhabitant of Great Britain.)

Up toward 900 there was, in miles, no further historically known progress in the unveiling of the New World. But there was other progress, growth of Icelandic population and navigation, which made the sighting of lands that lay near to the west inevitable.

The estimates of Iceland's population are usually as of the year 930, for that is the foundation date of the republic (the first meeting of the national parliament), when there are considered to have been around 50,000 people. It is likely that in 900 there were at least 25,000. A considerable number of these were on the west coast or on the north coast so located that a ship, whether coming from abroad or from other parts of Iceland, might pass on its way to them up along the west coast. With the square sails of that day almost any wind from shore was likely to drive a coasting vessel out to sea. For the first time on record it happened about the year 900 (the date may have been as early at 877) that one of them was blown so far out that its commander, Gunnbjorn, on making Iceland reported finding some skerries and that he had seen land to the west of them.

There has been dispute as to what land Gunnbjorn found. The general opinion was later, after Greenland became well known, that he must have seen islands that lay in the sea between Iceland and Greenland, and there his skerries appeared on the maps of the Middle Ages. But no such islands lie there now, and what he saw may have been something else than land. That suspicion arises from his having been apparently on his first voyage to Iceland when he reported the discovery.

If so, this was doubtless the first chance of his life to see an iceberg. If he had been in Iceland before he still may never have seen one, since they are rare visitors, and then only to a few parts of the country. Even sailors familiar with icebergs and expecting to see them have frequently taken them for islands or for headlands of a mainland, and have so reported them in their logs and set them down on charts. It appears likely enough, then, that what Gunnbjorn saw were drifting bergs of landlike configuration; perhaps moraine-covered or flecked and coated with wind-blown sand.

There is some doubt about Gunnbjorn's having reported other land west of the skerries. *Landnama* has an ambigious passage: "[Erik the Red] said he intended searching for that land which Gunnbjorn . . . saw when driven by storm into the sea west of Iceland when he found the Gunnbjorn skerries." Does this mean that he found skerries and saw another land or that he found land which was later named Gunnbjorn's Skerries? Most have favored the interpretation (as we did above) that the land and the skerries were two discoveries made at one time.

The foregoing is on the basis of the skerries being far from the land seen west of them, which was in the Middle Ages a usual view. Holm contends that the skerries were the islands of the Angmagssalik group. His interpretation of the sources which say or imply that the skerries were something like halfway from Iceland to Greenland is that by "Greenland" was meant not the whole land mass which bears that name today but only the colonized part of the west coast.

Around 950 a red-haired boy named Erik left the Jaeder District of Norway in the exiled family of his father Thorvald Asvaldsson who was guilty of manslaughter. They settled in Iceland and occupied various farms on the west coast, one of them so located that if they climbed the right peak in the right kind of weather they can have seen Greenland.

In what was apparently due course for that family, Erik

was outlawed from Iceland in 981 for three years because of manslaughter. He decided to spend those years in the exploration of the "land seen by Gunnbjorn." That is how the saga states it specifically. It is merely a brace of conjectures that Gunnbjorn's story had been reinforced since his time by at least somebody's seeing Greenland from Icelandic mountaintops, and that there had been other, though now lost, reports resembling the Gunnbjorn story of sailors who had seen skerries to the west (such reports being based either on mis-identification of icebergs with land or upon actual sight of the coast).

When Erik sailed for Greenland in 981 he had, considering the probabilities of the case, a ship between 70 and 100 feet long, partly decked, with oars, and with a square sail on a mast that could be stepped down. The vessel was clinker built and therefore, while otherwise seaworthy, badly suited for meeting the pressure of ice.

Using the methods of those who, from stray facts and reasonable conjecture, patch together lives of Jesus or of Shakespeare, we can piece out an account of the voyage which in the main is correct, although any single point may well be wrong.

The crew of the ship, then, consisted of Erik and his wife and children, his slaves and their children, and perhaps some freedmen with their families. There may have been a neighbor or two who wanted to come along, then similarly accompanied by family, slaves, and other dependents. The slaves and freed-men, and perhaps some of the others, will have been Irish, but most of the party were Icelanders of Norwegian ancestry or of Norwegian-Irish mixed. There were between twenty and forty people, and they carried most or all of the common Ice-landic domestic animals—horses, cattle, sheep, goats, dogs, pigs, and perhaps fowls. They had hay to feed the livestock. They carried some grain for food, but more of dried and other fish, and they probably caught fish over the side. They cooked

little on shipboard; if and when they did it was on an open fire
built on flat stones.

We have pointed out that the Norwegians knew nothing
about sea ice until they began their acquaintance with it west
of Iceland and that Gunnbjorn may be the first Norseman on
record to see an iceberg. The attempt by Erik to reach Greenland was, apparently, the first determined attack upon sea
ice in the recorded history of European civilization. For, to
judge by Pytheas and Dicuil, the Greeks, the Irish, and presumably everyone else before 981 turned back where they
met with the ice of the Greenland Current.

Erik sailed west from the Snaefell promontory of Iceland
and therefore approached Greenland near where now is the
Angmagssalik District. Coming to the edge of that stubborn
south-moving pack, which, to this day, makes it difficult for
ships to reach that coast, there were probably the same violent
local gales which we now have, and there was certainly fog
caused by warm waters sideswiping the ice and the cold of the
East Greenland Current. Whenever the weather cleared, there
would be the tantalizing sight of the coast line ten to thirty
miles away; between them and it was that heaving pack which
was more than capable of breaking ships much stronger than
any that existed in those days—indeed, capable of breaking,
if the nip is just right, any ship that was ever built.

It may have taken Erik's party several weeks to fight their
way slowly southwest along the edge of the Greenland shore
pack until they rounded Cape Farewell and were finally able
to make the beach, somewhere in what is now the Julianehaab
District. Then Erik put his ship broadside to the land; the
animals jumped or were pushed out and they swam or waded
ashore; the people landed, built houses and barns, made hay
for the stock, and spent the winter in the Icelandic fashion.

On the way to Greenland they had doubtless milked the
cows and perhaps the sheep and goats, and they had butchered
some animals as part of their food. They did similarly this

autumn and winter, shearing or plucking in the spring, and making clothes from the wool.

In the three years of banishment Erik explored the coast between the south end of Greenland and where now is the Godthaab District (around 64° N. Lat.), perhaps even well beyond. During this time he formed a colonizing plan. In that connection the saga has it that "he thought people would all the more desire to go there if the land had an attractive name," So he called it Green Land.

Erik's party returned to Iceland in 984. During the winter they "sold" Greenland so successfully to the Icelanders that in the spring of 985 twenty-five ships started back with him. Some were lost and some turned back, but fourteen won through. The average number aboard ship is believed to have been near twenty-five, so the colony numbered around 350. They reported no hardship and no loss of life the first season, nor did they until a ship, years later, brought from Europe an epidemic disease through which a number died.

It was the southern west coast and not the whole of the vast island continent which was named Green Land by Erik the Red. We think the naming pure salesmanship if our scale for comparison is the implication of John Davis who, in 1586, christened the same district Land of Desolation, and, indeed, if we accept for Greenland the conception that has been usual since Davis. But another Englishman came along a few years later and called the same region the Land of Comfort— James Hall in 1606.

Green Land, the Land of Desolation, the Land of Comfort —whichever you prefer, you will agree that calling it so takes no more poetic license with that shore than is required with the shore of Massachusetts to call it a "stern and rockbound coast." This, among other things, gives us reason to compare the first Norse colony in western Greenland with the first English colony in eastern Massachusetts.

But antecedent to a comparison between the colonies should

be a description of the colonists. Those of Plymouth are so
well known to every reader that we need not portray them;
those of Eriksfjord are less widely known.

For the period around 1000 we usually generalize about
Scandinavians by calling them Norsemen, whether they are
from Denmark, Iceland, Norway, or Sweden. These particular
Norsemen were from Iceland, but, like other Americans of
later times, they had a mixed ancestry.

We have pointed out that the first inhabitants of Thule
were, so far as we know, from Ireland. They are frequently
referred to as priests and anchorites, and some have jumped
to the conclusion, from the modern institution of Roman Catholic church celibacy, that only men were involved, or that, if
there were women, they were cloistered nuns. However,
celibacy had not come in as yet among these people. That an
Irishman was a priest had no more bearing upon his being
single or married than is the case today with Methodists or
Presbyterians. The Irish in Iceland, so far as we know, had
the usual proportions of men, women, and children. It is
recorded in the Icelandic literature, as quoted above, that most
of them left the country when the Norwegians came because
they were devout Christians who did not want to associate
with the heathen Scandinavians.

But many of the Norwegians came to Iceland by way of
Ireland, some of them having lived there two or more generations, perhaps from around 807 to the beginning of active
colonization in Iceland following 870. Some of the chieftains
are known to have had Irish wives. The immigrants had both
the institutions of polygamy and of slavery. Second wives as
well as concubines were frequently Irish; most of the slaves,
whether men or women, were Irish.

Then, as we said, there was friendly intercourse in Ireland
as well as hostility between the Norwegians and the Irish.
Wholly Irish families congenial to Norse chieftains would
accompany them to Iceland.

Many of the Icelandic colonists who had not resided in Ireland had resided in the Orkney Islands, the Shetlands, or in Scotland, there particularly in the region of Sutherland and Caithness. In these districts they had intermarried with Scots, some of whom, however, would probably be looked upon as Irish. A few of the colonists had lived in England.

During a century or more following 870 piracy was one of the chief occupations of Iceland. Then it was the equivalent of our college education, or of the Grand Tour of a century or two ago, for the sons of Icelandic chieftains to make expeditions of one, two, or several years with one, two, or several vessels. These were a combination of three things. They were frequently visits to kings, earls, and other nobles, particularly those related to the Icelandic chieftains; they were trading voyages, and they were buccaneering cruises. A man would, for instance, spend the winter at the court of the King of Norway, go to a British or continental shore for several weeks of trading, and then, his goods sold and his wares safely on board ship, he would start plundering.

It is considered that one of the commonest regions plundered was the coast of Ireland, where the freebooters went ashore and carried away practically an entire farm—the farmer with his wife, family, and servants, and with his domestic animals and household goods, the Vikings stealing at least enough of the hay and grain to feed the stock on the way to Iceland and likely tearing down the buildings for timber which, from the earliest time, was scarce in the northern island.

In Iceland the chief occupation was animal husbandry. There were other pursuits, but none of importance. Grain was cultivated but never very successfully; there was fishing but on a small scale only, nothing to approach an industry.

These, then, were the people who left Iceland for Greenland. It is believed by some that 90% of the blood of the modern Icelander is from Norway, the remaining 10% chiefly from Ireland. At least one authority, Gudbrandur Vigfusson, the famous lexicographer and translator into English of the Icelandic classics, believes that 50% came from Ireland. It is perhaps not far wrong to suggest that 60% is from Norway, 30% from Ireland, 4% from Scotland, with 2% each from England, Denmark, and Sweden. However, some of the Irish blood came in later than the colonization of Greenland; so that, although we know there were some Irish people along, the community of Erik the Red's time was in the main of Norwegian ancestry.

All but the few Irish, and a still smaller number of Norwegian converts, were heathen. The Christians were generally women; for in that day it was considered an effeminate or pusillanimous religion, appropriate for women, servants, and slaves.

The Greenland colonists were, as said, about 350, as against 102 for Plymouth. The Greenland records show that there was no famine the first winter, that there were no hardships to impress the colonists, and that the mortality rate was normal —the last we know because some years later an epidemic came, brought by an incoming ship. From the explicit record of the resulting deaths we feel sure that there would have been a similar account of deaths during the first or second years had they been numerous, or if they had been from an exceptional cause, such as scarcity of food or harshness of climate. In contrast the accounts of the Plymouth colony tell of hardship and of scarcity of food, resulting in the death of half the settlers during the first winter.

CHAPTER VI

The Greenlanders Discover America

THE DISCOVERIES of San Salvador and Haiti are to most of us the Columbian discovery of America. The discoveries of Iceland and Greenland are for the same reason the pre-Columbian discovery of America. For you cannot sail much around one of the Caribbean islands within finding a second and a third and at length the mainland; nor can you sail much around Greenland without finding Baffin Island and then the mainland.

Before the year 1000 there was a stereotyped way of sailing from Norway, or from Iceland, to Greenland. The Norwegians left their own country at some such place as Stad, nearly abreast of southeastern Iceland. Frequently they coasted Iceland, sometimes visiting or even spending a winter. But if they were in a hurry they sailed between Iceland and the Faeroes in such a way that "the horizon was halfway up the mountains" of the Icelandic south coast.

Whether from Iceland or thus from Norway, the course was westerly until you saw the first scattered floes in the Greenland Current, whereupon you sailed parallel to the coast, rounded Cape Farewell, and made your first landing probably at Herjolfsnes—at least the trading ships usually did.

It appears to have been a new departure when Leif, the son of Erik the Red, sailed in 999 from the northwest around Farewell, thence to the Hebrides, and from the Hebrides to

Norway. As was the custom of the Icelandic and Greenlandic nobility in those days, he went to the court of the Norwegian king. He was well received and spent the winter.

This king, Olaf Tryggvason, was an ardent proselyter. He had been busy the last few years converting, or at least baptizing, his fellow Norwegians, not seldom at the point of the spear. He had missionary designs upon Iceland and Greenland. The Olafssaga gives far more attention to his plans for Christianizing Iceland; but it mentions what concerns us, that he worked upon the young Greenlander through the winter and finally induced him to accept Christianity.

Now the king told Leif that since he was a Christian he ought to take missionaries with him for the conversion of the Greenlanders. The saga tells that Leif was reluctant, being skeptical on how pleased the Red Erik would be to have a member of his own family going over to the interests of what the old man looked upon as an alien and anemic creed, little suited to men of spirit.

But Leif agreed finally, and the king gave him two priests who were to help with the conversion.

Leif set sail in the spring of 1000 and took the direct route for Cape Farewell. None of the sagas which describe the voyage give the precise data for the sailing of his course, but the later Icelandic and Norwegian sailing directions which cover essentially the same voyage are that you pass not between Iceland and the Faeroes but between the Faeroes and the Shetlands, the Shetlands first on your left and presently the Faeroes on your right, giving them enough berth so that the sky line is halfway up their mountains.

We do not know whether Leif, after passing the Faeroes, took a course too far to the left for seeing Cape Farewell or whether he missed it because of fog. All we know is that when land came into view he recognized that it was not Greenland. They went ashore and found "wineberries," self-sown "wheat," and trees of various sorts, among them maples.

From the berries the land was named Vinland (Wine Land) or, from the berries and fertility combined, Vinland the Good.

They had overshot their mark and knew that the road home must be northeast. So they turned in that direction and reached Greenland during the summer.

In the summer of 1001 or 1002 an attempt was made by Thorstein, the eldest son of Erik, to reach the forested country his brother had reported. The members of this expedition were keen that the old man should go along, for they thought he would have his usual good fortune and they wanted to share in it. Erik was reluctant but was finally persuaded. His luck did not serve, for the ship was driven back and forth all summer by gales and they returned to Eriksfjord without success.

The next winter a pestilence swept the colony, carried there no doubt by a vessel from Europe. One of those who died was Thorstein, leaving a widow Gudrid.

Apparently the next summer, 1003 or 1004, the Icelander Thorfinn Karlsefni arrived in a ship that was large and especially seaworthy; another ship came with him. Thorfinn is described as an experienced navigator, which would likely mean that he had made voyages not merely to the Scandinavian countries and the British Isles but also south along the mainland coasts of Europe.

According to the grandiose custom of the time, Erik the Red invited Thorfinn and the whole company of both ships to be his guests at Brattahlid during the winter. There was much talk about the land discovered in the southwest and about the desirability that it be colonized. An expedition gradually took form, with three ships and 160 people. There were included a number of couples, among the women Gudrid, whom Thorfinn had married during the winter.

As we approach this, the chief voyage of attempted colonization beyond Greenland, we must note that the antiquarians, historians, and geographers have discussed in great detail the identification of the lands visited. However, they have devoted themselves chiefly to Vinland, the exotic country farthest from Greenland, a region of fruit, self-sown grain, and no winters. We cannot afford to get into that devious controversy and merely refer to what is no doubt the best of the many discussions, also one of the most recent, *The Problem of Wineland,* by Professor Halldor Hermannsson, 1936.

Most of the scholarly disputants have been so concerned in establishing that Vinland was in Georgia, in Virginia, in New York State, in Massachusetts, in Maine, in Nova Scotia, in the Gulf of St. Lawrence, or in James Bay at the southern tip of Hudson Bay, that they have been no more than casual about identifying the lands farther north. They usually say that the first seen by Thorfinn, Helluland, is Labrador, but admit in passing how strange it is that the saga tells us it was reached in two days from Disko Island, which means nearly 700 miles at an average sailing rate of fourteen or fifteen miles per hour, when eight was considered a high all-day speed for Scandinavian vessels of this period. Then, with Helluland (dubiously) settled as a part of the mainland, and with a paramount interest in Vinland farther south, Markland is to the commentators just an intervening stretch of forest country, Newfoundland or perhaps Nova Scotia.

Ours is a work on Greenland and we choose the reverse tack; we occupy ourselves most with what is near the main sphere of our discussion, the first and second lands rather than the third land reached by the Karlsefni expedition.

Many of the commentators on the narrative of the voyage have accepted the Icelandic word *sudur* as meaning south; which indeed it does, etymologically. But it is nearly or quite obvious that it cannot have this meaning here.

For if sudur means our south, then how can we explain the nomenclature of the sagas when they constantly speak of a western and an eastern colony on what to us is the west coast of Greenland? From discovering the house ruins we know where those colonies were; and, looking at the map, they seem to us to be a northern colony and a southern colony. The answer is that to the Scandinavians of the Middle Ages the coast from Cape Farewell to Disko Island ran east and west, although to us it runs north and south. A corollary to the solution is that medieval directional words did not mean in Greenland what their cognates mean to us now.

But in fact the coast is not east and west as the Scandinavians used to say, or north and south as we say, but halfway between, southeast and northwest.

There is a parallel modern case in New England, where people speak of going east from New Haven to Boston when actually they go northeast. And you will have a like experience if you visit the north coast of Alaska, where you hear everyone "speaking by compass." The compass around Point Barrow varies roughly 45° easterly, and the Alaskans of that coast say north when they mean northeast.

If you were to insist upon giving an etymological meaning to sudur, i.e., south, then you would be up against a difficulty when the saga tells you that steering sudur from Bear Island (Disko) they struck land in two days. It is scarcely conceivable that you could do that if you really steered south. But land would be reached in a moderate two days by steering southwest.

If we had nothing but our common sense to guide us, and were unfamiliar with the whole of northern literature except the Greenland and Vinland sagas, we would conclude that sudur would necessarily mean southwest. This happens to be also the conclusion of specialists in the eleventh-century meaning of directional words. For three of the outstanding contributors to this subject arrive at southwest as the meaning of sudur—that the variation from "true" was about 45°. A fourth authority makes the variation 60°. But whether 45° or 60°, either course will take you from Disko to Baffin Island in a reasonable two-day sail.

Changing each directional word, then, by 45°, we translate the directional passages for the Karlsefni voyage from the Saga of Erik the Red:

"Altogether the [Karlsefni] expedition had 160 people. They sailed first from Eriksfjord [in the Eastern Settlement, present Julianehaab] to the Western Settlement [present Godthaab] and then to Bear Island [Disko]. Thence they sailed two days southwestward, when they discovered land. They manned a boat and explored the land, finding large flat stones, some of them 12 ells [18 feet] wide. Foxes were numerous. They gave the land a name and called it Helluland [Flagstoneland].

"Thence they sailed two days, turning from their southwest course to a south course, and discovered a forested country with abundant game . . . [This was Markland, Forestland.]

"Thence they stood southwest along the coast for a long time."

A line drawn southwesterly from Disko will strike near Cape Dyer, the easternmost point of the Cumberland Peninsula of Baffin Island. So, in relation to the known speed of Scandinavian merchant vessels of the period, the speed of sailing to this point is moderate. For it is 270 miles from Disko to Cape Dyer, and in two days that is a daily average of 135 miles or five and a half miles per hour, when there were, according to Hovgaard, known cases of 170 miles per day, seven miles per hour.

Then Flagstoneland, where there were numerous foxes, is reasonably Baffin Island southward from Cape Dyer.

The southward course which the expedition now follows is from Dyer to Cape Chidley in Labrador. That direction fits the map, but the distance is 450 miles in two days, or an average of nine miles per hour—high, though well possible on account of the favoring Labrador Current.

But it would be strange if two centuries of oral transmission, before the story of Thorfinn was set on vellum, had not resulted in a number of unintentional changes. It is perhaps on the whole likeliest that these changes would be in numbers, in sailing days; figures are hard to remember, especially when they bear on things the memorizer does not understand, like distances between places where he has never been.

Besides, there is another way to interpret the distances in this saga. We cannot doubt that if the course was south in Greenland terms, southwest in ours, from Disko Island, then it will have to be Baffin, in the vicinity of Dyer or Walsingham, that was for Karlsefni the beginning of Helluland. It is possible to understand the saga as telling us that from the first place the expedition landed in Baffin Island to the first one where they stopped in Labrador is the two sailing days mentioned. But it is equally reasonable to consider that what the original narrator had in mind was the distance from the last place touched at in Helluland to the first place touched at in Markland.

It is true, moreover, that by calling a certain country as a whole Land of Forest you do not commit yourself to saying that it is forested throughout. It may very well be that after the navigators had crossed Hudson Strait they sensed a special continuity in the land, so that when they arrived at the first trees, and later at more of them, they gave the Forestland designation to the entire stretch that appeared to them continuous.

So the name Markland, Land of Forest, may well have begun to apply at the treeless northern point where Labrador starts for us. To earn the name, there was not even the need for continuous forest in any large fraction of the country. Names are not so fully descriptive. California is popularly known as the Golden State, and for a sufficient reason, but the gold is found only here and there. Iceland did not even get the name from snow on its high mountains, but from drifting cakes in the ocean, seen at a distance. You could name a country Land of Forest though you did not strike the first

bit of conspicuous woodland until you had coasted the shore
for some distance.

And then we must consider both that our explorers came
from a land without trees and that the word "forest" had a
meaning in their language quite different from ours. This
hinges upon their geography and history through the ninth
and tenth centuries.

The people to which the explorers belonged had been in
Iceland a little more than a hundred years when Erik sailed
for Greenland. Many of their forebears came from heavily
forested parts of Norway and from moderately forested parts
of Ireland. But there were many of them, also, who did not
come from either Ireland or Norway but from the slightly
wooded Sutherland and Caithness districts of Scotland or
from woodless island groups, the Shetlands, Orkneys, Hebrides, and Faeroes.

The sagas, written 200 and 300 years after the colonization,
speak of Iceland as having been forested when the settlers
arrived, but all the botanical and geographical indications are
that the "trees" and "woods" mentioned by the narratives were
only what we would think of as bushes and brush—alder and
willow and things of that sort. The tallest "trees" in Iceland
today are near thirty feet and people make long journeys to
see them. It is a forest there when bushes, few of them taller
than a man, cover fifty or a hundred acres. You even have
forests where the bushes are only waist-high. It was no doubt
like that in Greenland; they would have spoken of forest
when we would speak of brush.

To Greenlanders, and to Icelanders, then, you have forested
country in Labrador before you get a third of the way south
along the coast from Cape Chidley.

When the sagas enthuse about the trees of Markland they
say they are large enough for use in houses. But we learn from
the archaeologists that, while Greenland dwellings were moderately large in the aggregate of rooms, the individual rooms

were usually small; a rafter of twenty feet was a long one. So it would have been a big tree to a Greenlander that was more than half the size of one of our telegraph poles.

Markland was perhaps just Labrador. But it may have included Newfoundland, the Gulf of St. Lawrence, and Nova Scotia, perhaps going down well toward New England. Here they sailed by long reaches of forested shores. The sailing periods are not given in days, but they are rather obviously a good deal longer than the two days required from Disko to Baffin Island and the two from Baffin to Labrador (or to the first woods, in Labrador).

Ari the Wise tells us in his *Book of the Icelanders,* and a number of other sagas have like information, that when Thorfinn Karlsefni and his party saw the natives of Vinland they concluded that they were the same race as those whose remains Erik the Red's party had found when they first came to Greenland. It may be that Indians farther south than the Eskimos used skin boats and stoneware, but we know that the Eskimos used both and therefore have no reason to doubt the identification reached by Thorfinn and his party.

Another good Eskimo sign is that when a large number of the natives arrived at Thorfinn's camp the motion of their paddles gave the impression that staves were being waved in a circle; for this is just the impression you get when a number of Eskimo kayaks are approaching you with rapid use of the double-bladed paddle—you feel as if you were looking at the spokes of a revolving wheel. It is possible that more southerly Indians used the double paddle, but we know the Eskimos did; all of them did until recently and many still do.

The Karlsefni account mentions that the natives carried with them in boxes a mixture of blood and marrow. Travelers have described from the Eskimos, and apparently from no other American people, the custom of removing marrow from the long bones of animals killed and placing it in bags or boxes. Gradually the blood serum drains from the marrow, and when you open the bag or box you see the chunks of marrow awash in the red blood somewhat as if you were looking at cherries or other fruit bathed in its own red juice.

Another sign that we are probably dealing with Eskimos is the account of the battle which says that the natives used catapults. Here we must remember that the catapult was not a part of the war equipment of the Icelanders or Greenlanders and can hardly have been known to them except from hearsay —through being seen by the Vikings and other Norse travelers, such as Karlsefni himself, on their long voyages southward in the Old World.

And if the catapult was little known, the Eskimo throwing stick was wholly unknown. In the excitement of battle you do not perhaps observe so very closely. But you would notice strange things, particularly if they were effective against you. Some of Karlsefni's men were slain with missiles. It seems probable enough that when Thorfinn, years later, was trying in Iceland to describe the use of throwing sticks by the Skraelings he spoke of these people as using small catapults, hand catapults, or the like. In the verbal transmission of the battle narrative through two or several generations before it was transcribed the instruments would become just catapults. (It is obvious they could not have been regular catapults, for those were used in siege warfare; the saga describes the natives as scrambling up the beach and showering the Greenlanders with missiles.)

It seems fairly clear, then, that Markland was wooded country, and perhaps some country not wooded, farther north and east than New England. The location of Vinland is more doubtful. The chief talking points in that case are the maple trees, the self-sown wheat, and the wineberries of the narrative. Vinland is described as a country where all these grow.

It is agreed that maples are maples; they are readily identified but they do not mean much for identifying a country, for

they can be found in New England and as far north as Newfoundland. The general view is that the self-sown wheat is
wild rice and that this also may be found well into the section
called Markland. So far as wild rice and maple go, Vinland
and Markland can overlap.

The dispute, then, centers on the wineberry. No one disputes that usually, in the literature of the saga period, the
wineberry is a grape. The average translator of the Vinland
sagas just says "grape" and lets it go at that in the rendering
of his document; then he enters upon long discussions as to
how far north and east it is possible to encounter the wild
grape in North America now and how far north it may have
extended 900 years ago. This seldom takes the critic northeast
beyond the limits of New England. But it may enable him to
get into the St. Lawrence basin, and Vinland could perhaps
have been on a shore of the Gulf.

Since the main theme of our present work is Greenland,
we do not care to go far into the voluminous, tangled, and,
on the whole, fruitless Vinland controversy. Our one contribution is the note that it is rather arbitrary to demand that
grape shall be the translation of *vinber*. For, in daily speech,
a vinber is just a wineberry—whatever berry is commonly
used for wine making in a given locality. Vinber is, for instance, used for certain small red berries that grow in the
country around Narvik and Tromsö in northern Norway.

So far, then, as the mere case of the wineberry is concerned,
Vinland could have been farther north than Markland. Actually, of course, it was farther south; for the records are clear
that the progression was from Green Land to Flagstone Land
to Forest Land to Wine Land, which latter was some coastal
district still farther south than Markland, or farther west—
at any rate farthest of all the named places from Greenland
and most different in climate.

We barely mention the astronomical part of the Vinland
dispute, as to what the sagas tell about the length of day. The

Norsemen of this period, with all their seafaring, were not astronomers and mathematicians like Pytheas, and those are undoubtedly right who agree with the famous Norwegian scholar, Gustav Storm, that, so far as the length of day is concerned, Vinland could have been as far south as New England.

CHAPTER VII

Greenland Becomes a Christian Republic

THE RECORD of colonizing voyages, which began with Erik the Red's fourteen ships in 985, extends to the voyages of Einar Sokkason, with two ships, from Norway in 1124, one of them his own and Greenland-manned, the other a Norwegian vessel with a load of Norwegians who wanted to become colonists. However, the return of the Karlsefni expedition from Vinland in 1006 had marked the close of the most active period of Greenland's settlement.

It seems likely, then, that the period of comparatively large-scale immigration was less than one hundred and fifty years, although settlers would keep arriving sporadically in later centuries. As in Iceland, there was no doubt considerable addition to the population, after the main colonizing era, through merchants who came to trade but remained as permanent settlers. In Iceland such men sometimes remained because they liked country and climate; perhaps more often they stayed because they had married during the winter or had acquired other personal connections. Since most things we know were similar in the two countries, it is likely that in Greenland also there were these contributions to the population.

Similarly there is no doubt that every now and then Greenlanders emigrated. We have some specific accounts of returns to Iceland; others will have gone with Norwegian traders to Norway and (particularly in the fourteenth and fifteenth centuries) with English traders to England. There are, too, as we shall see later, accounts of captives being taken in Greenland and carried away by freebooters, probably English.

The most thoroughgoing student of medieval Greenland history was Dr. Finnur Jonsson of the University of Copenhagen, distinguished linguist, antiquarian, and historian, professor there of Scandinavian philology. He concluded, in a publication of 1928, that the greatest total population of the Eastern and Western Settlements combined was probably around 9000. He does not assign a year or decade for this highest population, but we would think it might have been during the second or third centuries of the Greenland republic.

As with the colonization of Iceland which followed 870, we have in the Greenland sagas an extensive listing of the noblemen involved, together with their wives in many cases. There is an occasional mention of special friends of theirs who, by statement or implication, are of lower rank; on rare occasions even a slave gets notice, but only for a very special reason— usually because he killed somebody or was himself killed in a way that started a feud. Broadly speaking, the sagas are chronicles of the wellborn.

Greenlandic political and social forms and ways of life are known from the literature and from archaeology to have been about the same as those of Iceland. We are safe, therefore, when we interpolate from the better-known record of Iceland to fill the gaps in our knowledge of Greenland.

In Iceland it took from 870 to 930 for the condition to develop which led to the establishment of a republic with a main parliament for the whole country, though with subsidiary parliaments. That was, shall we say, because the people had to evolve away from monarchistic concepts. In Greenland such an evolution was not required, for most of the settlers came from Iceland. It may be, then, that the Greenlanders called their first

parliament within, say, five years after 985. That is an inference, for we do not have, as we do from Iceland, any account
of the meeting of the first national assembly. What we do feel
sure of is that there was a parliament before 1000.

Politically, then, Greenland, though a republic, was a land
where only the nobility and gentry had an audible voice in lawmaking and in shaping affairs; no doubt women, freedmen, and
even slaves had minor powers, but only indirectly. The republic was elaborate in its codified law, and there were men of
learning who pronounced it, the law speakers, lawmen. The
difficulty was, as in Iceland, on a national scale what we have
recently seen on the international—the laws and other decisions of the supreme governing bodies of the republics were
what the decisions and proclamations of the League of Nations
have been—they were ever so just and legal but they had no
teeth in them. Not that these republics failed as quickly as the
League; for the Icelandic lasted from 930 to 1262 and the
Greenlandic from about 990 to 1261; but the seeds of decay,
and even of death, were congenital.

The parliament of Greenland had two names. One of them
was Althing, meaning supreme parliament, or parliament of all
(the nation); the other was the Gardar Thing, so called from
the place it met, Gardar, which was also (after 1126) the seat
of the Greenland bishopric. Like the parliament of Britain, the
Althing was both the supreme lawmaking body and the supreme court.

As we have implied, the chieftains were so jealous of their
power that they were nearly unanimous in not delegating any
of it to the government; they stood together and saw to it that
the legislature and judiciary developed no executive branch.

None of the chieftains, however, no matter what their
power or temperament, seem ever to have tried interfering
with the making of laws; they did not have to, for they could,
with sufficient force of arms, set at nought any decree of the
parliament as a supreme court or, indeed, the decree of any

court—for the subsidiary or local parliaments also had court functions.

The sagas of Iceland are full of law decisions interfered with by powerful chieftains through the use of force. In the Saga of Einar Sokkason is an example of how force was used in the Greenland parliament—in this case to prevent the court from rendering a decision rather than to upset a decision rendered.

In connection with the main parliament of Greenland, and no doubt the subsidiary parliaments as well, there was a law speaker, a man who knew and interpreted the law. He had great influence but no power beyond the reach of his persuasiveness and his friendship. The speaker might lay down the law, but a powerful chieftain would simply decide not to obey or not to pay attention. He would stop, if necessary, those who wanted to carry out the law.

This being the situation, those prominent men who had litigation before the Althing as a supreme court, or before another parliament as a subsidiary tribunal, would ride to the meetings under arms with as many of their retainers and their friends as they could muster. The parliament was, of course, aware of the comparative armed strength of the parties to the litigation. In some cases, therefore, they declined to render a decision, foreseeing it would be useless. In other cases they no doubt rendered decisions according to the man power of the litigants, but of this there is less clear evidence. Not infrequently a decision rendered was followed by a pitched battle, started by a loser before the court who thought himself able to win by the sword.

An informal function of the Thing was no less important than some of the formal, and this applied to the subsidiary and provisional gatherings as well as to the national parliament. People went to them in part as outings and to hear news. There would come for participation in the intellectual and social life men who had been on foreign voyages, those who had hunted far up the coast, anyone who had special things to relate, and there were the poets and half-professional raconteurs as well. There would be, of course, a certain amount of conversation and informal talk; but the main events were semiformal, when those with news, or the poets and the accomplished narrators of tradition, would hold forth to a circle, usually in the open air.

A thing which increased the value of these gatherings in the preservation of reliable history was that there were in nearly every group of listeners men well informed on the topic and as appreciative of the truth well stated as they were critical of any exaggeration or deviation from fact. This put every narrator upon his mettle and led besides to corrections when facts were mishandled. The corrections had at times startling accompaniment: if there was thought to be malice in a falsification the narrator had better look out. Fist fights were rare, it seems; but there were a lot of killings with sword, ax, or spear.

It was considered particularly appropriate in the blood feuds to attack or challenge a narrator who was holding forth about the things wherein you felt you had a duty of revenge. In this, as in the rest of Greenland life, there was a close parallel with Iceland. We have many instances from stories of the Icelandic parliament, and some from Greenland, where narrators were slain. A famous case is that of the Icelander Thormod Kolbrunarskald who spent three years in Greenland as part of a blood feud (1025 to 1027 inclusive) and finally killed his opponent, Thorgeir, as he was telling a circle at the Althing about his own prowess in an earlier stage of the dispute.

It is believed that in the establishment of the parliament, and during its first years, the laws of Greenland were identical with those of Iceland—that they were taken over somewhat as the American colonists took over the English common law. Presently there was, however, special Greenlandic legislation. We shall find an example of this in the Saga of Einar Sokkason, the case there being that special statutes had been passed in Greenland which made the laws of salvage and of flotsam and jetsam different from those of Norway. The Icelandic law under these heads was in this period the same as that of Norway, so we know that the Greenlanders must have passed their own legislation.

Of the two most important and most famous decisions made by the parliament of Iceland we have a known parallel in Greenland for one; there is an ill-supported case of probability for the other.

In the year 1000 messages arrived both in Iceland and in Greenland from Olaf Tryggvason, King of Norway, that he desired both countries to accept Christianity. Although in form no more than a wish, since the Norwegian king had no rights in either of the countries, there was behind it a threat of force. This king had in his own land a well-known propensity for suggesting baptism one year and forcing it the next at the point of a spear, so Icelanders and Greenlanders might have thought it the better part to accept the invitation rather than deal with a fleet of warships.

Both countries were already partly Christian at this meeting of the millenniums, although in both cases the religion was still unfashionable—looked upon as proper for women, slaves, and the lower grades generally but as effeminate and scarcely fitting to men of rank and spirit.

It is not clear from the voluminous Icelandic records to what extent the mailed fist in the velvet glove was responsible for the action of the parliament; the speechmaking was more to the effect that the country was seriously divided in factions between adherents to the old and new religions; that the heathen were tolerant and did not much care what people believed but that the Christians were fanatics and always nagging everybody about their religion. It would save trouble to decide in favor of the new religion, which was done.

Some have maintained that the case was probably similar in Greenland. They feel it reasonable that when Leif Eriksson came ashore in Greenland on his return from the mainland of North America the Althing may have been still in session; and that between his own persuasiveness and that of the two priests whom he brought with him they may have secured from the session of the year 1000 (more likely the one of the following year, 1001) a decision similar to the Icelandic—that, officially, the country should be Christian, without, however, placing penalties upon the heathen.

But the evidence seems rather against this. The weight of it seems to be that Christianity did not get full sway in Greenland until perhaps 1020, then probably through informal consent rather than by a parliamentary decree.

The momentous decisions of 1261 and 1262 are known to have been made through both the parliaments of Iceland and of Greenland. The actions of the two were, in effect, identical— each destroyed the independence of its country and made it a part of a foreign kingdom, Norway. Or, at least, that was Norway's contention—that Iceland and Greenland had voted themselves provinces subject to Norway.

The King of Norway had suggested to both countries the advantage of joining Norway. The arguments were several.

It seems in accord with the spirit of the time, although there is not much documentary evidence, that one of the reasons for the action of both parliaments was the sway of Christianity. Both Church and State had at this time an ideology and a setup fundamentally monarchic and dictatorial.

In the case of the thirteenth-century Church, authority came from God through Jesus, through Peter, through the bishops of Rome, through the popes, and from the popes through cardinals, archbishops, bishops, and lesser clergy. Like the Pope, the state derived authority from God by the prevalent doctrine of the divine right of kings and transmitted this downward through officials and through nobility and gentry. In essence, then, a republic was heretical; for it derived its authority from the people below, not from God above.

Then there was a tendency for small Scandinavian nations to want to identify themselves with the power and prestige of Norway. That country was in the thirteenth century no longer so powerful as it had been in the days when Scandinavians furnished Russia with its kingly house, when they took a large part of France to make it into Normandy, and when the Battle of Hastings was fought in England between kings, one of whom, the invader, was Norwegian on both sides while the other, who fought on the defense, was Scandinavian on one side. Still Norway was strong; the ties of blood and social organization were strong; commerce with her was more extensive than with any other country.

Commerce brings up the third of the main reasons for the fateful votes of the two republican parliaments, and doubtless the most important. The King of Norway promised the Icelanders and the Greenlanders that he would foster shipping, improve commercial relations generally. This was probably the main hope of both democracies.

At any rate, the Althings of Greenland and Iceland took parallel action in 1261 and 1262, each deciding that its country should join Norway.

We do not know the status on which the Greenlanders thought they were joining the Norwegian kingdom; we can say we know it for Iceland, but with the qualification that not all Icelandic authorities have agreed as to what the Icelandic position was. However, it is fair to say that through most of its history, perhaps through all its history since 1262, Iceland has steadfastly maintained that what they thought they were entering into was a partnership—their position, then, being similar to that of (no doubt) a majority of Scots when Scotland joined England.

With about as much consistency as the Scots, the Icelanders

have maintained since 1262 that any subservience has been due to force and not to law or justice.

It may well be, though the records are lost, that we could maintain for Greenland as for Iceland that although they became in effect a province, or a sort of colony, the original understanding had been that they should be partners, at the least a semi-independent country, with some such relation to Norway as Canada now has to Great Britain.

We suspect the Greenlanders were deceived about many, if not most, of the circumstances and probabilities of their agreement. We know they were deceived on the one that was to them the most important, commerce.

Before 1261 ships of all nations had been free in their sailings to Greenland. We learn from the Saga of Einar Sokkason that at least three (perhaps more) Norwegian ships were in the Western Settlement during one year, late in the first half of the eleventh century. We do not know what other ships may have been in the Eastern Settlement at the same time—the saga is not a commercial report for the year or the decade; it is a story of intrigue and battle and covers only the people involved in the dispute between the bishop of Greenland on one side, supported by Einar and the rest of the Greenlanders, and on the other men who had arrived from Norway to collect an inheritance and who were supported by the captains and complements of the three ships that are mentioned.

It has been considered that there may have been during the republic as many as six ships per year in Greenland from various countries, chiefly from Iceland and from Norway. Then the Greenlanders also possessed their own vessels, but they were not as large, and were presumably not quite so seaworthy, as the trading ships of the foreigners.

It was not long after Norway secured what she maintained was a legal right over Greenland before the Crown sold a trade monopoly to a firm of merchants in Bergen, and not so very long thereafter until one ship came in six years instead of six

ships in one year. The gap was sometimes even longer; for it
might be that a ship dispatched for Greenland would sink on
the way, and naturally it would in those days require a year
before the owners started worrying and two years before they
were willing to write vessel and cargo off as a loss.

The theory of trade under the crown monopoly, and indeed
the practice, was that the Greenlanders would exchange all
wares they had for all goods that were brought in, no matter
how small the quantity brought. This condition held down to
the last recorded Norwegian voyages, in the early fifteenth
century.

We see from the cumulative evidence that religion came to
play a big part in the lives of the Greenlanders.

The winter 999–1000 Leif, the son of Erik, had turned
Christian while at the court of Olaf Tryggvason to please the
Norwegian king. During the autumn of the year 1000 Leif's
mother, Thjodhild, accepted the new faith—perhaps for her
son's sake, perhaps because so many of the other women were
doing it. In any case she became almost at once a religious
fanatic and would no longer associate with her husband because he was a heathen. She built a church, near which she
erected her separate dwelling. Eventually she gave her property to the church which she had founded, and it looks as if
this may have been a considerable share of Erik's property.

In 1002 or 1003 Thorstein, the eldest son of Erik, gave
direction when he died that his property should go to the
Church. We see farther on, however, that his widow interpreted this rather liberally; perhaps she took it to mean only
his gold and silver. For the saga relates that when Thorfinn
married her she was owner of Thorstein's farm and property
in the Western Settlement.

Greenland was part of the Archbishopric of Hamburg.
This was by the arrangement which placed under Hamburg's
jurisdiction all continental Scandinavian countries and all
islands that were dominated by Scandinavians—the Shetlands,

Orkneys, Hebrides, Faeroes, Iceland, and Greenland. Vinland was also a part of the Hamburg domain, for it was considered by the Church (cf. Adam of Bremen) to be an island like Greenland and Iceland and a Scandinavian island in the sense that it had been discovered by Scandinavians.

By the records of Greenland, the first regular priest, apart from missionary priests, was ordained in Europe to the Greenland priesthood in 1055 but never got there. This corresponds with what Adam of Bremen tells us in his history, that messengers came to the Archbishop of Hamburg from Greenland and Iceland, among other countries, asking that clergymen be sent them. They asked for bishops as well as lesser priests; and, to hear Adam tell it, the requests were favorably received. However, it is pretty clear that none but missionary bishops can have penetrated as far west as Greenland that early. The Saga of Einar Sokkason is the recognized authority on this point and from its narrative, when collated with what we know from Sweden and Norway, it is clear that the first Greenland bishop was nominated by King Sigurd the Crusader either in 1123 or 1124, that he was consecrated bishop (by the Archbishop of Lund) in 1124, that he attempted to reach his seat in 1125 but got no farther than Iceland, and that he did reach Greenland in 1126.

In 1152 the bishopric of Greenland was transferred from the jurisdiction of Hamburg to that of Nidaros (the present Trondheim) in Norway. From that time most of the relations between the Vatican and Greenland were through the Archbishop of Nidaros.

A well-known exception is that in 1448 Pope Nicholas V tried to reach Greenland through a letter which he addressed jointly to the two bishops of Iceland, at Holar and at Skalholt. His doing so indicates not merely that the affairs of the Church were not taking a smooth routine way, from Pope to archbishop to bishop, but also that Rome was badly informed on political and economic conditions. In fact, they were more than a century behind the times; for it had by then been illegal for more than a hundred years for Icelanders to sail their vessels to Greenland, the privilege of navigating Greenland waters being reserved for the Bergen merchants who were holders of the monopoly grant from the King of Norway.

Generally speaking, then, the church administration of Greenland after 1152 was, like the political administration, in the hands of Norway.

Seemingly upon the authority of the Archbishop Adalbert, of Hamburg, Adam of Bremen says that both in Iceland and Greenland the bishops ruled as if they were kings. This is probably a little strong for 1075; but it was fairly well true later in Iceland, as we know from the complete records there. Likely it became true in Greenland, for it appears from the Saga of Einar Sokkason that the very first bishop to reach Greenland became, within a decade after his arrival in 1126, the most powerful man in the community.

That the Christian religious leaders should become secular leaders also was in the spirit of the old social organization and the previous religion; for the *godi* had been not merely priest and keeper of the temple but also a secular figure of the greatest prominence—equaled perhaps only by the law speaker of the parliament. There was only one speaker (except that there were subsidiary speakers for the lesser parliaments, or assizes) but there were many godis; and there came to be many priests, who worked with the bishop in things temporal as well as spiritual.

There were in Greenland sixteen churches, twelve in the Eastern Settlement and four in the Western. According to the topographic studies of Professor Finnur Jonsson their names and locations were:

Eastern Settlement

Herjolfsnes; present Ikigait.

Vik in Ketilsfjord, called Aroskirkja by Ivar Bardarson; in present Tasermiut Fjord.

Vatsdal (Vazdal) ; in present Tasermiut Fjord.
Vogar in Siglufjord; present Amitsuarssuk.
Höfdi in Austfjord; present Kagssiarssuk.
Hardsteinaberg, Dyrnes; present Sitdlisit.
Hvalseyjarfjord; present Kakortok.
Gardar in Einarsfjord; present Igaliko.
Brattahlid; present Kagssiarssuk.
Solarfjöll.
Isafjord; at western side of present Sermilik.
Gardanes in Midfirdir; at present Isaroq (?)

Western Settlement

Lysufjord; on Sandnes, near Qilaussarvik.
Hop; in Agnafjord.
Anavik; in Rangafjord.
Straumsfjord; was either at Andafjord or on Strömsnes in present Strömfjord.

These identifications are from the sagas and from other literary sources.

The archaeologists have been able to identify several of them. The Herjolfsnes church has been found; the waves of the sea have cut away much of the churchyard. The church at Höfdi has been located. So has the cathedral church at Gardar; it was dedicated to St. Nicholas. Of red sandstone, it was about seventy-five feet long but only twelve or fifteen feet wide. Near by were found the pieces of a large church bell.

The best preserved of all the ruins is that of the church at Hvalseyjarfjord, now called by the Eskimo name, Kakortok. This building was about fifty-two feet long and twenty-six feet wide; the walls, from four to five feet thick, are still standing to heights varying from nine to thirteen feet.

In addition to the churches there were at least two other religious institutions in Greenland: a monastery of the Augustinian order, dedicated to St. Olave and St. Augustine; and a nunnery of the Benedictine order. The former was at Ketilsfjord; the land around the inner part of that fjord was the property of the monastery. What are probably the ruins of its buildings have been found at Tasermiutsiaq. The Benedictine nunnery was at Hrafnsfjord, now called Unartoq.

It is considered that the population of Iceland was between 50,000 and 75,000 at the time when the Greenland population was around 8000 or 10,000. Yet the religious fervor, or at least the resulting construction activity, was so much higher in Greenland that there were not in Iceland, until well within the nineteenth century, churches as big as were two or more of the largest Greenland structures.

The situation was not one-sided. The Greenlanders were interested in the Church; the Church was interested in Greenland. Some of the Vatican's concern was distinctly practical; as a part of Christendom, the far northwestern land was required to help pay Christendom's bills. These were not merely the routine expenditures of the Church, but included were such special things as the financing of the Crusades.

Tithes were obviously paid in kind and naturally in those Greenland commodities which had a more ready sale in Europe.

We mention elsewhere that polar bears, the most valuable single item of Greenland export, were seldom if ever marketed; they were reserved for gifts, a sort of recognized and respectable form of bribery. Falcons were similarly used as gifts, but they were also sold and would then be available in the payment of tithes—all the more since princes of the Church shared with the temporal aristocracy in the cultivation of the sport.

However, the chief elements in the tithes were the same as in the commercial export. The largest contributor was the walrus, with ivory, a hide that made the favored thongs of the Middle Ages, and "fish" oil for the lamps of Europe. There were also the skins of the rest of the sea mammals and their fat; and then of course the furs from land mammals, as well as buckskin from reindeer. There may have been eider down and bird feathers generally as well.

One of the difficulties with the tithes, especially during the monopoly period after the Norwegian king sold the trading privilege of Greenland to the Bergen firm, was that all Greenland things delivered to Bergen were arriving in that port of all Europe which was most surfeited with their kind. For Greenland's sole competitors in the products of the Far North would be traders who went to the White and Kara Seas. On their return they would arrive at Bergen before they reached any of the other great commercial ports of northwestern Europe and would sell in competition with the transatlantic imports.

We shall see in a papal brief discussed hereafter that Norway's being glutted with Arctic produce was for Rome a serious problem. Or rather it was serious to the Archbishop of Trondhjem, for he was ashamed of how poor was his ability to cash in on Greenland wares for the account of the Church. The other horn of the dilemma was quite as sharp; for if he were to ship these things to countries farther south, where the price would be higher, the expense of transportation was great and the wares might spoil or be lost in transit.

One of the lights thrown upon the religious life of Greenland by the archaeologists is that they have shown a striking ascendancy of the Virgin Mary in the local development of Christianity. It is usual in the excavation of graves that you find a wooden cross, or a wooden slab, carved with devout runes; most frequent of all are references to the Virgin.

Not every grave inscription refers to a person buried there. For instance, one of the inscribed slabs found is a prayer for a woman who had been drowned at sea in a voyage toward Greenland.

Jonsson gives as sample inscriptions from the crosses and slabs: "God the Almighty guard Gudleif well," and "Thorleif made this cross in praise and worship of God the Almighty." There were occasional tombstones, and some of them were inscribed.

Most of the inscriptions are in Old Norse, the language which was then spoken both in Greenland and Iceland and which still is spoken in Iceland. Slight variations from the Icelandic are shown; but there is nothing to indicate that the two peoples had developed by 1300 or 1350 much more of a dialectic difference than there would be in Iceland itself between, say, the northwest and the southwest of that country.

In some of the inscriptions the Icelandic and Latin tongues are intermingled as, for instance: "Kristus natus est nobis [Christ was born for us]: Jesus Kristr hjalpi [may Jesus Christ be of help]."

It seems that the largest number of grave inscriptions is from around 1300. So it would appear that religious interest and fervor continued increasing through the first three centuries of the Greenland community and that it decreased thereafter. This meant, then, an upward slope from European heathenism from 1000 to 1300, and thereafter a downward slope toward the Eskimo heathenism of 1600.

CHAPTER VIII

Life and Letters in the Greenland Republic

THE GREENLANDERS seem to have been too busy between their first colonization in 985 and the year 999 to leave much record of their doings. Except for reasonable inferences, those thirteen or fourteen years are practically a blank.

By the rise of the curtain the district named the Eastern Settlement, which no doubt always contained at least three fourths of the population, had been fully colonized. Many if not most of the estates referred to in the literature of Greenland were already occupied. It is probable, of course, that some were divided and subdivided later.

In the beginning, at any rate, Greenland estates were always the property of aristocrats. Between saga accounts and the records of Church and commerce, the students of Greenland history have been able to determine that there were ninety or more estates in the Western Settlement and one hundred and ninety in the Eastern. Most of the people whose names are presented in the record were colonists of the Eastern district. A few names have come down to us from the Western Settlement, as, for instance, that of Thorstein, eldest son of Erik the Red, who had a property at Lysufjord; another Thorstein who was his partner, and those of their wives.

A collaboration of recent archaeologists and geographers with the historians has resulted in the identification of surely more than half, perhaps more than two thirds, of all the places named anywhere in the preserved written sources. What the identifications are we shall not develop beyond the use of maps for the two settlements where the chief ones have been inserted. The collaborators upon this study from the archaeological and geographic sides were numerous. The historical determination was chiefly the work of Finnur Jonsson.

We list from Jonsson ten of the leading men who settled the Eastern district, most of them companions of Erik the Red, with the places where their homesteads were:

1. Herjolf, in Herjolfsfjord, living at Herjolfsnes.
2. Ketil, in Ketilsfjord.
3. Hrafn, in Hrafnsfjord.
4. Sölvi, in Sölvadal.
5. Snorri (or Helgi) Thorbrandsson, in Alptafjord.
6. Thorbjörn Glora, in Siglufjord.
7. Einar, in Einarsfjord.
8. Hafgrim, in Hafgrimsfjord and Vatnahverfi.
9. Arnlaug, in Arnlaugsfjord.
10. Thorkell Farserk, in Hvalseyjarfjord.

It is the usual opinion that most of the best land in the Eastern Settlement was homesteaded before the year 1000 and that the Western Settlement was taken by latecomers during the eleventh century; but some of it, we know, was homesteaded by people from the Eastern Settlement—for instance, the mention of homesteading at Lysufjord by a son of Erik the Red.

The list of 190 farms in the Eastern Settlement and 90 in the Western is that of the historians; the archaeologists and geographers have been able to locate about 150 and 60. The determinations are based not only on the ruins of dwelling houses but also upon fences and upon the location of patches of agricultural land from which the stones were cleared by the medieval farmers.

The ruins of some of the churches are the best preserved of

all medieval Greenlandic structures. More instructive, how-ever, with regard to the lives of people has been the excavation of farmhouses and outbuildings, and particularly that of the graveyards. The results of these investigations fall in well with the written sources, whether annals, sagas, or church documents. For instance, the excavation of a barn with stalls for as many as 104 cows substantiates the record that milk and milk products were among the chief foods of the people; the exhumation of bodies clad in garments that have the striking continental fashions of about 1450 confirm the later frag-mentary accounts which speak of traders cultivating Greenland around the time when Columbus and Cabot were making their voyages.

The people lived in the Icelandic fashion; we read that from the sagas and confirm it by archaeology.

The dwellings in the later period had a considerable number of rooms, but none of them large. Timber was scarce, as in Iceland, and had to be imported. Much of it came from Nor-way, but it seems clear that at least as late as 1347 voyages were made by the Greenlanders to the forested sections of the American mainland or to Newfoundland, chiefly no doubt for house timber and for wood needed for utensils.

There were also sections of the Greenland coast, more espe-cially along farther north than the northern end of the West-ern Settlement, where driftwood was abundant; and ships went to fetch it. The sagas explain that this timber drifted to Greenland from the sections we call Labrador and Newfound-land, which to them were Markland. As we now know, the timber actually came chiefly from the Mackenzie River of Canada and then from the rivers of European Russia and of Arctic Siberia. In a drift of perhaps five or ten years the logs eddied through and crossed the polar basin; they came southwest along eastern Greenland, transported in the Green-land Current; they rounded Cape Farewell and passed the Eastern Settlement too far offshore for many of them to find lodging. There seems to have been considerable driftwood in the Western Settlement; but, as said, it was north of that district where most of the logs came ashore.

The walls of the houses were thick, their materials sod and stones. The more stones you have the more permanent the wall, but also that much colder the house, for a rock is a better conductor than sod. Because of the scarcity of fuel it was more important that the wall should be a good insulator than that it should be lasting. Accordingly, the proportion of stones to sod was small; many of the walls were wholly of sod, like the sod cabins of the pioneers of the nineteenth century on the prairies of our Middle West. The roofs, as in our West, were sodded.

It did not matter quite so much that churches should be warm, but it mattered that they should endure. Therefore, church walls were often wholly of stone, or with no more sod than was needed as a kind of mortar, to fill in the crevices both so as to keep the wind out and to hold the stones in place, or at least to give some of them a kind of bedding.

At Brattahlid, Nörlund excavated the ruins of a one-room house, or hall, that is probably typical of those in use during the early period of Greenland colonization. The site of the house, which may even have been Erik the Red's own dwelling, was well chosen, with the mountains at its back and in front a full view of the fjord below. The single room, which served for kitchen, dining room, living and bedroom, measures about fifty-two by sixteen feet. Flagstones are scattered here and there about the hard dirt floor, the blackened stones indicating that fires were burned at one time or another at almost any place within the dwelling. However, there is a main cooking hearth near the back wall, opposite the door.

While the cooking and heating arrangements appear primitive, a modern note is struck by equipment for running water. A spring which rises by the rear wall flows through a stone gutter to a basin in the middle of the floor, whence the overflow

Photo by S. Bengtsson

Robes found at Herjolfsnes; the man's garb is on the left
and the woman's on the right.

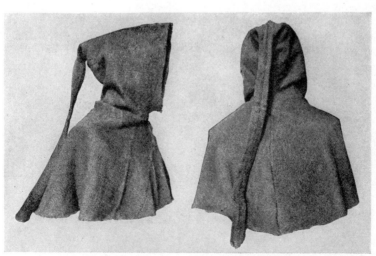

Photo by S. Bengtsson

Hoods found at Herjolfsnes, like the robes above, date from
the fifteenth century.

is carried by a narrow stone channel across the room and out under the wall near the door. The water channel was covered over with stones, which could be removed at will.

In his *Viking Settlers in Greenland,* Nörlund speculates on the purpose of this arrangement. Aside from the obvious convenience of "piped" running water within the house, there may have been the motive of having an assured supply of water in case of attack by a belligerent neighbor during one of the frequent blood feuds.

Not all buildings were equipped with this type of water supply, although most were situated so as to take advantage of springs rather than rivers. An arrangement, almost as convenient but lacking the security of an indoor reservoir, was having the spring, with a trap for catching the water, just outside the door.

From about the year 1100 the long-hall type of house began to go out of fashion. The change appears to have been gradual. At first the long hall was divided into two or three rooms; then, as need arose, smaller rooms were built on to the back of the house. Finally there was evolved the "passage house," a type characteristic of Iceland and Greenland and perhaps invented in one of these countries, with rooms opening off both sides of a corridor, much like the arrangement in many modern apartments and with similar resulting convenience to the occupants. The greatest advantage of this kind of house, particularly to people living in a country where fuel is scarce, was that not all of the rooms would need to be heated, thus requiring less fuel than one great hall. Nörlund describes a house of seven rooms which had only three very small cooking pits and no real fireplace.

However, there may have been more facilities for heating than this would indicate, for Nörlund adds that no doubt they gradually adopted the Eskimo fashion of using seal-oil lamps for illumination, for heating, and for cooking.

It has been said of Greenland farms that many of them were

equipped with bathrooms; it is more accurate to say there were bathhouses. These were small, individual structures, a few paces from the main dwelling; and, like most baths of northern Europe in this period, they were for stimulant purposes rather than for cleanliness and used steam, not water. Fire was built under large flat stones; when these and the room were terrifically hot, and with the bathers stripped, water was cast upon the stones, filling the room with steam.

Probably the steam bathers, when overheated, dashed out and rolled in the snow, if it was wintertime, or jumped into cold water—at least that is the practice with such bathhouses to this day in northerly Old World countries and was with the Eskimos of northwestern Canada and Alaska until the last decades of the nineteenth century.

The chill of jumping into water is comparable to that of passing under a shower in a Turkish bath. There is no comparable shock from rolling in snow, at least not when the snow is very dry, for it does not melt fast enough for transmitting to the sensory nerves of the skin that chill which is necessary for producing the shock familiar to city water shower bathers. It need not be thought, then, that the Greenlandic and other northern customs of bathing require greater hardihood than that of the tired businessman who relaxes in a New York Turkish bath.

From the written records and from archaeology we know that the food of the Greenlanders was at first nearly identical with that of Iceland; but there was a steady change in the direction of more dependence on hunting.

The colonists brought with them from Iceland horses, cattle, sheep, goats, and the domestic hen. There were a few pigs and there may have been some geese.

The most important animal, on the whole, was the sheep. As in Iceland and in modern Greenland, as indeed in Wyoming and Montana, they were able to feed out all winter, though it was advisable to lay up some hay in case of a spell of particularly bad weather. The sheep gave wool for most of the clothing of Greenland, and there appears to have been some for export at times, chiefly in the form of cloth. The sheep gave meat as part of the flesh food of the country; its milk was used for ordinary dairy purposes. There were barns for them, but it is pretty clear that these were in large part emergency structures—permanent buildings but for emergency use.

Like the Norwegians and the Icelanders of today, the Greenlanders used to drive their herds of sheep to considerable distances into the mountains for summer grazing. This was to reserve the home pasture for milk cows and to give the meadows a chance in the production of hay.

Again as in Iceland, the meadows were of two kinds: First came the home field, from which stones had been removed, which had been leveled and which was systematically manured, producing a heavier crop of hay and of better quality. Then there were the wild meadows with the stones still in them, without leveling or manuring, the producers of second-class hay.

From the home field, if it was of any size, and from the wild meadow, the hay was brought home in pairs of huge bundles carried by the horses. These were in Greenland the same sturdy ponies we have today in Iceland—you may think of them as larger and stouter Shetlands. They carry a man, at reasonable galloping and other speeds, perhaps twenty or thirty miles a day. If you want to go farther, or if the journey is to be a long one, you have two ponies, riding them alternately.

Horses were important in Greenland, then, as pack animals rather than for drawing sledges or wagons, and as steeds. They had a beef value, too; for in common with the north of Europe in this period the Scandinavians, both at home and in the American islands, liked the flesh of the horse and the steer equally. There are, indeed, references in the sagas to men who preferred horseflesh.

We judge by inference from Iceland that following the adoption of Christianity in Greenland there developed gradually a campaign against the horse as a food animal—under the prohibition of Deuteronomy that you must not eat of a beast unless it both splits the hoof and chews the cud. In Iceland, and perhaps, then, in Greenland, it became necessary to invoke heavy penalties against inveterate horse eaters, until finally the practice was stamped out. The last to give up horse eating, Scandinavians are today far behind most of Europe in the re-adoption of horse beef.

It is likely that horse eating was never wholly discarded by the Greenlanders. We know, from evidence which we present in discussing the relation between Greenland and the Church of Rome, that the Vatican was grieved in the fourteenth and fifteenth centuries at the failure of its bishopric west of the Atlantic to observe some of the Church prohibitions. It seems likely (if the Greenlanders were as fond of horse meat as the Icelanders, and we cannot see why they would not be) that horse-beef eating may have persisted down to the very extinction of European culture in Greenland, down to the finally complete shift of the European Greenlanders from a life of husbandry to that of the huntsman.

Cattle were chiefly dairy animals. Calves were eaten, and some steers and bulls; but the aim of the management was always that of the dairy farmer, the meat and hide being treated as by-products.

The Greenlanders produced a lot of butter. The Saga of Einar Sokkason tells that a farmer, and evidently not one of the big farmers, had in storage at one time twelve *vaettir* of butter. This unit is considered to have approximated eighty pounds, which would mean just under a thousand pounds of butter in this one storehouse of a small, or let us say, ordinary farm.

We have little specific information about cheese, but we know it was produced.

As in most northern countries of long winters of fairly steady cold, it was customary in Greenland to butcher in the fall meat needed for the whole winter. The butchering is, then, just at that stage of autumn when sheep are fattest from grazing, and the same with cattle. The above-mentioned small farmer is said to have had in the storehouse along with the thousand pounds of butter sixty dressed sheep and "a large quantity of dried fish." Beef is not mentioned; our source is not a report but a narrative and it can well have been that the farmer had his beef in another place or that he had not yet butchered—the latter is reasonable, for we infer from the rest of this narrative that the time was about the first of September, which is early for the beginning of autumn and of autumn butchering in southern West Greenland. Still we would not have expected a record of much beef, if one had been set down; for, as said, cattle were maintained chiefly for dairy purposes.

The written sources do not tell much of chicken culture. We have in some places, as, for instance, in the Erik saga, references to the use of their down for pillows and cushions—prohibitions against the use of feathers of wild birds under certain circumstances; preferment of the use of domestic feathers. Chicken bones are found in some of the refuse heaps of the farms. Swine also are little mentioned, and it may be that they were a rarity. We do find some pig bones in refuse heaps but it is not impossible that these were brought from Europe as salt pork, or even as live animals aboard ship to be butchered on arrival in Greenland, somewhat as customary in our own and other merchant marines down toward the end of the nineteenth century. Indeed, the practice of butchering live animals at the end of a voyage, instead of bringing in their meat, comes down within the last few years and within the field of aviation. For beef animals have been flown into Hudson's Bay Company posts in the Canadian Arctic to be slaughtered.

From the beginning the Greenlanders made some use of fish; but, once more as in Iceland, there was nothing like a fishing industry, nor was there probably even a single family in all of Greenland during the first century of the republic which secured any considerable part of its food from either salt or fresh water.

The hunting of the caribou was more important than fishing, right from the start; there are more references to it in the literature than to fishing, and there are more bones in the refuse piles. However, with these as with the rest of the finds in kitchen middens, it must be remembered that the Greenlanders had dogs, traditional devourers of bones. That is one of the things which makes the bone pile an uncertain record of just what was eaten. A dog cannot very well get away with the entire head of a caribou, but he may eat every last scrap of a chicken, including bill and claws.

It seems that from the beginning there was less dependence on husbandry and more on hunting in the Western Settlement. This was only partly because the grazing facilities were less; it was rather because the hunting was better.

Indeed it was not long, as we can tell from the sagas, before the Norsemen discovered that the farther north they went the better the hunting. Within the first century it was customary to make voyages far north beyond the last farming settlement. These were no doubt at first mere summer excursions, but at any rate by the fourteenth century the hunters were spending the winter. One of the proofs of this is the runic stone found north of present Upernivik, near Lat. 73° N., about 450 miles north of the Arctic Circle, which tells of three men who had wintered there.

As Jonsson points out, the records are clear in that the seasonal round of work in Greenland was the same as in Iceland. During summer haymaking was the chief occupation. At the proper seasons were fishing, whaling, and the hunt for land animals. During the winter the men fed the stock and looked after them; the women did spinning and weaving.

A peculiar occupation developed in Greenland, that of whittling utensils and appliances from soapstone. We find in the house ruins and middens fragments of stone pots; the spindle whorls were of soapstone when in Iceland they would have been of some other material.

In the island of Hreinsey, at present called by its Eskimo name Akia, is one of the main soapstone quarries. Ivar Bardarson says of the stone from this quarry that it is the best in Greenland and that it is "so firm that fire cannot destroy it." The comparative excellence of stone from this quarry is supported by our present knowledge of Greenland. But it is a little hard to credit Bardarson when he goes on to say that the largest of the jars made from it would hold forty and even forty-eight bushels.

The clothes of the Greenlanders were in the main woven and sewed during winter. There were also garments of tanned skins. The supply of weapons and of armor seems to have been limited from the earliest time. Note, for instance, when reading our translation of the Saga of Einar Sokkason, that the Greenlanders brought out as a thing of considerable value a suit of armor so poor that it angered the Norwegians to have it suggested to them that it had value.

Iron was, beyond everything but timber, the needed import of the Greenlanders. The sagas do not tell it and the Church records, the *King's Mirror,* and other sources are alike silent, but the archaeologists have demonstrated that the Greenlanders attempted to smelt iron from local sources and had at least a slight success therein. It is not easy to date the remains of this enterprise, but the attempts were probably in the twelfth or thirteenth centuries.

We hear in the sagas much talk of the desire for corn from which to make intoxicants, but there is never talk of wanting the corn for bread or porridge. We know from papal documents and from the *King's Mirror* that many did not see bread during their whole lives; this would be, however, in the later period, after Greenland had become a Norwegian province and had fallen under the trade monopoly.

There are many sources from which we learn about the exports of Greenland, but they are scattered and the record is fragmentary. The sagas mention now and then what the merchants received in exchange for the cargoes they brought; later, when the Church began to collect tithes, we have an enumeration of the goods in which these taxes were paid. Every now and then from remote fields we get bits of information. For instance (as we shall dwell upon later) a Saracen leader who has taken prisoner a Christian prince demands, and receives, a ransom in Greenland falcons; and Scandinavian kings present to their royal cousins of southern Europe polar bears and Greenland falcons, for which they get in return supplies of port and other wines.

Greenland's chief exports were derived from the walrus. Ivory had a comparatively higher value then than it has now, and the "teeth" of these animals, as a single commodity, may have ranked highest as a source of gross revenue; but "ropes" of walrus hide will have been a close second, for these obtained a European reputation as the best in the world. Entire walrus hides were also shipped and used, no doubt, for a variety of purposes. There were also the skins of seals and of reindeer. The domestic hides were exported, those of cattle and sheep. Seal "tar" was an export commodity, and so was the fat of the whale and walrus. Woolen cloth was exported, but doubtless in small quantities. It is uncertain whether butter and cheese were real exports, but traders would buy enough of them to provision the voyage home.

All sorts of Greenland wares had to be purchased by those traders who wintered—except in the grandiose early days when it was customary, as we gather from a number of the sagas, for prominent chieftains to invite an entire ship's company to spend the winter. However, merchants so invited were apparently in the habit of giving their hosts such handsome gifts that perhaps the cost of entertainment may not have been much lower than if they had bought the necessities in the open market.

One of the difficulties in telling the story of Greenland, from its settlement by the Icelanders during and following 985 to the disappearance of the colonists around 1500, is that the chief element in the source material is the Icelandic saga and that many readers, especially American, think that a saga is folklore or fiction. This idea has become even more prevalent through the success of Galsworthy's *Forsyte Saga*, whereupon every third piece of fiction suddenly became a saga.

In truth the expression "Icelandic saga" means simply "Icelandic prose writing" or "Iceland prose narrative." The term is noncommittal on subject matter. One saga may be so lacking foundation in historical fact that you might use for it a novel foreword, that any resemblance to historical characters or events is purely coincidental; another may be as factual as a newspaper report of a train wreck or a political convention. A saga may be anything between these two extremes.

Perhaps the clearest and least biased statement on the saga that has ever been published in English is by a man whose training especially qualifies him to make it, Sir William Craigie. There can be no better testimonial to his research qualifications and sound judgment than two facts about him, that he was editor of the great Oxford Dictionary in its final stages and has now been selected by the University of Chicago to edit what promises to be a correspondingly great dictionary of the American language.

Craigie's little book, *The Icelandic Sagas,* published by the Cambridge University Press in 1913, gives the low-down on Icelandic literature of the Middle Ages. It deals out the praise with the blame and establishes what we began by saying, that the name saga carries no implication of truth or falsehood but is merely descriptive of a style of presentation, that of terse narrative prose with a minimum of coloring by exposition.

Craigie explains the cosmopolitan relationship of the Icelanders—that although they dwelt in a comparatively remote island they were great travelers and were welcomed not only at the courts of the Scandinavian kings and those in the British Isles but also on the Continent. He emphasizes that numbers of them even used to visit Constantinople, where some remained for years as members of the bodyguard of the Emperor of the East or in other positions related to the court. These travelers found it a way of increased distinction, when they returned to their homes in Iceland, to be able to tell in an attractive and entertaining way what they had seen and learned, blending the events and their ideas about them into what eventually became contributions to the written prose histories of foreign lands, the Utlandasögur.

Some of the Icelandic sagas, like the Heimskringla, are indispensable source material for the history of the Scandinavian countries, Ireland, Great Britain, and the smaller surrounding islands; they also have a bearing, some of them, on the Baltic states, including Russia. They have at least some value now and then for the history of more southerly countries.

But deep as was the interest for things abroad, the Icelanders reserved their keenest attention for the sagas of their own country. And this sphere embraced the sister republic of Greenland.

Craigie discusses the turbulent conditions in Iceland, the blood feuds and the struggles of chieftains which gave unlimited material for truthful and stirring prose narrative. He points out that some of these stories were gradually fictionized through the centuries, until a few of them became practically historical novels; but he says that the books of pure fiction are chiefly those related to heroes abroad, as, for instance, the Nibelung sagas and those of other ancient heroes and gods.

One of the great services of the Icelandic saga was to preserve the religious history and other knowledge of foreign lands when the memory of these things had died out and the records had disappeared in the countries of origin.

It is not merely true, as Wagner himself said, that he had to come to Iceland for the source material of his Nibelung cycle; there is also the same kind of truth in a statement issued by one of the officers of the present German government, a year or two after Hitler came into power, that just as German Christians used to visit Palestine as the Holy Land of their religion so should those Germans who want to build up the Teutonic religion visit Iceland as their Holy Land and the source of their holy books. For surely three fourths of all we know about the immediate pre-Christian religion of the so-called Germanic, Teutonic, or Nordic peoples would disappear if the literature of Iceland could be wiped out.

However, what concerns us here is that most of what we know of the history, customs, laws, and social conditions of Greenland as well as Iceland we know through the Icelandic saga.

Craigie says that out of the knowledge gained in foreign lands by the Icelanders, out of the traditions brought with them originally by the settlers, and out of the things which happened in Iceland and Greenland ". . . there gradually grew up in Iceland a rich body of genuine historical tradition, beginning from at least the days of King Harald and the settlement of the island, and becoming fuller and more accurate in proportion as the events were more recent." He classifies the narratives into groups or cycles and considers to be one of the most important the body of sagas related to Greenland.

The winter 1117–18 is given by Craigie as the date for the first complete book written in Iceland. Before this time writing had been of small literary value; for the runes, although familiar for centuries, were not adapted to the pen and brush, or at least were not so used, but were cut into stone or wood and used only for brief messages or for short compositions like spells and charms.

However, the work of 1117 was not a saga; it was a book of law. The proper recording of history began with Saemund the Wise (1056–1133) who is credited with writing the great religious work "The Elder Edda," the Bible of the Nordic faith.

Next after Saemund came Ari, also called the Wise (1067–1148). After describing him as a critical and judicious historian, Craigie has a passage which refers to Greenland:

"Ari's chief work was one entitled *Islendinga-bok* or *Book of Icelanders,* of which only a second and shorter recension, made by the author himself about 1130, has come down to us. This is a concise account of the settlement and early history of Iceland, in which special prominence is given to legal and ecclesiastical matters. Ari made special efforts to fix the exact date of every important event which he mentions, and his chronology was usually accepted as authoritative by later writers. He was also very careful to base his statements on the best authority available and constantly gives the names of the persons on whom he relied for each particular piece of information. Thus he fixed the date of the settlement of Greenland from information given by his uncle Thorkel, and he again had it from a man who went there with Eirik the Red."

In his chapter "Historical Sagas Relating to Iceland and Greenland," Craigie says:

"The contents of Ari's *Islendinga-bok,* and of *Landnama-bok,* would be sufficient in themselves to show that a very great knowledge of the past history of the island existed in Iceland in the twelfth century; but it would have been impossible to imagine how rich and full the traditions actually were, if so many of them had not formed the bases of separate sagas. In almost every district of Iceland, but especially (as we have already said) in the west and north, the memory of

great men and distinguished families had been handed down,
and out of these traditions came the collection of sagas now
commonly grouped under the name of *Islendinga sögur*. Although they may thus be classed under a common title, and
have certain characteristic features in common, these sagas
differ greatly from each other in length, and in the extent
to which they can be regarded as having a genuinely historical
character."

Craigie discusses most of the sagas which relate to Greenland. His verdict on some, among them the *Saga of the Blood
Brothers,* the *Saga of Erik the Red,* and generally the ones we
cite in this volume, is that they are historical documents of
importance. He says their main accuracy is not reasonably to
be doubted, although fictions have crept in here and there.
We do not rule Washington off the historical stage through
disbelief in the yarn about the cherry tree, nor do we seriously
impugn the general truthfulness of a number of writers from
colonial New England just because we do not take seriously
everything they say about witchcraft and the comparative
efficacy of different kinds of wood fire in driving away evil
spirits.

We should always keep in mind, with regard to the saga
literature, that while some are wholly fictitious, other sagas are
as nearly factual as any connected narratives which we derive
from antiquity or from the Middle Ages; and that a story
which was originally truthful throughout may have had ex-
traneous matter grafted upon it not merely by narrators before the work was inscribed on vellum but also by copyists.

In the frequently recopied Icelandic sagas we must be
chiefly on guard against additions. Particular care must be
taken against those well-intentioned medieval scribes who were
constantly "improving" the manuscripts as they transferred
the contents from one sheet of vellum to another. Fortunately
these improvements seldom consist of leaving things out, so
that most of the truth is likely to be carried over through sev-

eral recopyings—except, of course, for actual mistakes, as where a word is wrongly deciphered or where passages are inadvertently omitted or transposed.

The additions can often be detected by their religious flavor, for it was one of the main purposes of the scribes to benefit their readers, and clearly they thought that the more there was of godliness and of miracle the better. This had its reverse side. They would not merely bestow devout thoughts and actions upon their heroes and on the characters that were said to be good Christians, but would also suggest or state about less desirable characters that they had dealings with evil spirits, usually with deposed heathen gods.

On our guard, then, against religious, miraculous, and superstitious interpolations, we may treat the sagas as valuable sources. We must use them, of course, with the same discretion as we do other historical material. Some of them resemble the Brendan legends in having scarce more than a trellis of fact over and through which the vines of fancy climb and weave; some, on the other hand, are at least as reliable as Tacitus on Germany or Herodotus on Greece.

As material for Greenland history, next in combined importance, after the sagas, are the various documents that come from the Church of Rome, directly or indirectly. First of these are the letters of the popes themselves; documents which still exist, as originals or authentic copies, in the Vatican archives.

Of greatest weight, following the papal letters, is the history of the Archbishopric of Hamburg, *Historia Hammaburgensis Ecclesiae,* written by Adam of Bremen and completed about 1075. This has long been recognized as one of the main sources of North European church history and its credibility has, therefore, been assessed by scholars of competence again and again. This book contains, so far as we have yet found out, the first written reference to the mainland of North

America, under the name of Wineland, as well as the first reference to Greenland as Green Land.

But while we do get invaluable knowledge of the establishment of the Christian church in Greenland through the writings of Adam of Bremen, we get far more detailed information concerning land and people from the *Konungs Skuggsja, Speculum Regale,* the *King's Mirror,* which was written in Norway sometime between 1220 and 1260 and which circulated thereafter in a number of manuscripts in at least three different languages, Latin, vernacular Norwegian, and Old Norse (Icelandic). The *Mirror* carries its own evidence of reliability, for its detailed descriptions of natural conditions in Greenland have been found accurate.

The last of the important manuscript sources are the annals kept at various places in Iceland. These have about the usual reliability of North European medieval annals.

There are a number of minor sources as, for instance, the treaties made between England and the Scandinavian countries involving Greenland and the records of commerce that give some knowledge of imports and exports.

As we get nearer to the period of the Columbus-Cabot revival of sailings, the authorities become more numerous and are scattered through various countries, from Italy and Portugal to Denmark, Norway, and Iceland.

After the three voyages of Sir Martin Frobisher, 1576–7–8, the literature on Greenland became voluminous and commonplace. It was now chiefly in English, Dutch, and Danish, but there are contributions from nearly every European tongue.

CHAPTER IX

The Sagas of Erik the Red and Einar Sokkason

SINCE THERE ARE TWO SAGAS which have especial bearing on Greenland and seem indeed to belong in this book, it may well be that here is the place where they best fit. The Saga of Erik the Red is the better known, since it has been heavily leaned on in most of the historical novels as well as the histories which have dealt with the pre-Columbian discovery of America. The Saga of Einar Sokkason, less known, gives a clear and concise picture of life in Greenland.

The Saga of Erik covers the last half of the tenth century and the first part of the eleventh. The Saga of Einar is from the early part of the twelfth century. We translate both of them from the Icelandic of the Reykjavik, 1935, edition.

SAGA OF ERIK THE RED

CHAPTER I

This chapter is not worth translating for any but the professional reader. It is a maze of genealogy, of which there is at least enough for our purposes in Chapter II.

CHAPTER II

A man was named Thorvald. He was the son of Asvald, the son of Ulf, the son of Ox-Thorir. His son was named Erik

the Red. Father and son had to leave the Jadar (section of
Norway) because of some killings. They homesteaded land
at the Hornstrands, where they made their home at Drangar.
Thorvald died there.

Erik secured as wife, Thjodhild, the daughter of Jörund,
the son of Ulf, and of his wife Thorbjörg Shipsbreast, who
was at this time married to Thorbjörn from Haukdale. Erik
then moved north and cleared land at Haukdale and dwelt
at Eriksstead near Vatnshorn.

Now it happened that some slaves belonging to Erik set
going a landslide down upon the home of Valthjof at Valth-
jofsstead. Eyjolf the Dirty, a relative of Valthjof, killed the
slaves at Skeidsbrekka up by Vatnshorn. For that reason Erik
slew Eyjolf the Dirty. He also killed Hrafn the Duellist at
Leikskalar.

Geirsteinn and Odd from Jörvi, relatives of Eyjolf, took
up the cause and Erik was banished from Haukdale. Then
he homesteaded Brok and Ox Islands and lived at Tröd in
South Island during the first winter.

At that stage Erik lent his hall posts to Thorgest. Later
he moved to Ox Island and dwelt at Eriksstead. Then he
asked for the hall posts back, but they were not returned to
him.

Erik then went to Breidabolstead and seized the hall posts.
Thorgest pursued him. The battle between them took place
near the farm at Drangar. Two sons of Thorgest fell, and
several other men.

After this both sides kept large numbers around them.
Styrr supported Erik; so did Eyjolf from Swine Island, Thor-
björn Vifilsson, and the sons of Thorbrand from Alptafjord.
The sons of Thorir Gellir supported Thorgest, and so did
Thorgeir from Hitardale, Aslak from Longdale, and his
son Illugi.

Erik and his men (those originally involved in the fight)
were outlawed at the Thorsnes assizes. He got a ship ready

in Erik's Harbor, after which Eyjolf kept him in hiding in Dimun's Harbor while Thorgest and his men searched for them throughout the islands.

Thorbjörn, Eyjolf and Styrr accompanied Erik beyond the islands, and they parted with the greatest friendship. Erik vowed that he would as best he could support them in any way they might ever need. He told them that his purpose was to search for the land which Gunnbjörn, the son of Ulf the Crow, saw when he was driven westward into the ocean, at the time that he discovered the Gunnbjörn Skerries. He added that he would return eventually to his friends if he found the land.

Erik now stood out to sea abreast of Snaefellsjokul. He reached land opposite that glacier (in Greenland) which is named Blaserk (Blue Sark). He followed the land south to discover if it were suitable for habitation. He spent the first winter at Erik's Island which is near the middle of the Eastern Colony (i.e., near the middle of what was later so-called).

Next spring he went to Eriksfjord where he took a homestead. That same summer he continued to the western uninhabited country where he gave names to features of the coast. He spent the second winter at Erik's Holm, by Mount Hvarf. During the third summer he sailed all the way north to Snaefell and into Hrafnsfjord, whereupon he considered he had reached the head of Eriksfjord.

Now he turned back and spent the third winter on Erik's Island, which is at the mouth of Eriksfjord. Later that summer he went to Iceland, landing at Breidafjord. He spent the winter with Ingolf at Holmlatri.

The next spring there was a battle between his forces and those of Thorgest, and Erik's side got the worst of it. A settlement was then arranged between them.

That summer Erik sailed to colonize the land he had found and which he had called Green Land because, as he said, men would desire to go there if it had an attractive name.

According to Ari Thorgilsson, 25 ships sailed that summer for Greenland from Breidafjord and Borgarfjord; but only 14 got through. Some of the others were driven back and some were lost. This was 15 years before Christianity was legally adopted in Iceland [i.e., 15 years before 1000 A.D.]. Erik homesteaded Eriksfjord and his home was at Brattahlid.

CHAPTER III

More than half of Chapter III is about the friendship of Orm and Thorbjörn, and about Thorbjörn's especially beautiful daughter, Gudrid. Thorbjörn was a popular man but land-poor; and he was under pressure to marry off his daughter to a wealthy man who, however, was not considered to be of noble descent.

That spring Thorbjörn gave a reception to his friends, and many came. It was a sumptuous banquet. During the festivities Thorbjörn asked for silence that he might address them:

"Here I have dwelt until toward the end of a long life and have experienced friendship from my neighbors and the greatest affection. I consider that our dealings have been satisfactory on all sides. But I am growing land-poor and cannot maintain standards at the accustomed level. I would rather abandon my land than dwell unfittingly there; I would rather leave the country than shame my relatives. So I intend to follow up the pledges of my friend Erik the Red, the ones he made me when we parted in Breidafjord. I shall go out to Greenland this summer, if I can at all manage."

There was regret at these proposals, for Thorbjörn was looked upon with affection; however, it was considered that he would not have spoken at all but that his mind was so made up that there was no use trying to change it.

Thorbjörn distributed gifts among his friends, and the banquet was over. All left, each going to his own home.

Thorbjörn sold his land and bought a ship which was lying at Hraunhafnaros. Thirty people decided to accompany him, among them Orm from Arnarstapi, and his wife and other friends of Thorbjörn who loved him so that they would not part with him.

They stood offshore. When the ship was well at sea the sky darkened. They did not know which way to steer and wandered about during the summer. A disease broke out. Orm and his wife, Halldis, died, and half the people aboard. The sea was rough. The company endured cold and wet and hardship of many kinds. Still they reached Herjolfsnes in Greenland, but only when winter was setting in.

A man named Thorkel then dwelt at Herjolfsnes, a most prosperous farmer. He received Thorbjörn and all his companions, who spent the winter with him. He entertained them handsomely.

CHAPTER IV

At this time there was a serious scarcity of food (farm produce) in Greenland and those had also been unlucky who devoted themselves to hunting. Some of them had not returned from the hunt.

There was a woman in the settlement called Thorbjörg. She was a fortuneteller and was called the Little Witch. She had had nine sisters, all of them similarly gifted, but she was the only one still living. It was her custom in winter that she accepted invitations to banquets; those most curious about their own fortunes or the weather of the approaching seasons were most likely to give her these invitations.

Now Thorkel was the largest farmer in the neighborhood and it was considered his responsibility to find out when would be the ending of the hard times from which all were suffering. It was for this reason that he invited the fortuneteller to his house.

When the witch arrived she was welcomed heartily, as was the custom when women of her type were being received. A high seat was prepared and a cushion was placed thereon; it was required that it should be stuffed with the feathers of domestic chickens.

The witch arrived in the evening, and with her the herald who had been sent to meet her. Her costume was such that she wore a blue mantle with buckles at the neck; it was decorated with precious stones all the way down to its hem. She wore a necklace of glass beads, and the sort of low cap of lambskin which both men and women used; it was black outside but lined inside with white catskin. She had a staff and a knob on it which was decorated with brass and set with gems. She wore a belt from which was suspended a large pouch where she kept the magical appliances she needed in performing her mysteries. On her feet were calfskin shoes with the hair on, fastened with long laces that had big knobs of tin at their ends. She wore gloves of catskin; the hair on them was white and was turned in toward the hand.

It was considered that when the fortuneteller entered everyone should greet her handsomely, each in his own way. She received greetings according to how she felt about those who spoke to her. The head of the house, Thorkel, took her by the hand and led her to the seat which had been prepared for her. He asked her to look over his servants, his domestic animals and his house and outbuildings. To this she made little response.

The table was set for dinner, and we should tell what food was prepared for the witch. They made her porridge with the milk of goats, and they served her dishes containing the cooked hearts of every different kind of animal they had been able to secure. She had a brass spoon and a knife hafted in walrus ivory, the handle twice ringed with copper; the point of the blade had been broken off.

When the table was set the master of the house, Thorkel, went and stood before Thorbjörg and asked how she liked everything she could see and how well she was suited by the

rooms and by the deportment of the people, and how soon
she thought she would have the knowledge to answer what
he had asked her about, the thing that everyone was most
concerned to know. She replied that she would have nothing
to say until morning; she would first have to sleep there
overnight.

Next morning, when the day was somewhat advanced, there
were made for the witch those preparations which were necessary in order that she might be able to perform her witchcraft. She asked that there should be found women who knew
the spell which was necessary for the witchcraft and which is
named *vardlokur* (warlock). But such women could not be
found. They asked everyone around the house whether anybody knew anything of the sort.

At last Gudrid spoke up: "I am not very well informed (on
witchcraft), nor am I a witch, but it is true that Halldis, my
foster mother, taught me in Iceland a verse which she called
vardlokur." Thorkel said she was fortunate in her knowledge
but she replied: "These are goings-on with which I want nothing
to do; for I am a Christian."

Thorbjörg then said to her: "You might be no worse than
you were before and still be of help to the community; however, I consider it Thorkel's responsibility to furnish me with
everything I need." Hereupon Thorkel brought pressure upon
Gudrid and at last she yielded.

The women now made a ring around the platform on which
Thorbjörg sat. Gudrid sang the stanzas so pleasingly and so
well that no one there present felt he had ever heard them
sung with a more beautiful voice. The sybil thanked her for
the song and remarked that many powers had now gathered
around to whom it was agreeable to hear the song so well
rendered—"powers which up to then wanted to keep away from
us and to yield us no obedience. Now I can clearly see many
things which were previously dark to me and to many another.

"I can inform you, Thorkel, that the present famine will

not last more than through this winter; good conditions will come with the spring. The epidemic which has been upon us will be ameliorated sooner than you would expect. But you, Gudrid, I can reward out of hand for the assistance we have derived from you; for your fate is now clear to me. You will make the best kind of match here in Greenland; but it will not endure many years, for your path lies to Iceland where there will be derived from you a large and eminent family; over the path of your descendants shine brighter lights than I am able to describe to you. Bless you, my daughter!"

Now everyone crowded up to the witch, each asking the things he was most eager to know. She answered them readily; and few were her prophecies that did not come true.

Now people arrived from a neighboring estate to fetch her. When she had gone with them Thorbjörn came back to the house, in which he had refused to remain while these ceremonies were being performed, which he considered abominable.

Conditions improved quickly, as Thorbjörg had forecast.

CHAPTER V

The wife of Erik was Thjodhild and they had two sons, Thorstein and Leif. They were both promising young men. Thorstein remained at home with his father and it was considered that not in all of Greenland was there a man of his quality.

Leif sailed to Norway [by way of the Hebrides] . . . arriving there in the autumn. He went to the court of Olaf Tryggvason. The King showed him much consideration and evidently thought him a man of ability.

At one time the King said to Leif: "Are you returning to Greenland next summer?" "That is my plan," said Leif, "if it meets with your approval." The King replied: "I do approve, and you shall be my messenger to spread the faith of Christianity."

Leif said that of course he would follow the King's direction but this kind of mission to Greenland he thought would be difficult. The King replied he knew of no one better suited for the undertaking, "and I feel sure your fortune will carry you to success." "That will happen," said Leif, "only if I have your support."

Leif set out upon his voyage. They were a long time at sea and finally struck a land they had not expected. It had fields of self-sown wheat, and wine berries. Among the trees were maples. Of all these things they took aboard specimens, including beams so long that they were suitable for house building.

[On his way back to Greenland] Leif found men on a stranded ship and took them home with him. In the rescue he showed those personal qualities which distinguished him in many other things, like those which made him instrumental in Christianizing the country. He was ever after called Leif the Lucky.

Leif struck the coast of Greenland at Eriksfjord and went home to Brattahlid. Everybody was delighted to see him. He began preaching Christianity through the land immediately. When proclaiming the faith he showed people the tokens he had from Olaf Tryggvason, explaining how excellent and how glorious was the new religion.

His father, Erik, was not inclined to be much impressed with the new ideas; but his mother, Thjodhild, accepted them readily and had a church built near the farm. This building was thereafter called the Church of Thjodhild. Here she worshiped, and so did the rest of those who accepted Christianity. She would not associate with Erik after she was converted, which annoyed him.

Now there was great talk that people ought to seek out the land which had been discovered by Leif. The leader in this was the accomplished and popular Thorstein, Erik's son. People wanted Erik to come along, for they had the greatest confidence in his foresight and his good luck. He was reluctant; but he finally refrained from saying no when his friends beseeched him.

The ship which Thorbjörn had brought with him [from Iceland] was now made ready. Twenty men were chosen for the voyage, which was to carry little trade goods, only weapons and provisions.

The morning Erik left the house he took a box which contained gold and silver and hid it. Riding along toward the ship he fell off his horse, breaking some ribs and injuring his shoulder. This led him to tell his wife, Thjodhild, that she might have the treasure; he considered the accident a visitation, the result of having secreted the valuables.

Amidst great rejoicing the ship stood out from Eriksfjord; everybody was much pleased with how things were going. But they encountered difficulties at sea, were much delayed, and did not attain to where they wanted to go. At one time they had a view of Iceland; at another they saw birds from Ireland. Their ship kept being driven back and forth across the sea. Toward autumn they returned to Greenland, discouraged and tired. Winter was already beginning when they reached Eriksfjord.

Now Erik said: "There was more jollity when we sailed out of the fjord last summer than there is now, but still we are not so badly off." Thorstein replied: "It is our responsibility as leaders to make some provision for all these men who are now without resources. We must find them a home for the winter." Erik remarked: "There is much truth in the saying that no one knows the reply to his question till he gets the answer, and that is how things are now. I shall do as you suggest." Everyone who had no other home went with Erik and his son. They proceeded to Brattahlid and spent the winter.

Chapter VI

Now we have to tell that Thorstein Eriksson sought the hand of Gudrid, which was well received both by her and her father. The arrangements were made and they were married at Brattahlid in the autumn. The wedding was seemly and was well attended.

Thorstein had a farm in the Western Settlement, the name of which was Lysufjord. Another man owned half of that farm, whose name was also Thorstein; his wife was Sigrid.

When Thorstein Eriksson and his wife arrived at Lysufjord in the fall they were well received and they spent there the winter.

An epidemic was sweeping the district and reached their farm early in the winter. Gardar, the superintendent of the farm, an unpopular man, was the first taken ill, and he died. Thereafter it was not far between one death and the next.

Among those who became ill were Thorstein Eriksson and Sigrid, the wife of the other Thorstein.

One evening Sigrid was going out of doors, and Gudrid with her. They had just gone out beyond the front door when Sigrid screamed. Gudrid said: "We are being careless in going out; you must not get chilled. Let us go right back into the house." Sigrid replied: "We can't do that, for all the dead men are standing lined up in front of the door, barring it, and Thorstein, your husband, is among them. I can also see myself among them, and that I don't like." After a moment, however, the vision departed and she said: "Let us go back in, Gudrid; now I cannot see the dead men barring our way."

Here follows a long and circumstantial account of ghosts and marvels —dead men coming to life and falling back dead again, visions and prodigies. The last part of the chapter tells that Thorstein Eriksson had been dead for some time when he sat up and spoke to his wife Gudrid.

"It is not proper, as has been the case here in Greenland since we became Christian, that men should be buried in ground not consecrated and with scant singing of the mass. I desire that I be carried to a proper church, and so with the others who have died here. However, the body of Gardar should be burned in a great fire as soon as possible; for he is responsible for all the supernatural things which have been happening this winter." He also told her about her future, that her career would be remarkable, and begged her to refrain from being married to a Greenlander. He asked her to see to it that their money went as a gift to the church, but that some of it should go to the poor. Having spoken, he fell down dead a second time.

It had been the custom in Greenland since Christianity that men were buried near the farms where they had died, and in unconsecrated ground. The practice was to set a rod upright upon the breast of the corpse; later when a priest came the rod was pulled up and holy water poured down through the hole, and then there were masses said, although it might be long after the burial.

The bodies of Thorstein and the rest who had died were brought to the church at Eriksfjord and were there properly buried, with masses sung by the correct religious functionaries. Erik received Gudrid into his home as if he had been her father. . . .

CHAPTER VII

A man named Thord dwelt at Höfdi in Höfdaströnd [in Iceland]. [Here follows a genealogy tracing the ancestry of his wife to one of the kings of Ireland.] A son of Thord was named Thorfinn Karlsefni. He was customarily on merchant voyages and was considered a good navigator.

One summer Karlsefni prepared his ship for a voyage to

Greenland. With him went Snorri Thorbrandsson from Alpta-fjord, and there were forty men on that ship.

Another man was named Bjarni Grimolfsson from Breida-fjord; still another was Thorhall Gamlason from the eastern fjords. That same summer they also were getting a ship ready for Greenland which likewise had a crew of forty.

The two ships set out together. It is not reported how long they were at sea but only that both reached Eriksfjord by autumn.

Erik the Red and a number of other Greenlanders rode down to meet the ships, and there was brisk trading. The captains of the two vessels offered Erik whatever goods he wanted from their cargoes. To show equal generosity he invited the entire crews of both to be his guests for the winter. The merchants accepted gratefully. Hereupon their goods were transported to Brattahlid where there were ample vacant storehouses for accommodation. Erik's guests found that his home was well provided, and they spent a pleasant winter.

But when it drew toward Christmas Erik began to seem depressed, much more gloomy than was his nature. So one day Karlsefni asked him what the trouble was: "Why are you sad, Erik? Everybody seems to feel that you are more depressed than is your nature. You have been generous to us and it is our duty to reciprocate as best we can. Do tell us what is the trouble."

Erik replied: "Your whole attitude is proper and is to your credit; I am much concerned that you shall not get the worst of our exchanges. Besides I cannot be happy to think that when you go elsewhere it shall become known that you have nowhere had a worse Yule than this which is now approaching, when Erik the Red was your host at Brattahlid in Greenland."

"That will never be the case, my dear sir," said Karlsefni. "We have in our cargoes both malt and corn and you shall have of these as much as you like to use in as rich a banquet as you care to arrange."

The offer was accepted by Erik, and a Yule feast prepared such that those who were there could not imagine anything more sumptuous in a land of so few resources.

After the feast Karlsefni sought the hand of Gudrid, for he had reason to believe he would be successful. Erik received his proposal favorably and said that she would have to yield to her fate [i.e., the above prophecy of Erik's dead son, Thorstein, and his warning that she must not marry a Greenlander]. Besides, he said, he had heard nothing but good of Karlsefni. The outcome was that Thorfinn and Gudrid were married, whereupon the Yule festivities were prolonged into a wedding feast. They dwelt at Brattahlid the rest of the winter.

CHAPTER VIII

At Brattahlid was great talk that there ought to be a search for Wineland the Good, for it was said that the conditions there were favorable in soil and climate. The upshot was that Karlsefni and Snorri prepared their ship for a voyage which was to search for that country in the spring.

Bjarni and Thorhall decided to join the expedition with their ship and the crew which had accompanied them. A man named Thorvard, whose wife was a natural daughter of Erik the Red, went with the expedition, and so did Thorvald, the son of Erik, and Thorhall, who was called "the hunter." He had been with Erik a long time as a hunter during the summer and as a steward in winter. He was a large man, strong and uncouth, usually silent but ill-spoken when he was not silent. He ever tried to persuade Erik to the less desirable of two courses. He had not become a real Christian. His knowledge of the wilderness was extensive. He was on the ship of Thorvard and Thorvald, which was the vessel that Thorbjörn had brought [from Iceland]. Altogether the expedition had 160 people.

They sailed first to the Western Settlement and then to Bear

Island (Disko). Thence they sailed two days southwestward, when they discovered land. They manned a boat and explored it, finding large flat stones, some of them 12 ells [18 feet]. Foxes were numerous. They gave the land a name and called it Helluland (Land of Flat Stones; Flagstoneland).

Thence they sailed a day and a night, turning from southwest to south, and discovered a forested country with abundant game. An island lay to the south; there they killed a bear and so they named it Bjarney (Bear Island). But the land they called Markland (Land of Forest).

Thence they stood southwest along the coast for a long time and came to a ness; here the land was on the starboard. The beaches were long and there were sands. They rowed ashore and found on the ness the keel of a ship, wherefore they named it Kjalarnes (Keelness). Also they gave to the coast the name Furdustrandir (Wonder Strands), for it took so long to sail past them.

Now the coast began to be deeply cut up with bays. They steered the ships into one of the bays.

King Olaf Tryggvason had assigned to Leif two Scots: the man was named Haki and the woman Hekja. They could run faster than reindeer. They were on Karlsefni's ship. When the expedition had passed Wonder Strands they put the Scots ashore and asked them to run southwest into the country to find out the quality of the land. They were to be gone two days and the intervening night. They had a garment named a kjafal [Irish cabhal]; it was so designed that it had a hood and was slit at the sides, without sleeves, and was fastened together between their legs with a button and a loop. Apart from this both of them were unclad.

The expedition waited. When the messengers returned one of them carried a twig with wine berries, another carried an ear of self-sown wheat. They went aboard ship and the expedition proceeded.

They stood into a fjord. Outside its mouth was an island

around which were strong currents. Therefore they named it Straumey (the Island of the Violent Currents). The eider ducks were so numerous on this island that one could hardly step without breaking an egg. They named the bay Straumfjord (Fjord of the Strong Currents).

Here they unloaded their ships and made preparations for residence. They had with them every kind of domestic animal. It was a fair country and they paid attention to nothing much but exploring [i.e., neglected haying, etc.]. They wintered there, although they had not made suitable preparation during the summer. The hunting became poor and food started running short.

Now Thorhall the Hunter disappeared. Up to this time they had been praying to God [the Christian God] for food, but the response to their prayers had not been as prompt as they would have liked. They searched for Thorhall for three days and found him at last high up on a cliff. There he lay with his face toward the sky, mouth and nostrils wide, mumbling. They asked why he was there, which he said was none of their business. Then they asked him to come home with them, and he did.

A little hereafter they secured a whale which they cut up, not being able to recognize, however, what kind of whale it was. The cooks boiled the meat, but when they ate of it everyone became ill. Then said Thorhall: "Redbeard [the heathen god Thor] turned out to be a better provider than your Christ. This [whale] is what I got for composing a poem to Thor, the most dependable of gods; he has seldom failed me."

When the people heard this they turned the whale adrift upon the sea, and put their trust in the Lord. Then the weather improved so that they were able to row out (for fish or sea game). There was no longer a scarcity, with hunting on the land, eggs upon the island and fish in the sea.

CHAPTER IX

Thorhall the Hunter wanted to go north beyond Wonder Strands and Keelness in search of Vinland, but Karlsefni wanted to go south. Thorhall made his preparations in the shelter of the island and there were only nine that accompanied him; all the rest went with Karlsefni. As Thorhall was watering his ship he composed a stanza. [We use the Reeves translation]:

> *When I came, these brave men told me,*
> *Here the best of drink I'd get,*
> *Now with water-pail behold me,—*
> *Wine and I are strangers yet.*
> *Stooping at the spring, I've tested*
> *All the wine this land affords;*
> *Of its vaunted charms divested,*
> *Poor indeed are its rewards.*

When the ship was fully prepared they hoisted sail. Thorhall composed a stanza:

> *Comrades, let us now be faring*
> *Homeward to our own again!*
> *Let us try the sea-steed's daring,*
> *Give the chafing courser rein.*
> *Those who will may bide in quiet,*
> *Let them praise their chosen land,*
> *Feasting on a whale-steak diet,*
> *In their home by Wonder-strand.*

Then they sailed beyond Wonder Strands and Keelness and desired to head west; but there came against them a west wind and they were driven to Ireland, where they were beaten and enslaved. Thorhall lost his life there, according to the report of merchants. [These would be Irish merchants who came to Iceland; many Irish trading ships did in this period.]

A fleet of Eskimo kayaks; early Icelandic voyagers to the North American mainland (Labrador) recorded the same memorable sight in their sagas.

Chapter X

The story about Karlsefni is that he stood southwest along the coast, as well as Snorri and Bjarni, with their companions. They sailed a long time, even till they came to a river that flowed from the land into a lake and thence into the sea. There were extensive gravel bars so that it was not possible for the ships to enter the river except at the highest tide.

Karlsefni and his men sailed into the mouth of the river, which they called Hop.* In this country they discovered fields of self-sown wheat wherever the land was low but wine wood [possibly grape vines] wherever there were hills. Their brook was full of fish. They dug pits where the land met the most frequent high tide currents; when the tide fell these pits contained halibut. There were great numbers of wild animals of every kind in the forest.

The party remained a half month, enjoyed themselves well and saw no signs of natives. They had their domestic animals with them.

Early one morning as they looked around they saw a great number of skin boats. Pieces of wood were waved from the boats as if grain were beaten with flails, and the motion was sunwise.

Then spoke Karlsefni: "What would be the meaning of that sign?" Snorri Thorbrandsson answered: "It may be that this is a peace signal. Let us take a white shield and carry it toward them." They did so.

The visitors came rowing toward them and marveled at them as they scrambled ashore. They were dark and villainous looking, with coarse hair on their heads; their eyes were conspicuous and they were broad across the cheeks. They stayed awhile marveling, and then rowed away south beyond the ness.

*The word is pronounced like our hope. It is the Icelandic word for a small, landlocked bay that is salt with the high tide but fresh with low tide; cf. English place names like Stanhope, Easthope.

The Karlsefni party had built their dwellings on a slope by the lake and some of the buildings were near the water, others farther away. They spent the winter. There was no snow* and the domestic animals fared out all winter.

Chapter XI

That spring they saw early one morning that a multitude of skin boats came rowing past the ness, as many as if charcoal had been scattered over the whole estuary. As before, staves were waving from every boat. Karlsefni's party raised their shields aloft. When the two parties met they started trading.

What these people most desired was red cloth. They had for exchange peltries and skins that were uniformly gray. They also wanted to buy swords and spears but the sale of these was forbidden by Karlsefni and Snorri. The natives, whom the Norsemen called Skraelings, took a span's breadth of red cloth in exchange for a good pelt, and they bound the pieces of cloth around their heads. That is how the trading went for some time. When the cloth which the Karlsefni party had with them became scarce, they began to cut it into smaller pieces, so that finally some of them were no more than a finger's breadth, but the natives paid as much for these as they had paid for the larger pieces, and even more.

It happened that a bull which belonged to the Karlsefni party came running down from the woods, bellowing loudly. This frightened the natives; they ran to their boats and rowed southward around the cape.

Now there was no sign of the natives for three weeks to-

*This is no doubt another case of alteration during oral transmission, before the narrative was written down. Probably what Karlsefni said was that there was so little snow it did not interfere with the grazing of his animals. That this might be true in New England will perhaps seem strange to New Englanders today; but it will not seem a bit strange to Icelanders or to people who have been living on the Eskimo stock farms that now flourish in Greenland; nor will it seem strange to ranchers from Montana and Wyoming. Both in Iceland and in Wyoming sheep will feed out all winter under conditions more severe than those of New England.

gether. Thereupon, however, Karlsefni's people saw a multitude of boats coming from the south, moving forward as in a steady stream. This time all the staves were being waved counter-sunwise and everybody was screaming at the top of their voices. In reply Karlsefni's people raised a red shield and carried it toward them. The natives jumped from their boats and the two parties met in battle. There came a shower of missiles, for the natives used war slings (catapults).

Karlsefni's people saw that the natives were raising a large sphere on a pole. This was about as big as the [inflated] stomach of a sheep, seemed bluish in color, and was thrown from the pole up on the land above the heads of Karlsefni's people. There was a terrifying sound when it struck the earth. This frightened Karlsefni's men so that they had no desire but to flee and to retreat upstream along the river. It seemed to them that the natives were approaching from all sides; so they did not stop retreating until they came to some cliffs, where they made a resolute stand.

The woman Freydis now came out from her house and saw that Karlsefni and his men were retreating. "Why do you flee from these wretches? Such stout fellows as you are, it seems to me you could just butcher them as if they were domestic animals. It looks to me that if I only had weapons I could make a better fight than any of you are doing." They paid no attention to what she said.

Freydis tried to follow them; but was slow, for she was with child. Still she reached the forest, with the natives attacking her. She came upon a dead man. He was Thorbrand Snorrason and there was a flat stone sticking in his head. His unsheathed sword lay beside him. She took this up and prepared to defend herself. When the natives approached her she exposed her bare breast and whetted the sword on it. This proceeding frightened the natives; they went to their ships and rowed away.

Karlsefni and his companions went up to her and praised her

stratagem. Two of their men had been killed and many of the natives. The Karlsefni party had been greatly outnumbered.

They returned to their houses, dressed their wounds and considered what the multitude could have been which came toward them from inland. Finally they concluded that the only people actually in the fight had been those who came from the ships, and that those who appeared to be coming from inland were figures of their imagination.

The [retreating] natives found a dead man, and there lay an ax beside him. One of them took the ax and chopped with it into a tree, and so did one after another; evidently they thought it was a marvel of sharpness. Then one of them tried to chop a stone with it and the ax broke. Apparently they decided it was worthless, when it could not stand being used chopping rocks; and they threw it away.

Karlsefni and his men decided that although the land was fertile there would always be fear of the natives, and strife with them. So they prepared to leave, intending to sail for home, and stood northeast along the coast, where they found five natives sleeping under fur robes near the sea. They had with them boxes containing deer marrow mixed with blood. Karlsefni's party thought it probable that these men were outlaws; they killed them.

Now the party came to a ness on which there were many animals; the whole ness was one cake of manure, for the deer had spent the nights there.

The Karlsefni party arrived at Straumfjord where they found awaiting them an abundance of everything they needed.

It is one variant of the story that Bjarni and Gudrid had remained behind there with a hundred people, not having gone farther, and that it was only Karlsefni and Snorri who went farther south, accompanied by forty men, that they did not stay at Hop more than a scant two months, and that they returned [to where Bjarni and Gudrid were] the same summer.

Now Karlsefni took a single vessel to go in search of Thorhall the Hunter, the rest staying behind. They went northeast beyond Kjalarnes and advanced to the northwest, with the land on their port side. Here they found nothing but uninhabited forests, so far as they could see, with never a clearing. When they had traveled a long way they found a river which entered the sea coming from the southeast and flowing northwest. They went into the mouth of this river and placed their ship along the southwestern bank.

CHAPTER XII

One morning Karlsefni and his men saw on the other side of a clearing something that glittered, and they gave a shout. It moved and turned out to be a uniped which scuttled down the river bank where the ship lay. Thorvald, the son of Erik the Red, sat at the helm. The uniped shot an arrow into his abdomen. Thorvald pulled out the arrow and said: "There is a lot of fat around my guts. We have certainly discovered a good country, but we do not seem likely to have long use of it." He died of the wound some time later. The uniped ran off north.*

Karlsefni and his party gave chase and caught sight of the uniped now and then. The last they saw was that he disappeared into a ravine. Thereupon they turned back. One of the men composed this stanza:

> Eager, our men, up hill, down dell,
>   Hunted a Uniped;
> Hearken, Karlsefni, while they tell
>   How swift the quarry fled!

Now they stood toward the northeast and thought they could see the land of the unipeds.† They decided not to risk

*Both manuscripts of this saga have the word north. The editors of the edition we are following consider this an error in view of the previous statement that the ship was lying by the southwestern bank of the river.

†Meaning seems to be they were so far from shore that it was doubtful whether or not what they saw in the distance was land.

the lives of their company further. In their opinion those were the same mountains which they saw here and which were at Hop, and they concluded that the distance either way from Straumfjord was about the same.

They spent the third winter at Straumfjord. The party became divided into cliques and the women were the cause of it. Those who were unmarried wanted to get them away from those who were married, which caused the greatest disorder.

It had been during the first winter that Snorri was born, the son of Karlsefni. He was three years of age when they took their departure.

When they sailed from Vinland they got a southerly wind. They reached Markland where they met with five natives, one of whom was bearded. There were two women and two children. The Karlsefni party captured the two boys but the rest escaped, disappeared into the ground. They took the boys along with them, taught them to speak [Norse], and they were baptized. They called their mother Vethildi, their father Ovaegi. They said that two kings governed the natives, one of them named Avaldamon, the other Avaldidida. They explained there were no proper houses; people dwelt in caves or in holes in the ground. They said that across the water opposite to their country was a land with people dressed in white clothes who carried long staves, to which cloths were fastened [i.e., flags], and that they made great outcries. It is considered that this must have been the Land of the White Men, or Ireland the Great.

They reached Greenland and spent the winter with Erik the Red.

CHAPTER XIII

This chapter is, so far as we are concerned, a digression. It tells about the ship of Bjarni Grimolfsson being lost in the Irish Sea and half the men with it, including Bjarni himself—who nobly permitted a young man to take his place in the ship's boat because of a promise to his father in Iceland that he would keep the youngster as safe as he could.

Chapter XIV

The second summer thereafter Karlsefni went to Iceland, to his home in Reynines, and with him Gudrid. His mother felt he had married beneath him and so refused to live with him the first winter. But experience showed her that Gudrid was an able woman, so she returned home; they got along well thereafter.

The daughter of Snorri, the son of Karlsefni, was Hallfrid, the mother of Bishop Thorlak Runolfsson. They had a son named Thorbjörn whose daughter Thorun was the mother of Bishop Bjarni.

The son of Snorri was Thorgeir, the father of Yngvild who was the mother of Bishop Brand the First.

Here ends this saga.

We have included this final genealogy to explain how it is that so many people in Iceland trace their descent from that Snorri who was born on the mainland of North America.

Snorri's having been born outside the country will have been, if anything, a handicap. But in the Middle Ages, and especially in Iceland, bishops were prominent. Within a few generations came three bishops descended from Snorri. This gave the families such a start of prominence that in Iceland, which has always specialized in genealogy, it is considered particularly easy to trace descendants in this family back to the eleventh century.

SAGA OF EINAR SOKKASON

Chapter I

A man was named Sokki, the son of Thorir. He dwelt at Brattahlid in Greenland, an eminent and popular man. He had a promising son named Einar. Between them father and son were powerful in Greenland; decidedly they were the leading men.

Sokki sent out a call for the meeting of a parliament where he explained that in his opinion the country should no longer remain without a bishop of its own, and proposed that everybody in the whole country should contribute so that a bishop's seat might be erected. All the assembled squires agreed.

Sokki asked his son Einar to make the required journey to Norway, saying that he was the best ambassador they could send for the purpose. His son agreed.

Einar took with him a large quantity of walrus ivory and of walrus rope to use for gifts to influence leaders with whom he would have to deal.

When they reached Norway Sigurd the Crusader was King. Einar advanced his cause by the distribution of gifts, went to see the King, explained his mission and requested the King's support toward attaining what he sought for the good of the country. The King agreed that the plan would be to the advantage of Greenland.

Now the King summoned a man named Arnald. He was learned and well suited to be a teacher of religion. The monarch bade him undertake this difficult task for the sake of God and King. "Carrying letters from me, as well as my seal, you shall go to Denmark to Archbishop Össur at Lund."

Arnald said he was reluctant to accept, for two reasons: on his own account since he considered himself ill-adapted for the position, and also because he did not want to be separated from his friends and relatives. A third difficulty was that he thought he would find the people of Greenland hard to deal with. The King replied that his merit would be greater the more sorely he would be tried by his parishioners.

Arnald then said he would not refuse, since the King wished it. "But," he continued, "if it should happen that I am consecrated bishop, then it shall be a condition that Einar swear me an oath to support and strengthen the bishopric, and to protect those properties which are given to God, to punish those who try to deprive the bishopric of its property, and that he shall be protector in every respect." The King told Einar that he should agree to this, which he did.

The candidate for the bishopric now went to see Archbishop Össur, explained his mission and delivered the letter from the King. The Archbishop welcomed him and fell in with the plan. He saw that the candidate was well qualified for the proposed dignity, so he consecrated Arnald a bishop and gave him gifts. [According to the Annals of Iceland, this was in 1124; Össur was Archbishop at Lund 1103–1137.]

Bishop Arnald now returned to the King, who received him well. Einar had brought with him a polar bear from Greenland which he gave King Sigurd. In return the King honored and decorated him.

Now they sailed for Greenland on one ship, the bishop and Einar; on another sailed the Norwegian Arnbjörn and other Norwegians with him who wanted to settle in Greenland. When they stood out to sea the winds were not very favorable, so that at last the bishop and Einar came ashore at Holtavatnsos, below Eyjafjöll, in Iceland.

At this time Saemund the Wise dwelt at Odd. He came down to meet the bishop and invited him to spend the winter, to which he agreed with thanks. Einar also spent the winter beneath Eyjafjöll.

It is said that when the bishop was riding with his men from the ship they came to a certain farm in the Landcy district, pausing outside the farm house. An old woman came out who had been carding wool and had the comb in her hand. She went up to one of the visitors and said: "My man, will you be so good as to fasten one of the teeth of my comb?" The man took the comb and said he would do his best. He took a hammer from a bag and made the repairs with it so that the old lady was well pleased. The man who did this was the bishop who was handy with tools. We tell the story to show what a modest man he was.

The bishop spent the winter at Odd. He and Saemund got

along very well together. Nobody had any news of Arnbjörn and his ship. The bishop's party assumed that he must have reached Greenland.

The next summer the bishop and Einar left Iceland. They reached Greenland at Eriksfjord, where people gave them a fine reception. Even here they were unable to get news of Arnbjörn, which seemed strange, nor did they have news during the next several years. It was now the general talk that the party must have been lost at sea.

The bishop decided to have his seat at Gardar, and moved to that estate. Einar supported him, and so did his father. The bishop had a higher regard for them than for any other men.

CHAPTER II

A certain Greenlander was named Sigurd Njalsson. He used to go on autumn hunts in the uninhabited districts. He was also a very fine sailor. On the journey we speak of he had 15 men with him.

That summer the party reached the glacier Hvitserk [so they must have gone southeast around Cape Farewell and then some distance northeast, up the east coast]. They found certain fireplaces, and signs that people had been hunting.

Sigurd asked his men: "Which do you prefer, to return home or to go on farther? There is little left of the summer and our success in the hunt has been small so far." His men said they would rather turn home, for they considered it very dangerous to cross the large fjords beneath the glaciers [i.e., because the glaciers might calve, producing dangerous waves]. He said it was true (about the danger) but that he thought they would get home with little booty if they turned back now. So his men asked him to decide, saying they had long trusted his judgment and with good results. He decided they should proceed, and they did so.

One of their shipmates was named Steinthor. He said: "I

dreamt last night, Sigurd, and I would like to tell you the dream. It seemed to me we were going into this great fjord just ahead of us and that I got in between some gigantic cliffs and I cried out for help." Sigurd said that the dream might have a moderately good significance . . .

As they proceeded into the fjord Sigurd remarked: "Is it as it seems to me that there is a ship there in the fjord?" His men agreed he was right. Sigurd remarked he thought there would be a tale to tell from this.

They kept on into the fjord and found that the ship was in the mouth of a river, and fenced. It was a fine seagoing vessel.

When they went on shore they found a house with a tent near it. Sigurd said they ought to pitch their own tent before making any investigations; "It is now late in the day and I want everybody quiet and careful." They followed his directions.

In the morning they went out to look around. They found a log with an ax sticking in it and a corpse near by. Sigurd considered that the man had been at work chopping the log and that he had died of starvation. Then they went up to the house, where they saw another corpse. Of him Sigurd remarked that he must have kept walking as long as he could. "These must have been the servants of those who are within the house." There was an ax beside this corpse.

Sigurd then said: "I consider it advisable to make a rift in the wall of the house so that the evil smell from the corpses within may escape, for they must be badly decayed, having lain there so long. Everybody should be careful about breathing this air, for it is not unlikely that illness may result. But it is likely that these men will do us no harm" [i.e., no supernatural harm; as by haunting them later]. Steinthor said he thought it strange for them to make useless work for themselves by tearing a special hole in the wall. He pushed in the door as they were at work tearing a gap in the wall.

When Steinthor came out, Sigurd looked at him and said:

"That man certainly has had a change of countenance." Steinthor screamed and started running away, his companions pursuing him. He jumped into a cleft between rocks where no one could get at him, and there he lost his life. Sigurd remarked that Steinthor had made the mistake of dreaming too true.

After this the men obeyed the orders of Sigurd. They tore open the house (so that the foul air could get out) and no one took harm from it. They found within a number of dead men and a great deal of property.

Then remarked Sigurd: "It seems to me most practical that we remove the flesh from the bones through the use of their own cooking pots, for in that way it will be easier to get their bones to the church for burial. It seems to me most likely that this is Arnbjörn's party; for, according to my information, he was the owner of this beautiful ship which we find here standing up on the land."

The vessel had a carved figurehead, was inlaid with stones and was a remarkable craft. Her boat was rather badly damaged on its bottom, so that Sigurd judged it to be of no value. They therefore pulled out the nails, after which they burned the vessel. As they returned toward the settlements they had with them fully loaded their own ship, Arnbjörn's ship, and the dinghy.

At the colony they went to see the bishop at Gardar. Sigurd told him the news and about the discovery of all the property. Sigurd said: "I cannot see it any other way than that the part of their property is best employed which is used for their bones [i.e., to purchase ground in the cemetery, pay for masses, etc.] and, if I have any control, that is what is going to be done with it." The bishop said he had spoken well and wisely; so said everybody else.

It was a great treasure which went with the bones. The bishop said that the ship was a particularly fine one. Sigurd felt it would also be reasonable that the ship should go to the bishopric as payment for masses for the souls of the dead. The rest of the property was divided between those who had made the find, according to Greenlandic law.

When this news reached Norway it came to the ears of a man named Össur who was a nephew of Arnbjörn. There were also others who had lost relatives on that ship and who wanted to make a claim for the property. They sailed and reached Eriksfjord. People went down to trade with them, after which the ship's company took lodging with the local people for the winter.

Össur, as commander, went to Gardar to spend the winter with the bishop. At this time there was another merchant ship wintering in the Western Settlement, commanded by a Norwegian Kolbein Thorljotsson. A third ship was commanded by two men, Hermund Kodransson and his brother Thorgils. They had a large crew.

<h3 style="text-align:center">Chapter III</h3>

During the winter Össur told the bishop that he was there in hopes of getting some property which had belonged to his relative Arnbjörn, asking that this be cleared up both on the bishop's part and that of others. The bishop replied that he had received the properties according to the laws of Greenland applicable to the case and that he had done nothing arbitrarily. He said it was most proper that the money should be used for the benefit of the souls of those dead who had been the owners, as well as for the church where their bones were now buried. He said, too, it was an unworthy thing now to be trying to get hold of this property.

After this talk Össur did not want to be the guest of the bishop any longer at Gardar, so he went to his own men. He and they kept together in a body during the rest of the winter.

That spring Össur prepared to present his case before the spring assizes at Gardar. To this gathering went the bishop and Einar Sokkason; and they had a large number of men with them for support. Össur was there also, with his shipmates. When the meeting assembled for judgment, Einar came to court with his large retinue and made the point that they should make this kind of suit as difficult for Norwegians to win in Greenland as it would be for Greenlanders to win another like it before a Norwegian court. "We think we should be subject only to Greenlandic laws here in Greenland," said Einar.

The Norwegians did not succeed in winning their case and they left.

Össur was now ill-pleased. He felt it keenly that he had received only slights where he expected to receive property. So what he did was to go where the [disputed] ship lay and to chop two planks from its bottom, one from either side of the keel. Then he sailed for the Western Settlement where he met Kolbein and Ketil Kalfsson, to whom he explained the position.

Kolbein said that an unseemly thing had happened, but also that he did not approve of what Össur had done [breaking up the ship]. Ketil said: "I am in favor of your joining forces with us, for I know about the bargain between the bishop and Einar; you by yourself will not be able to oppose the machinations of the bishop and their execution by Einar. Let us all join forces." He felt it most likely that in this way they could manage. One of those who was in the party of the merchants was named Icy Steingrim.

Össur went back to Kidjaberg, where he had been with his men after he left the bishop's.

CHAPTER IV

The bishop was seriously angered when he learned that the ship had been damaged and he called Einar Sokkason to him saying: "Now has come the time for you to make good the oath you swore as we were leaving Norway to revenge upon those guilty whatever harm was suffered by the bishopric or its property. I now declare that Össur is guilty in that he has damaged our property and has shown himself ungrateful toward us in every way. I do not conceal from you that the situation, as it is, does not suit me at all. If you leave things be I shall say that you have broken your oath."

Einar replied: "You have been ill-treated, my lord; but some will maintain that there is at least an excuse for Össur, considering how great his loss. Things have not been well managed when these Norwegians have been given a chance to see in the hands of others valuable property which they recognized as having belonged to their dead relatives, and they unable to get possession of it. I am puzzled just what decision to make on these issues." They parted, each with ill grace, the bishop looking angry.

People gathered for the celebration that was held on the anniversary of the dedication of the Langanes church. The bishop and Einar were both at the banquet. Many had come to receive the sacrament; and the bishop intoned the mass. Among those present was Össur. He stood under the south wall of the church where a man named Brand Thordarson was talking with him; he was one of the bishop's employees. This man begged Össur to give in to the bishop. "Then I think everything will go well," he said; "but as things are it looks like trouble." Össur replied that he could not bring himself to yield, as badly as he had been treated. They kept talking back and forth about this.

Now the bishop and several others walked from the church to the adjoining farm, with Einar a member of the party. When they reached the door of the farm house Einar separated from them, walking back alone to the churchyard. There he took an ax from the hand of one of the worshipers and walked around to the south side of the church. Össur was standing there leaning upon the handle of his ax. Einar struck him at once a death blow, going then immediately back to the farm. The tables had been set there and he seated himself across from the bishop; however, without saying a word.

Some time later Brand Thordarson came into the hall, approached the bishop, and asked: "Has anyone told you any news, my lord?" The bishop replied he had heard nothing— "or have you something to tell me?" He replied: "A man fell, out here." The bishop asked: "Who is responsible, and who was the victim?" Brand said that not far from the bishop was somebody who could tell him. Then the bishop turned to Einar: "Are you responsible for the death of Össur?" He replied: "No doubt I am responsible." "Such deeds are not right," said the bishop, "but one can understand."*

Brand asked that the corpse should be bathed and that a mass should be sung over it. The bishop replied he would give people an opportunity to do that. They sat silent at the table and everything was quiet.

When the meal was over the bishop secured men to conduct the burial ceremony. Einar supported this request and asked that the burial service be seemly. The bishop commented it would really be more proper not to bury the man in the churchyard; "but still, since you ask it, he shall be buried at the church, since there is no chaplain available." He was not able to secure clergymen to preform the burial ceremony until after the corpse had been prepared for the burial.

Einar remarked: "Serious things have now happened, due not a little to your [i.e., the bishop's] arrangement. Violent men are here involved and I foresee that a good deal of trouble is going to be stirred up against us." The bishop replied he expected they would be able to stave off this violence [of the Norwegians] and that the prestige of the Greenlanders would increase in connection with this action, if moderation were maintained.

*Since we know from the rest of the account that the bishop had to gain from Össur's death, some commentators have considered that what the bishop meant by the critical part of his remark was that it was improper to do the killing in the churchyard, or so near the church.

CHAPTER V

The news spread and reached the merchants. Then spoke Ketil Kalfsson: "I did not guess far wrong when I said that he would be likely to be killed."

A tall and strong man named Simon was a relative of Össur. Ketil said it well might prove that Simon would find use for some of his prowess and that he would keep in mind the slaying of his relative. Simon replied he would not use any big words about that just now.

Ketil made their ship ready and also sent some men to Kolbein, the master of the other ship, to tell him the news. "Tell him I plan to bring an action against Einar, for I am familiar with the laws of Greenland and am well prepared to deal with them. Also, we have a goodly company of fighting men, if it comes to that."

Saying that he would take advice from Ketil, Simon went to Kolbein, told him about the slaying, and gave him the message from Ketil that the merchants should come from the Vestribyggd to support them in the parliament of the Greenlanders.

Kolbein replied he would of course come if he could. He said it was his desire that it should not turn out profitable for the Greenlanders to kill Norwegian traders. Ketil immediately followed the advice of Simon and started with a small company, telling the merchants that the rest of them should follow as soon as they could, "and bring all your trade goods with you."

Kolbein started as soon as the message came to him, asking his companions to go to the parliament and saying that if they did they would have so powerful a support that it was doubtful whether the Greenlanders would be able to have their way.

Kolbein and Ketil met and consulted together. Both of them were able men. When they started the weather was unfavorable. They did get through with a large company, but not with as many men as they had expected.

Now people gathered at the Althing. Sokki Thorisson was there. He was a wise man, now elderly, and was accustomed to being arbitrator in disputes between people. He went to see Kolbein and Ketil, telling them he desired to arrive at a settlement. "I offer myself as an arbitrator. True, I am connected with my son Einar; but still I shall so decide the case as will meet the approval not only of myself but of other judicious men."

Ketil replied that they intended to press their suit to the limit of the law; but that still he did not want to make it impossible to arrive at a compromise. "But we have been badly treated, and we have not hitherto been accustomed to yielding our rights to anybody." Sokki replied that it seemed to him they were not in a very strong position; he thought it doubtful they would be better off otherwise than if it were he who made the decision.

The merchants went to court and Ketil brought the action against Einar. Then said Einar: "The news will spread far if they succeed with overbearance against us." He went to the court and broke up its sitting by violence, so that no session could be held.

Sokki spoke: "My offer still stands, that I arbitrate this case." Ketil was against his being arbitrator, "for your award will amount to being the same injustice that Einar is now bringing about in this case." So they parted.

The reason why the company of merchants at the parliament had been so small was that some of the traders who were in the Western Settlement had not been able to get there. This was because headwinds had developed when they got two of their ships ready.

In midsummer there was to be [evidently by an agreement reached at the parliament subsequent to the brawls we have described] an arbitration meeting at Eid. Now the merchants came from the western colony, the ships gathering at a certain

ness; and now they were all together for a consultation. Kolbein said there would never have been this arrangement for arbitration if all the merchants had been together at the parliament; "and now I think we should all go together to this arbitration meeting, with such forces as we can muster." What they actually did was that they went and hid in a certain ravine, a short distance from the bishop's seat.

Two things happened together at the bishopric, that there was ringing for the high mass and that Einar Sokkason arrived. When the merchants heard this they said it was a great reception for Einar that the bells were so rung in his honor. They thought this an extraordinary proceeding and were displeased by it. But Kolbein said: "Don't be so displeased; perhaps, before evening, it will have turned out that these are funeral bells."

Einar now came with his party and they sat down on a slope. Sokki put forward certain articles for the appraisal of their value, for they were intended as payment of the damages (which the arbitrator would award). Ketil said: "My desire is that Hermund Kodransson and I be the ones to value these articles." Sokki agreed. Simon, the relative of Össur, looked displeased, and kept walking back and forth while the articles were being valued.

An old suit of plate armor was brought forward. Then spoke Simon: "It is a disgrace that such things should be offered in compensation for the life of so important a man as Össur was." He tossed the armor to one side and walked up toward those who sat on the slope. When the Greenlanders saw him coming they jumped up and stood looking down-slope in the direction of Simon. This enabled Kolbein, who had separated from his companions, to walk up behind them; they were all looking away from where he now was, and that enabled him to get in right behind them.

The two things happened together that he came up behind Einar and struck him with an ax between the shoulders, and that Einar's ax struck the head of Simon; so that both received death blows.

Einar said as he fell: "This was to be expected."

Now Thord, foster brother of Einar, ran toward Kolbein and was going to strike him with an ax, but Kolbein turned around so quickly that he was able to stick the spear point of his ax into Thord's wind pipe. The wound proved fatal.

Now there was a general battle while the bishop sat by Einar, who died with his head in the bishop's lap.

A man named Steingrim spoke up saying they ought to stop fighting, and he walked in between the two parties; both were so excited that he was pierced by swords from two sides.

Many were now wounded. Kolbein and his people got back to the ships, having lost 30 of their men. They sailed across Einarsfjord to Skjalgsbud. The merchant ships were there and were nearly ready to sail.

Kolbein reported there had been something of a disturbance, "and it is my opinion that the Greenlanders are not better satisfied now than they were before." Ketil remarked: "Those proved true words of yours, Kolbein, that we would hear funeral bells before we left. I think that right now Einar is dead and is being carried toward the church." Kolbein replied that he had done his best to secure that result.

Ketil said: "It is to be expected that the Greenlanders will be trying to get in touch with us. It is my advice that all of us keep our trade goods well in hand and that we all spend the nights aboard ships." That was what they did.

Sokki grieved over these events and asked people to support him in the coming battles.

CHAPTER VI

A man was named Hall. He dwelt at Solarfjöll, a wise man and a good husbandman. He was a supporter of Sokki and was the last to bring his support (when they were gathering to re-

venge Einar). He said to Sokki: "I do not think well of your
plan to attack the great Norwegian ships with our small vessels
and with such preparations as I suppose they must have made
against us; besides, I do not know how reliable are some of
your fighting men. The good fighters will not be slack; but
there will be others who will keep in the background so that
the more aggressive fighters will be killed. In that case our
situation will be even worse than before. It seems best to me
that we propose that oaths shall be exchanged among us, every
man swearing that he will either lose his life or be victorious."

At the speech of Hall many became discouraged. Sokki
spoke: "Still we cannot stop at a point where a settlement of
the case has not been reached." Hall offered to try to arrange a
settlement. He shouted to the merchants asking: "Am I free to
come and have a discussion with you?" Kolbein and Ketil answered that he was free to come. Hall then went to confer, and
said that it was necessary a settlement should be arrived at
after such serious deeds. The merchants replied that they were
prepared to settle if others were. They said that all the difficulties had been started by the Greenlanders, "but now when you
show such good will we are satisfied to let you arbitrate between us." He said he would do this and would make his decisions as right as he could, whether either side liked them
or not.

Now Sokki was consulted. He agreed to rest with the judgments of Hall. But the merchants were to make preparations
[for sailing] during the night, for it was said that Sokki would
not be pleased with anything except that they should leave the
country as soon as possible, "for if they delay in their preparations for sailing, to my annoyance, then it is to be expected that
any men they lose will be lost without compensation."

They now parted and an arrangement was made for an ad-
judication meeting.

Ketil said: "It does not look as if our preparations for sailing would be very rapid, and our food is running low. It is my

advice that we search for food. I know where a farmer lives
who has a lot of provisions. I think we should see if we can get
hold of them." Everybody said they were ready to try.

So one night 30 men, well armed, left the ships and went to
the farm in company, but they found everything bare. Thorarin was the name of the farmer who lived there. Ketil admitted
his advice had not turned out so very well. They left the farm
and were on their way back to the ship when they went through
a patch of bushes. Ketil then said he was sleepy and would
have to take a nap. He was told this was inadvisable, but still
he lay down and fell asleep, they watching him. He soon woke
up, saying: "Many things have I seen [in a dream]. How
would it be if we were to pull up by the roots the bush that I
rested my head on while I slept?" They pulled it up and beneath was an underground storehouse.

Ketil said: "Let us see, first thing, what there is to be had
here." They found 60 dressed sheep, 12 vaettir (each of about
80 pounds) of butter, and a large supply of dried fish. Ketil
then said: "It is lucky for me that I did not mislead you."
They went back to the ship with all this booty.

Now came the arbitration meeting. Both parties arrived
there, the traders and the Greenlanders. Then spoke Hall: "It
is my arbitration between you that I want to have reckoned
equal the killing of Össur and the killing of Einar. But on
account of difference in rank, it shall be a penalty upon the
Norwegians that they shall have no shelter or rights here in
the country [i.e., they must go and not come back]. The killings of Steingrim and of Simon shall be charged even against
each other; so also those of the Norwegian Krak and the
Greenlander Thorfinn, the Norwegian Vighvat and the Greenlander Bjarni, and the slayings of Thorir and of Thord. Now
remains uncompensated for one of our people named Thorarin,
a man of large family. For him a compensation shall be paid
in money."

Sokki expressed himself as disappointed with the arbitration; and so did other Greenlanders when they considered how the men lost by the two sides were valued according to rank. Hall said that they should nevertheless abide by his word, and they decided to do so.

Now the sea ice came in and all the water of all the fjords was covered. The Greenlanders thought the prospect good that they would capture the merchants who now would be unable to abide by that term of the judgment which required that they quit Greenland; but just as the month ended the ice all drifted away, giving the traders a chance to sail from Greenland. So that is how they parted.

The merchants arrived in Norway. Kolbein had brought with him from Greenland a polar bear and now went with it to King Harald Gilli. He gave him the bear and explained to the King what heavy punishment the Greenlanders deserved. He berated them severely. However, the King heard another story later on, from which it seemed that Kolbein had tried to deceive him; therefore the King did not recompense Kolbein for the polar bear.

Hereupon Kolbein decided to take the part of Sigurd, the Sham Deacon, and attacked King Harald Gilli, and wounded him [i.e., was one of several who together murdered the King]. Later, as they were going past Denmark, sailing with great speed, Kolbein was in a boat towed behind the ship. The weather was stormy and the boat broke loose, so that Kolbein was drowned. But Hermund and his companions returned to Iceland, their native land.

Here ends this saga.

CHAPTER X

The Decline and Disappearance
of the Colony

IT TAKES STRENGTH OF WILL to be brief when we come to the fascinating historical mystery of what finally did become of the Greenland colonists. We touch on only a few of the more important things which are known and bring out only a few of the chief inferences.

Greenland was a republic until 1261 when, a year earlier than Iceland, it elected to join Norway. Because of the monopoly of the Greenland trade granted merchants in Bergen, it became against the law for anyone else to sail a ship in Greenland waters, at least for trade, so the colonists were virtual prisoners. There seem to have continued, to or beyond 1347, the journeys to Labrador for cargoes of timber to trade in Iceland; but eventually nothing remained except what was possible along shore with small boats and what might be accomplished (as, for instance, a passage to Europe) through the kindness of the legal traders from Bergen or of traders who flouted the law. As our studies advance we have increasing reason to believe that there was a good deal of illicit voyaging to Greenland, perhaps Hanseatic or Basque and Portuguese but likely most of it British, from Lynn and Bristol.

At first there were legal ships most years from Bergen to Greenland, but eventually there was only one every few years. The last undisputed Norwegian voyage took place in 1410;

though there may have been unrecorded Norwegian voyages later. In fact there is reason to believe that they continued down to 1484 when "Hanseatic pirates" are said to have killed in Bergen forty men, the last in that port who knew how to sail to Greenland.

In 1432 a treaty was signed between King Henry VI of England and King Eric of Pomerania, ruler of the three Scandinavian countries, by which the English king promised to forbid his subjects trading in Iceland or Greenland. We know that the promise was not kept with regard to Iceland. Nansen says that by 1451 "the English merchants, some of whom were no doubt Norwegians established in Bristol, seem to have seized upon nearly the whole trade of Iceland."

Some historians have naïvely assumed that the English agreement of abstinence from trade, broken with regard to Iceland, was nevertheless kept with regard to Greenland. By the nature of the Greenland situation, positive evidence for or against this is hard to come by. Nor is the trouble solely Greenlandic, for in the fifteenth century there were much secrecy and camouflage about sea-borne commerce in general. The merchant did not want his competitors to know how or where he got his profits. Voyages were made in the greatest possible secrecy, sometimes helped out by issuing false statements on destination and purpose. After such a treaty as that of 1432 English traders had a further reason for secrecy, particularly if the king's real sentiment perhaps was that he did not mind his subjects trading with Greenland so long as he did not officially know about it.

One school of commentators feels that after 1412, or at least by 1430 or 1448, the Greenland colony was entirely cut off from Europe and that it became extinct through two main causes, (1) malnutrition resulting from lack of imported cereals and other foods of vegetable nature, and (2) attacks on the weakened population by Eskimos. We have space here to examine only some of the main contentions.

During the last few years, since historians have become vitamin-conscious, it has been maintained that the colonists died out through deficiency diseases. A proof of this was alleged to have been discovered by Dr. Poul Nörlund at Herjolfsnes in 1921. The skeletons there undoubtedly showed evidence of rickets and similar troubles. The weakness of the interpretation of the evidence, indeed its susceptibility to a reverse conclusion, appears from conditions in Greenland today.

The Danish physician Alfred Bertelsen showed, in his *Sanitation and Health Conditions in Greenland,* published in 1928, that rickets is common among Greenland children in the families of Danish officials, but practically unknown in "Eskimo" families. This might be interpreted as showing the Eskimos to be racially immune, but that view does not fit the results of studies elsewhere. Speaking of Labrador children varying from pure Eskimo through mixed European, to almost pure white, Dr. William A. Thomas, in his *Health of a Carnivorous Race,* says that among those who are carnivorous "there is neither scurvy nor rickets." But speaking of those pure and mixed Eskimo children who live in a Europeanized way largely on European food, he says that "scurvy, rickets, and a combination of the two are universal." So in Greenland, where also it is food and not race that makes the Danes rickety when the Eskimos are sound.

Really the deficiency-disease portion of the Herjolfsnes investigation contributes nothing to the solution of why the colony disappeared. Herjolfsnes was the first port of call for ships from Europe. Nörlund himself has shown that people who died there around 1400 and 1450 were buried in clothes of recent European fashion. Beyond every other place in Greenland this community fed on a European diet. If an application is insisted upon, then it surely must be that European food was detrimental and that the Norse were here killed off by commerce. But if the conclusion is pushed that far it becomes an absurdity.

The contention that the Norse were exterminated by the Eskimos depends mainly on two things, the allegation that we have an account of the destruction of the northerly settlement from Ivar Bardarson, and the claim that the Eskimos told Hans Egede and others, following 1721, that such a destruction had occurred.

Nansen, foremost critic of the destruction-by-Eskimos view, dwells on the absurdity of the Bardarson account when it states in substance that men sent (around 1345) to spy out conditions in the northern colony had found dwellings surrounded by domestic livestock but with no people and had concluded from this that the Europeans had been killed by Eskimos.

The Bardarson party, Nansen maintains, were in no position to know the whites had been killed by Eskimos. That the Eskimos, not warlike but a race of hunters, had killed the people *and left the domestic animals grazing about* was contrary to common sense. What they might have done was to kill the animals and not the people; certainly if they had killed the people they would have killed the animals, too, and eaten them. Indeed, Nansen could have made that contention stronger; for it is the Eskimo way to kill all animals they can get at, whether they eat them or not.

Nansen advances as the reasonable hypothesis (supported by considerable evidence) that the colonists of the Western Settlement by this time had begun to depend on hunting for a livelihood to a much greater extent than formerly and to a much greater extent than in the Eastern Settlement. What they had then done (in the situation which Bardarson misunderstood) was to leave the farm animals grazing safely about while they went off to more favorable hunting districts, the intention being, no doubt, to return in time to make hay and take care of the livestock before winter. A wrong interpretation of the evidence by Bardarson, Nansen feels, is the more likely because he, as he himself admits, was afraid to go ashore and merely reported that he had seen from shipboard grazing farm beasts but no people.

The view for which Nansen was a prominent contender is that there disappeared from Greenland the civilization of the Europeans, not their blood. The main points are four:

1. Wherever they have been in contact, whites have intermarried with Eskimos about as readily as with any nonwhite people in the world. There must have been constant intermarriages in medieval Greenland.

2. In Greenland the Eskimo way of life was better adapted to the environment and resources than the Norse. The only things which might have preserved European culture would have been a larger population of Europeans than Eskimos and a constant reinforcement of the Norse culture from Europe through commerce. But it is unlikely, even if the Scandinavians may have numbered ten thousand, that this total was greater than that of the Eskimos; and we know that the commerce, which had been decreasing even under the republic, fell off sharply after the 1261 union with Norway. Norwegian commerce disappeared early in the fifteenth century, and the only contact with Europe thereafter was (probably) an occasional ship from Bristol and Lynn, with some Hansa or Basque and Portuguese relations a possibility.

3. During the latter part of the historical period the Church of Rome complained frequently about the apostasy of the Greenlanders. One part of this apostasy, Nansen suggests, may have been intermarriage with the heathen Eskimos. Such blending of the racial strains would promote that Eskimoization of the culture which is shown by the considerable percentage of bones of game animals in the late middens. This increase in the reliance on hunting must have necessitated a movement from the fjord heads, which were suited chiefly to husbandry pursuits, toward promontories where the sea-mammal hunting was better and where the relation with the hunting Eskimos would have been closer. The evidence is also

that the *nordurseta* hunting excursions, bringing still more
Eskimo contacts, went farther north in the middle (and perhaps the later) period of the colony than they did in the early
part. This northward extension was not primarily because
game had been killed off by excessive hunting in the south, but
mainly because the north, then as now, was by nature a better
hunting country.

4. There is so much obvious white blood in Greenland today
that it cannot well be explained as having resulted from the
European revival of the sixteenth and seventeenth centuries in
which Frobisher was a pioneer. Of the eighteen thousand
"Eskimos" now in Greenland, from a quarter to a half could
be so dressed and prepared that they would pass racially unnoticed in London or New York. Some of them would look to
you like Scandinavians, some like just anybody, and it might
occur to you that a few of them looked like Italians. There has
been no approach to such a Europeanization of Eskimos anywhere else in the world. Greenland is, moreover, the only country where marriages of white women with Eskimos can have
been common.

The high if not supreme standing of Dr. Fridtjof Nansen
as an authority on the history of northern exploration, and his
challenge to what was in his day the majority view, that the
Eskimos were known to have exterminated the Greenlandic
Europeans, leads us to keep referring to the race amalgamation theory as that of Nansen. But we must not let it seem that
he was the inventor of it.

Throughout the fifteenth and sixteenth centuries it was the
uniform opinion, from Rome to Reykjavik, that a European
community and a Christian church still existed in Greenland.

The last Greenland message of the popes, with which we
shall deal at some length hereafter, was that of Alexander VI,
written either late in 1492 or early in 1493 and still preserved
as an original document in the Vatican archives. It speaks of
the lifelong interest of that pope in the church west of the

Atlantic (then dating back some forty years, to his early priest-hood); it details efforts that had been made and should be made to get in touch with the bishopric at Gardar and assumes that the Greenlanders were clinging to an admittedly some-what contaminated form of Christianity.

The people of Iceland, as we bring out elsewhere through quotations from their annals, were in at least some contact with Greenland after 1500, and they continued to assume until well in the eighteenth century that a Norse Greenlandic community existed.

Churchmen and others in the continental Scandinavias planned a Greenland expedition every now and then, and even secured royal support, but something always happened so that these expeditions did not sail. From the writings of the pro-moters it appears they were certain that Europeans were still living in Greenland but uncertain whether they were still Christian. The talk was for the need to sustain and revive their faith or to reconvert them to Christianity.

Later, after the Reformation, there was some agitation for expeditions from the then Lutheranized Scandinavian coun-tries on the theory that the Greenlanders were still Roman Catholic and that they needed saving from the errors of Popery.

Following 1721 the devoted Norwegian missionary, Hans Egede, reported to his Danish superiors that he had traveled many hundreds of miles along the shore line of Greenland, finding many ruins of farms and churches but no surviving Europeans. Being a Norwegian himself, he naturally had clear ideas of what Norsemen would be like; being wholly un-familiar with the North American Indian type, and finding people unlike Scandinavians, he took them to be wholly non-European, even though his actual descriptions of some of them indicate to us a mixed-blood population.

Egede knew the Bardarson report, that Eskimos had de-stroyed the Western Settlement. Believing the Eastern Settlement to be on the east coast of Greenland, he thought himself in the Western Settlement and concluded that Bardarson had been right about the destruction. He took the people whom he saw around him to be the race Karlsefni had seen in Vinland and whom Bardarson had accused. Egede still thought there might be Catholic Christians in Greenland; but, if so, they were in that Eastern Settlement.

Disappointed in not finding Europeans to convert from Roman Catholicism or from heathenism, Egede devoted himself to learning the Eskimo language so he could convert the heathen he did find. It cannot have been long from the time when he first commanded enough of the language to make himself understood until he began to give the Eskimos some intimation of his theory about the part their ancestors must have played in the disappearance of the Norsemen.

Travelers and ethnologists report from primitive people in many lands, including various Eskimo groups, that it is a part of their ethics to answer a leading question according to what they think to be the desire of the questioner, so as to be in agreement with him. That Egede did ask leading questions about the disappearance of the Norsemen is made probable by his own statement of the case. For after remarking that the Eskimos of southwest Greenland had little detailed information about the Europeans who had been there two or three hundred years before, he says that they did confirm that their forefathers made war upon the Norsemen and destroyed them.

It can have been true, as we suggest, but it need not have been, that Eskimos who previously knew nothing about the destruction of the Norsemen by their ancestors would agree with Egede about his theory just to please him. For there is another trait of primitive man, frequently reported from Eskimo communities, which gives us an even better solution.

In explanation, we take an instance from the Eskimos of Coronation Gulf. When first visited by an anthropologist, in 1910, the people there had never seen a bowhead whale and were unaware from tradition that their forefathers had ever hunted whales. During May of that year several of them, replying to questions at different times, said all they knew of the bowhead was its Eskimo name and that certain large bones found on their shore line were from the animals to which that name belonged.

But in March 1911 a member of this same Eskimo community was heard telling a circumstantial and localized story about how a great whale hunter, by name Kaplavinna, had been out in a kayak (these Eskimos do not have the umiak), had harpooned a bowhead, and had towed it ashore at a certain named point where he cut it up.

When asked why he had not admitted this knowledge the previous spring the narrator replied it was because at that time he had not known the story. From whom, then, had he learned it since? He had heard it from one of the local Eskimos who had joined the party of the white men the previous summer and had spent with them several weeks.

Later, when this second man was questioned, he said he got the story from an Alaska Eskimo who was a companion of the white men. The Alaskan, in his turn, said he had been telling the local people about a whaling voyage in which he had taken part. The captain of the ship was Leavitt (of Portland, Maine), and it was his name, "Cap" Leavitt, that had become Kaplavinna in the local story. The Alaskan's account of lowering a boat, shooting the whale, bringing it alongside the ship, and cutting it up had been transmuted into the story of a single hunter in a kayak, Kaplavinna, harpooning the whale as if it had been a seal and pulling it ashore for the cutting up.

Nothing will seem likelier to those intimately familiar with primitive Eskimos than what we think to be the probable Greenland sequence, followng 1721. We think Egede told the Eskimos his view that their ancestors had killed the last Norsemen; from this the Eskimos would normally develop, in their own terms, a story (with names and places) that was, so far as they understood it, the substance of what Egede had told them, which they had taken not as a theory but as a tradition of the white men. The final stage would be that the missionaries were told these stories and welcomed them as corroboration of what they themselves felt sure must be the truth. Following the Egede report there was throughout the Scandinavias, and eventually throughout Europe, a shocked acceptance of the view which Egede and the rest of the early Danish missionaries advanced, that the Christian Norsemen had been exterminated by the heathen Eskimos.

The extermination view seems to have gone unchallenged for half a century. Then the Danish mission sent to Greenland the Icelander Eigil Thorhallason, the first man to go there who was thoroughly familiar with the history of the Greenland republic and who understood the relations between Iceland and Greenland from the time of Erik the Red until the fifteenth and even the sixteenth centuries. With that knowledge to fortify him against the ready assumption that the Norse became extinct through the causes which were then adduced, Thorhallason developed his own tentative solution of the problem.

In 1776 this Icelandic missionary published at Copenhagen in Danish his work *Rudera*. It deals in the main with the archaeological remains found in Greenland, the ruins of churches and farms, but it has a supplement on the question of how and why the Europeans disappeared.

This book is one of the least known in the whole literature of the disappearance problem. Nansen does not seem to have been aware of its existence. So far as we have seen, it is not mentioned in his thousands of footnotes or anywhere else in his voluminous text, nor is it listed in any of his available bibliographies. Few applicable books are so seldom noted in any branch of the Greenland literature. The discovered references all concern themselves with the archaeological descriptions of the *Rudera;* none have yet been found giving Thorhallason's views on the problem of the colony's disappearance. Therefore, instead of summarizing, we present here in translation, with some digressions omitted, the said appendix. It gives in essence what later became known as the Nansen theory of race amalgamation:

A SHORT SUPPLEMENT
ABOUT THE DESTRUCTION OF THE OLD
NORWEGIANS AND ICELANDERS IN THE
WESTERN SETTLEMENT*

The later writers of Greenland's history are of different opinions regarding the destruction [of the Europeans]. Some of them say that according to the old accounts they were destroyed by the Eskimos in the fourteenth century; others that they died from starvation. Still others say that the plague which swept over the North in 1350, and was called the Black Death, killed them all.

1. The first opinion is based on accounts which are not clear. Ivar Beer [Ivar Bardarson] says at the end of his history of Greenland that "the Western Settlement is now possessed by the Eskimos alone."

But history does not give any account of a war between the peoples, except when the Eskimos killed 18 Norsemen and took two boys prisoners, which event Torfeus refers to the year 1379. It is not easily understandable, in view of what we know from history about the old Norwegians, their courage and experience in war, that they should be completely destroyed by the unaggressive, inexperienced and practically defenseless Eskimos, unless the latter found a chance to sneak upon them murderously, which is their style when they have a killing in mind. But in that way they could not have destroyed all the Norse who, at that time, had about 100 farms spread

*Translated from: *Efterretning om Rudera Eller Levninger af de Gamle Nordmaends og Islænderes Bygninger paa Grönlands Vester-Side, Tilligemed et Anhang om Deres Undergang Sammesteds,* Kjöbenhavn, 1776.

over the Western Settlement;* some places, for instance in
Angmagssalik, the farms were so close together that the farmers could easily come to each other's assistance.

If you say that the Eskimos could shoot the Norwegians
down with their bows and arrows, before the latter could
reach them with their weapons, then you should be told that
the Norwegians also used bows in war; they also had shields
for defense. The opinion is, in any case, rejected by Dr. Kranz
(4th book, paragraph 9, p. 338, 1st edit.) as unfounded.

But it is peculiar that the Greenlanders up to this day tell
stories about and are proud of their ancestors having destroyed
the old Kablunaet [white men]. A certain place in the Godthaab Fjord is called Pissikfarbik, i.e., a place where to shoot
with bows and arrows,† and it is said to have derived its name
from the war waged between the Eskimos and the Kablunaet.
But even if they conquered them there they did not necessarily
destroy them in the whole of the Western Settlement. Perhaps
the Eskimos did not know there were more Norwegians than
those living in this immediate neighborhood, in the Kappisselikfjord, where there have been found ruins of other farms. Who
knows whether the Greenlandic account does not just refer to
the 18 men [killed by Eskimos] whom our history mentions?

2. The opinion which states that the old Norsemen . . .
died of starvation is still less well founded. The answers are:

(a) In the beginning of the colony there was perhaps danger
of starvation; but this did not occur the first years and after that
the colonists could take precautions. The Norsemen lived here
a long time, as can be seen by the remains of their buildings.

---

*This was written at the time when it was believed that the Eastern Settle-
ment was on the east coast; consequently Thorhallason believed himself to have
seen only the Western Settlement.

†*Note by translator:* Pissikfarbik (Pisiksiarvik) does not as a name imply
that men were killed with arrows there any more than "shooting gallery" is a
place where Americans are shot with rifles. The word, of itself, has no implication of killing. Throughout the Eskimo world the expression means "a place
where people shoot at targets with bow and arrow," or where they try out their
bows to see who can shoot farthest. There are many similar Eskimo place names.

(b) Most of the livelihood of the colonists was derived from domestic animals, for which end they had erected good-sized farm buildings, cleared big fields, and established themselves well, as can still be seen. Most of the farms are situated near salmon rivers and near the coast where there are herring, spawning fish, crabs and sea scorpions in abundance, besides hunting grounds and other fishing. In the country there were reindeer, hares, ptarmigan and Iceland moss [a well-known Icelandic food source] in great quantities, so that they cannot have died from starvation; at least, this could not have happened to them all at the same time, so that those who needed help could have gone to their neighbors for it. Old stories also tell that when the [Ivar Bardarson] relief party came from the Eastern Settlement they found both sheep and cattle in quantities. The owners of these, then, could not have died from starvation. But the above-mentioned relief party found no people. How did they then perish?

3. Did they perish by the plague? Dr. Kranz says in the place I have quoted that this is the most likely reason for their destruction and that the savages would then have been able to put an end to them more easily. But the Icelandic Annals state that in the year 1350, when the plague was at its worst in Norway, there came no ship to Iceland and they expressly state that this plague did not reach Iceland.

It must be presumed that the government of Norway used the same precautions with regard to Greenland, and this seems to be confirmed by the fact that the annals mention neither Greenland nor Iceland in their narrative about this plague, which the annals say raged in the Hebrides, the Orkneys, the Shetlands, and the Faeroes. However, the annal writers do say something about the plague years. They state that in 1347 there came a ship from Greenland to Iceland; and in 1359 Jon Skalli (John the Bald) who earlier had been ordained Bishop of Greenland came to Iceland and had then received the bishopric of Holar. He had presumably returned from Greenland to Norway at the time of the plague; for his predecessor, Bishop Arni, was still alive when Jon Skalli was ordained, without Archbishop Poul knowing it. Jon Skalli was ordained bishop in 1343.

Bishop Egede proves in his *Natural History,* p. 13, that voyages to Greenland continued long after the plague. And thereto could be added this: In 1383 a ship came to Norway from Greenland where it had been for two winters. It carried a number of people from the bishopric Skalholt that had been shipwrecked the previous year but had escaped in a boat to Greenland. They brought the news that Bishop Olaf (others called him Alf) of Greenland had died six years before. During the lifetime of this bishop the fatal war between the Eskimos and the Norwegians is said to have taken place (1379). That was many years after the plague.

And why should the plague, if it came to Greenland, spare the Eskimos and not the Norse?

Still I cannot find better means to combine the truthfulness of our old history with the Eskimo stories that they fought and conquered the old Kablunaet than this: that the Eskimos took advantage of the general disease among the Norwegians, attacked them murderously, and destroyed as many as they could; the surviving Norse [of the Western Settlement] would then partly have fled to the Eastern Settlement and partly have been obliged to make friends with the Eskimos and take up their way of life. Or perhaps the Eskimos, killing the old, spared the young and adopted them.

You can still find among the Eskimos several signs of their having had close connection with the Old Norse. Among these are:

(a) Words and names which resemble the Old Norse, as for instance: Hvann (Hvonn) [The Icelandic words in parenthesis], *Angelica;* Kollek (Kola), *a lamp;* Nisa (Hnisa), *a porpoise;* Nouk (Hnukur), *a high point or ness.* Terkelin,

Olak, Uttuk, Sunnilik, I think, mean Thorkell, Oli, Otto, Gunnhildur.*

(b) The Eskimos have several games that to this day are played in Iceland; as, for instance, *Hnappleikur,* where all stand in a row and everyone tries to get hold of the one ahead of him; but one stands apart from the others, facing the ones in the first row and tries to get hold of the one in the back row. Also they play *Vikivaka,* where a number of people hold hands and walk around in a circle, hop on one foot and at the same time sing to each other, or answer each other with song. The difference is that the Greenlanders play this game without sense or order.

(c) The cadence of the Eskimo song is not unlike the Icelandic chanting of *rimur.* When they sing to each other, or on other occasions play the drums and sing, the player speaks some words that are supposed to resemble a verse, and then everybody answers in a monotonous sound with Amna aja ajaaja, which lasts until the player again speaks some words, that then give the song renewed force in Amna aja aja ajaaa.

The whole proceeding is rather like that which the Icelanders call to "kveda undir"; that is to repeat the refrain, when the *rimur* are sung.

Kranz states in his fifth book, pgf. 3, p. 505, first edition, that you could see where the Greenlanders had brought an old woman, not yet dead, to the grave. They had made the sign of the cross all the way in the snow, so that her spirit should not come back and disturb them.

---

*This is perhaps Thorhallason's weakest paragraph; and still he may be right in perhaps a third of his cases. But falling down here does not much weaken his argument, for it is not necessarily true that words (except names) survive when two linguistic stocks amalgamate in culture and blood. Anything between 10% and 30% of the Icelandic ancestry is Irish and there is a great deal of Irish material in the literature, but there are surely less than a dozen Irish words in the Icelandic language, other than names. New York City was once a Dutch town, and we still have many Dutch place and family names; but there are probably less than a dozen other words from the Dutch language that remain in the current speech of New York.

The Greenlanders have no superstition about the cross, have not even a name for it, nor can they understand what it means, so I should think that one of the company, without meaning anything by it or as a joke, swung his arrow or walking stick, making thereby some signs in the snow. But as it is stated that this was done in order that the spirit of the deceased should not come back this must be a remnant of the cross ceremonies of the Roman Catholic Norsemen, if the story is true. The Greenlanders will not acknowledge it. . . .

Still another reason for the destruction of the old Norsemen is found in a letter which Pope Nicolaus V wrote in 1448, 12. Cal. Octobris (i.e., the 18th of September) to the Bishops at Skalholt and Holar in Iceland . . . And as I do not know that it has been published in Danish I will give my readers a translation of it. [Translation omitted, because we quote this papal document elsewhere.]

[Like Nansen 135 years later, Thorhallason devotes his criticism of this papal letter, and of its then current interpretation, chiefly to the statement that the Christian community in Greenland had been attacked by barbarians (which the interpreters said meant Eskimos), that many had been carried away as prisoners, but that some of these had been repatriated in Greenland by the barbarians, and that the barbarians had destroyed those churches which were in accessible places but had been unable to reach the ones that were in the depth of the valleys, thus leaving them uninjured. We give Thorhallason's comments on these points.]

The question is, then: What barbarian neighboring nations attacked the Greenland Norsemen with a fleet? The nearest nations were the Eskimos, whom the Norse called Skraelings. If you assume that it was they who, in this manner, attacked the Norse, and at the same time settled in Greenland, it fits quite well with regard to time, i.e., first in the fifteenth century does our history [i.e., Bardarson] state that the Western Settlement was no longer peopled by the Norse but inhabited by the Eskimos alone. But then these questions arise:

1. From where did the Eskimos get such an enormous fleet? The Eskimos have to this day only fragile skin boats which, they say, were no stronger in olden times, and these could hardly be called a fleet without great exaggeration. But, admittedly, it is far from Greenland to Rome, and the story may have become exaggerated on the way there.

2. It does not seem to fit in with the nature of the Eskimos to spare the parish churches that were farthest away, "as they could not get at them because of the steepness of the mountains."

3. The defeated Norsemen were said to have been carried away to slavery, and yet the majority returned to their homes after some time. This and other things show that some other nation than the Eskimos must have captured them. It will always be uncertain which nation it is, but I think you would not do injustice to the nation which is known to have sailed to Greenland for a long time [i.e., England], if you thought that they had taken the opportunity, when the voyages from Norway to Greenland suddenly stopped, or at least were neglected for many years in succession, to acquire a trade monopoly with the Eskimos. To that end they may have tried to destroy the Norse in Greenland. . . . But this undertaking of theirs did not probably meet eventual approval [by the English nation], so the captured Norse were sent back to their homes.

4. The papal brief says, in effect, that although the barbarian attack was cruel and destructive it did not completely destroy the Norse. On the contrary, the parishes farthest inland are said to have escaped destruction. Most of the prisoners [according to the Pope's letter] came back and rebuilt some of the ruined places. So this attack cannot be a sufficient reason for the disappearance of the colony. . . .

(End of Thorhallason translation)

In comparison with the speculations on the disappearance of the Norsemen from Greenland which appeared during the following hundred years, this 1776 document of Thorhallason's makes a remarkable showing. We emphasize two of the points:

Through a century of comment on Greenland after 1776 we meet again and again the idea that a plague crossed the Atlantic to Greenland and killed off most of the Europeans, leaving the remnant an easy prey for the Eskimos. It was not until the last fifty years, or more nearly the last twenty-five, that this argument was generally dropped; there had finally penetrated to the historians and antiquaries the conclusion of the epidemiologists that European contagious diseases are usually much more fatal to the people of the Americas and the Pacific oceanic islands than they are to those of the Old World.

Thorhallason, then, was at least one hundred years ahead of the average Greenland commentator when he wrote what now seems a mild protest, that he could not see why a disease would attack Norsemen and leave Eskimos be. Today we would write that if the plague crossed to Greenland the chances were that the death rate would be at least twice as heavy among the Eskimos as the Europeans, even granting that the Europeans had lost some of their immunity through centuries of comparative isolation. Relatively the Norse should have been stronger after the plague than before it.

The only possible counterargument now is that perhaps the Eskimos were geographically so far removed from the Norse that the disease was unable to leap the gap. But history and probability were always against that. Recently have come along the archaeologists who show that in this period, or a little later, Eskimos with a partly Europeanized culture, or Europeans largely Eskimoized, were occupying the whole northern half of the west coast of Greenland as far at least as Inglefield Land, some 800 miles north of the Arctic Circle, which would give the two peoples several hundred miles of overlapping. Race blending was no doubt in rapid progress everywhere, except just possibly in the most southerly districts of the Eastern Settlement.

The second thing we underscore is how Thorhallason reasoned out, with nothing but general knowledge to support him, that the "barbarians" who attacked the Greenlanders, who destroyed the churches in the open fjords and on the promontories but could not reach those of the deep fjords, who carried away prisoners and repatriated them years afterward, must have been the English. One hundred and thirty-five years after him Nansen was able to document the same contention with a treaty between the English and Scandinavian kings where the English promised to restrain the depredations of their freebooters in outlying places, and to repatriate those who had been carried away as prisoners from a number of dependencies of the Scandinavian kingdom, among them Greenland.

A direct statement that Eskimos and whites fraternized is found in Bishop Gisli Oddsson's annals for 1342. "The inhabitants of Greenland voluntarily abandoned the true faith and the Christian religion, having already abandoned all good customs and true virtues, and amalgamated themselves with the people of America *(ad Americae populos se converterunt)*."

The use of "the people of America" is explained by the fact that these annals were written up from old Norse language sources by an Icelandic Latinist about 1637. He was probably, at the point here in question, paraphrasing from memory documents which had been lost when the Skalholt Library was burned in 1630. That a learned Icelander should in that period translate the Norse word for Eskimo, *Skraeling,* by "the people of America" is more than natural, since the first and best known of Icelandic references to the Eskimos is the one which specifically states that the natives of Green-

land were the same kind of people as those whom the Greenlanders met in Markland. Well before 1637 the Icelanders
would have arrived at the conclusion that the Markland of
their sagas was part of the country which, in post-Columbian
times, had come to be known as America.

In his *Klima-Vekslinger i Historisk og postglacial Tid,*
Nansen has well said that he is unable to think so badly of
his own countrymen of the Middle Ages as to assume that
none of them were adaptable enough to learn the, for the
country, admirable ways of the Eskimos, by which they could
survive in Greenland and prosper. He goes on to add that
he knows no reason to think that there would have been any
reluctance on the part of the Norsemen to intermarry among
a people so attractive, who must have seemed doubly admirable
against the Greenlandic background where they were so com-
petently at home.

Nansen says that race consciousness and discrimination
against so-called "inferior" peoples is a relatively modern
development, the result of the post-Renaissance ascendancy of
Europe and the political and economic supremacy of the whites
over colored types. It hardly actuated the medieval Norsemen
in their contact with the Eskimos of Greenland. Whatever
objection the former had against intimate relations with the
latter must have been on cultural, not racial, grounds. When,
therefore, during the later isolation of the Greenland settlements from Europe around 1350, the Eskimo culture proved
itself to be better adapted to the environment than the im-
migrant and stranded Norse culture, the superiority-complex
hindrance against racial intermarriages, if it existed, must
have grown weak.

Nansen's monumental study, the two quarto volumes *In
Northern Mists,* with his other writings, is basic to our sum-
mary here of what we call the Nansen view of how the Europeans disappeared. In it he is careful, as one must be writing
a work intended primarily for scholars, to buttress his every

statement with footnotes and to give credit to all his sources. But nowhere, so far as we can see, has he mentioned in this connection the well-known Norwegian sociologist and historian, Eilert Sunt. Yet this fellow countryman of Nansen's was a pioneer, after the likewise unmentioned Thorhallason, in maintaining that it was more probable the Norsemen in Greenland had disappeared by amalgamation than through extermination.

In *Egedes Dagbok i Udtag,* Christiania, 1860, the Norwegian sociologist is commenting on the diary which Hans Egede, Norwegian missionary in Danish service, kept during the first few years of the Greenland mission, following 1721:

"It is by no means settled that the Norwegian population was completely destroyed by the Eskimos . . . When the connection with the mother country stopped so that the Norsemen (in Greenland) had to get along without such things as iron for tools and clergymen for the maintenance of divine service, it will be understood that the Norse culture and way of living was no longer possible. But it was possible to live in the Eskimo manner. Then it could have happened—although it is very embarrassing for us to think about it—that one and another of the Norse families had to make friends with the Eskimos, take up their manner of living, and begin to travel with them along the coast where there is most food. With this way of life all better things would soon be forgotten, and now it might happen that a Norse girl preferred an Eskimo kayak paddler as a suitor and master to a less successful family supporter of Norse descent. . . .

"While the genuine Eskimos are very easy [for Egede] to recognise from their black, stiff hair, a rather dark complexion, low stature and an inclination to fatness, Rink found so much European appearance among the Greenlanders that he assumes there has been a considerable mixing with Norse blood from the time of the old settlement . . .

"We are not accustomed to think that a population of

higher education, Christian and relatively civilized, would fall so low and disappear in mixing with a crude race. But that a population like the Norse in Greenland, which had been living there 400 years, should disappear completely is just as rare an occurrence . . . And when we, in our own time and in our own country, learn that the Norwegians in small out-of-the-way districts in Finmark mix with the Laplanders in marriage and associate with them so that the Laplanders' language and way of life becomes prevalent among the children, or at least the grandchildren, of the mixed families (cf. my book: *Om Aedruelighedstilstanden i Norge,* 1859, p. 112), then you can understand that this may also have been the case with our former countrymen in the desperate circumstances of Greenland . . .

"Egede had probably expected to find recognisable countrymen of his own; but the indefatigable way in which he took care of the 'savages' that he found there will please us still more when there is a reason to think that the remains of the Norse population really had assimilated with the Eskimos, so that he—though without understanding what he saw—had on his journey south a glimpse of his countrymen's fair hair and blue eyes."

Even before 1410 and the nearly complete isolation from the countries previously most intimate, Norway and Iceland, there could have been a deal of blood mixture, since race consciousness does not ordinarily prevent concubinage or in general the relation of the "superior" men with the "inferior" women. It is the unions of men previously social inferiors with the women of the previously superior race which, so far as the probabilities go, might be supposed to have increased in Greenland with the deterioration of European commerce.

Southernmost Greenland, more populous, comparatively successful in husbandry, and relatively in close touch with Europe, would have shown the greatest resistance to Eskimo relations on terms of equality. The less numerous Norsemen in the more northerly colony, less in touch with Europe, less successful with their cattle and sheep, and more dependent on hunting, would, for those reasons and because they met the Eskimos more frequently, come much more readily to a feeling of tolerance and later of equality. Those hunters of both settlements who penetrated occasionally or habitually to the game districts still farther north would have increasing reason to adopt Eskimo ways and views, until in great probability a majority of the farthest pioneers had Eskimo wives, just as the majority of northerly Canadian and Alaskan white trappers have Eskimo wives today.

It is, then, in the most northerly districts that the marrying of Eskimo men and white women would have started; but likely the beginning of the Church protests against apostasy coincided with the arrival of the race-mingling wave in the southern district of Greenland, the vicinity of the bishop's seat. Around the middle of the fourteenth century Eskimoization of the ways of life had progressed, in all likelihood peaceably, to a stage where the Western Settlement was no longer an outpost either of European culture or of the Christian religion. Ivar Bardarson, who had been in Greenland about twenty years following 1341, wrote in Norway about 1370 (we translate): "The Skraelings now hold the entire Western Settlement. Still there are [in that district] plenty of horses, goats, cattle, and sheep; but [they are] all wild and there are no people, either Christian or heathen." This would seem reasonably interpreted as meaning that the people had sort of walked out of the farmer life as an institution at the same time as they moved out of the farmlands of the Western Settlement northward into the hunting country. Still, the narrower interpretation a few pages *ante* is all that Bardarson's testimony demands.

Part of the fourteenth- and fifteenth-century transformation in Greenland would have been the adoption of Eskimo culture by members of the Eastern Settlement who went north on nordurseta expeditions. Those who liked hunting would no doubt stay in the north, while the misfits (from the hunter point of view) returned to the peasant life of the Eastern Settlement. In that sense the most southerly districts of Greenland were being subjected to a reversed natural selection. The adventurous, those of restless energy, the pioneer type, would have been eliminated gradually by emigration, leaving behind the conservative and, in certain respects at least, the weaker. Because of that conservatism, because they were by choice farmers, hostilities in the south were likely to take the place of the peaceable amalgamation in the north.

The farthest poleward extension of European activity west of the Atlantic before Columbus is that indicated by certain discoveries of the Nares expedition in 1876, by folklore recordings of Rasmussen during the second decade of the twentieth century, and by Danish archaeological work in Inglefield Land, a little farther north and east than the Nares and Rasmussen findings. Some maintain, however, that the proof of Norse penetration does not extend beyond 73° N. Lat.

By account in the sagas, and elsewhere, the Greenlanders very soon after the colonization, perhaps before 1000, and at any rate immediately thereafter, hunted in the uninhabited region north beyond Disko. The districts in which the hunting was done had in the records two names, Greipar and Kroksfjardarheidi.

To go on the northern quest had what was in practice a technical designation: *"ad fara i nordrsetu," "ad vera a nordrsetu."* *Nordrseta,* or, literally, "sitting north," was apparently at first spending the summer on the northern hunt; later it might mean spending the whole year. [In this book we use generally the modern Icelandic spelling, *Nordurseta.*]

When once the practice of wintering had developed, it was a logical extension to spend several years; to make a semi-permanent if not a permanent residence. As we show presently, we know the practice of wintering had started by 1266.

It is difficult for the archaeologists to check up on this extension of the Norse activity. There were no farm animals and consequently no stables to fall in ruin for the edification of later scientists. If human nature was the same in those days as it is now (and, curiously enough, Fridtjof Nansen, as we have stated before, is about the only writer on Greenland who keeps insisting that it must have been) then these pioneers toward the north would have adopted Eskimo methods of housing, camping, and hunting, just as modern pioneers in the far north are doing now. That makes for the archaeologists a double trouble—the Eskimo type of housing that is used

RUNIC STONE FOUND AT KINGIKTORSUAK, LAT. 72° 55′

on hunting expeditions leaves few remains, and such remains as are left by Europeans using Eskimo technique are hard to distinguish from the same kind of remains left by the Eskimos themselves.

Until about a hundred years ago we had no real evidence beyond literary sources that this sporadic (and perhaps later semipermanent or permanent) hunt extended beyond Disko. But then was found near 73° N. Lat., some twenty miles north of the present Danish colony of Upernivik, a rune stone with an inscription: "Erling Sigvatsson and Bjarne Thordsson and Enridi Oddsson on the Saturday before Gangdag [April 24] made this [these] cairns." From the style of the runes and language, scholars believe the inscription to be from the year 1333. The month, April, shows the party had wintered in the locality—some four hundred miles north of the Arctic Circle.

The Eskimo traditions gathered by Knud Rasmussen would seem to indicate that the excursions of the Norse Greenlanders, during the prosperous days when they still had large wooden ships, extended a good deal farther north than where the rune stone was found, occasionally to the Smith Sound district around 77° N. Lat. After relating the tales in his *Myter og Sagn fra Grönland,* Rasmussen concludes that: "Likely enough there is concealed in these race memories a testimonial that the Icelanders of the saga time used to reach Smith Sound on their journeys along the coast of Greenland. Nagivators who could reach Upernivik, where one of their rune stones has been discovered, would find nothing to prevent them from crossing Melville Bay when the ice conditions were favorable."

For the year 1266 we have from the Norse record the account of what may have been the first voyage, probably was, of the medieval Greenlanders north to that section of North Greenland, near N. Lat. 76°, where Rasmussen heard the traditions from the Eskimos. The Norse account, which is from the Greenlandic Annals that were compiled in Iceland near 1640 by Björn Jonsson, tells that the Greenlandic Europeans wanted to find out where the Eskimos were then living (1266). So they made a voyage which apparently took them to the head of Baffin Bay—to the region of Jones Sound, the waters that narrow toward Smith Sound, and the bight which is now called Melville Bay.

As we have explained elsewhere, Jonsson compiled the Greenlandic Annals from old manuscripts which he had before him, from his memory of other manuscripts that he had read in previous years, and from tradition that had survived verbally in Iceland, the main dependence being on the manuscripts.

In 1876 Sir George Nares was in command of an expedition that was attempting to reach the Pole. They did make a journey a hundred miles or so north over the pack from Ellesmere Island, but their geographically important work was done mapping the coasts of that island and those of north-western Greenland. Archaeologically and historically their most suggestive discovery was of two beacons, or monuments, on Washington Irving Island, a tiny high islet on the east coast of Ellesmere Island at 79° 35′. That the monuments are of medieval Norse building gets inferential support from Nares, who speaks of them as "ancient cairns, far too old to have been erected by Dr. Hayes, the only traveler known to have visited the neighborhood."

A perhaps even more suggestive discovery than that of the monuments is not mentioned by Nares, only by Dr. Edward L. Moss, physician on the expedition. They found, he says in his *Shores of the Polar Sea,* an eider-duck nest in a shelter which he describes verbally and by a drawing so as to indicate that it is the typical shelter built for eider ducks by the Norse people.

". . . A little further inland (on Norman Lockyer Island) we came upon a bird-shelter, such as the natives of Danish Greenland still use to encourage geese and ducks to settle on their shores. It consisted of four stones piled together like a miniature 'Druid's altar,' so as to form a chamber large enough to shelter a nest. Generations of eider duck had been hatched in it in security since the last wild hunter left the shore. When we found it, it held a deep nest of eider down with three eggs, fresh, but cold, probably belonging to a duck we had killed before landing."

The key to the discovery is in one of the fundamental differences between Norse and Eskimo culture. The Norse are husbandmen, only secondarily hunters; the Eskimos (with the sole exception of their relation to the dog) are hunters only. The Eskimos own no birds and protect none; the Norse own barnyard fowl and protect the eider duck. The Eskimos use the skins of dead birds for clothes; the Norse use the down of live birds for quilts and in other ways. Eskimos kill eider ducks if they can; they may or may not eat their eggs. The

CAIRNS ON WASHINGTON IRVING ISLAND

187

Norse sometimes kill eiders when they are on a journey; but when they live in eider districts they kill no birds and gather no eggs, for to them the down of present and prospective birds is of more value than the meat and eggs would be as food. In Norse communities it is anti-social, if not a crime, to kill eiders or destroy their eggs.

EIDER DUCK SHELTER

But in order that you may gather down successfully you must make your locality attractive to the ducks and you must protect the down from being carried away by the wind. Therefore you build shelters for the nests. These, called "houses," have been consistent in form, though of more than one type, in Scandinavian lands for a thousand years, perhaps much longer.

It seems obvious, then, that *if* this was an eider-duck shelter then it was built either by white men from the northwest of Europe or by Eskimos who had adopted the custom from them. But such Eskimos could have been only those with whom the Scandinavians had mingled at least enough culturally so as to give them the idea of protecting the duck—more probably, in our view, the mingling was both through cultural and blood mixtures.

Support for the view that the Moss report shows the northward extension of Europeans, or Europeanized Eskimos, this far north in the Middle Ages came by implication from a discovery almost as far north and considerably farther west by the Otto Sverdrup expedition of 1898–1902.

When Sverdrup reached Jones Sound (1899) on his long expedition his former chief, Nansen, had not yet published *In Northern Mists;* the ideas were not much abroad that the Greenlanders had either traveled as far in various directions as we now believe or that they had blended with the Eskimos and adopted to an extent their hunting culture.

Sverdrup found no living people in Jones Sound, but the ruins of former habitations were scattered about. It did not occur to the Norwegian explorers that the ruins could be of any but Eskimo derivation, but there came discoveries which puzzled them. Sverdrup relates of St. Helena:

"The gulls were nesting; in the clefts and fissures lived thousands of black guillemots, and well sheltered under the sides of the mountain were long rows of eider ducks' nests. The sites of several tents told us, too, that some time or other the Eskimo must have been here. As far as I could understand, they had even built nests for the ducks of the same construction that is in vogue to this day up in Nordland (the Nordland section of Norway). Certainly I have never heard that the Eskimo were in the habit of protecting the birds in this fashion."

Sverdrup's *New Land* was hurriedly published, as stories of polar journeys usually are, to catch readers before the news value of the expedition disappeared. So this first publication expresses merely the surprise, which was felt at the time of discovery, that Eskimos should here have gone against their nature in building shelters for birds—and building them in Norse style at that!

But the years brought leisure for thought and study. The result was crystallized in 1932 by Sverdrup's second-in-command, then become a distinguished polar authority in his own right, Captain Gunnar Isachsen, who published an article in which he maintained that no eider-duck shelters could be of Eskimo origin and that no chance of European post-Columbian origin was known or suspected. So these remains, Norse in type, must be of pre-Columbian Norse origin. They were derivable only from the Icelandic Greenlanders of the late Middle Ages, reasoned Isachsen.

Pondering on the bird shelters, Isachsen realized another thing of similar import. He had seen Norse cairns in Jones Sound!

Norsemen build cairns wherever they go—to mark the farthest attained within a cave, up a slope, or along a coast. They build them, too, as mementos of stirring deeds, of evil or good fortune. And these cairns are not like anything built by Eskimos. Two such cairns, centuries old and of Norse type, had been found near Björneborg, well along westward on the south shore of Ellesmere Island (across Jones Sound northeast from St. Helena). Specifically these cairns resembled in appearance and age three cairns found at 72° 58′ N. Lat., on the west coast of Greenland—structures known to be of Norse origin because one of them contained, as we have discussed elsewhere, a stone with a runic inscription.

It would seem, then, that (apart from the possibility of Eskimos borrowing cairn building and eider culture from the Norse) we have a demonstrated northwesting for the white Greenlanders of beyond 79° N. (Nares) and beyond 89° W. (Sverdrup).

During recent decades archaeologists supported by the Danish Administration of Greenland and by Danish scientific and philanthropic organizations have contributed increasingly toward filling the gaps of the historical record for the Greenland coast southward from Smith and Jones Sounds.

During 1935–37 a Danish archaeological expedition worked on the Inglefield coast, which lies northeast from Admiral Peary's customary expedition base at Etah between latitudes 78° and 79° N., therefore more than eight hundred miles north of the Arctic Circle. At the southern entrance of Marshall Bay was found the site of an old Eskimo settlement of

about thirty houses. Among articles excavated from the ruins
were a few Norse relics. About two miles to the west, on a
rocky islet in Marshall Bay, the ruins of five houses were
found on a moss-covered plateau. Here, too, were Norse
relics, including a comb that was reminiscent of one found at
Sandnaes in the Godthaab District. Speaking of these archaeological findings, Dr. Erik Holtved has said that his studies
were not complete, and that he was not yet prepared to say
whether the remains were those of Eskimos heavily influenced
by medieval Norse culture or of Norsemen who had largely
adopted an Eskimo way of life.

This might perhaps appear a distinction without a difference.
For, if the relations of whites and Eskimos in all other parts
of the world are any guide, the blood and the cultural mixtures
always go together.

The mentioned runic inscription some twenty miles north
of Upernivik shows that in the thirteenth or fourteenth centuries Europeans, occasionally if not regularly, wintered more
than four hundred miles north of the Circle, therefore wholly
divorced from European pastoral methods of breadwinning.

From Upernivik southward the excavations of medieval
"Eskimo" ruins show either that the Eskimos had been influenced by European culture or else that these people were
Eskimoized Europeans—for instance, there are pre-Cabot
dolls and human figures portraying Europeans and showing
other European influence. Still farther south the kitchen middens reveal an increasing Norseman use of wild animals and
decreasing reliance on sheep and cattle as time advanced. The
literary records confirm this and particularly show that the
Eskimoization proceeded more rapidly in the more northerly
districts.

It seems on the whole as if toward the Columbus-Cabot
period European trade with the northern settlement, and
perhaps with the northern portions of the southern district,
had dwindled to a point where it resembled the nineteenth-

century trade of Americans with the Eskimos of Alaska, or
of England (the Hudson's Bay Company) with the Eskimos
of Baffin Island. But at least one place was so steadily and
fully supplied that it kept its European character—Herjolfsnes, near the southern edge of the southern settlement. This
has been shown by Nörlund. He depends on all sources, naturally, but his most striking proofs came from European fashions
in dress. Garments of European cut preserved by the frozen
soil have demonstrated the fashion dependence of Herjolfsnes
on Europe well into the fifteenth century. Nörlund has extended the time of high probability beyond the firm demonstration so that, under date 1935, his second edition of *De Gamle
Nordbobygder* summarizes (we translate from the Danish
text) :

"Around 1500 or somewhat later, medieval Norse culture
definitely perished from Greenland. The last who may be considered to have seen the old Greenlandic Norsemen is the Icelandic Jon the Greenlander, who in ships which plied between
Hamburg and Iceland visited the Greenland coast several
times during the years around 1540—we know from other
sources that Hamburg ships were driven to Greenland in 1537
and 1539. The last record is that a caravel was sent from Hamburg under command of Gert Mestermaker; they reached land
but were unable to discover any people and accordingly turned
back."

Thirty-nine years after Nörlund's last date for a Hamburg
voyage, in 1578, the English landed under Frobisher. They
discovered an encampment whose people had fled at their
approach. Best's narrative says:

"They left in their tents all their furniture for haste behinde
them, where amongst other things were found a boxe of small
nayles, and certayne redde Hearings, boordes of Fyrre tree
well cutte, with dyuers other things artificially wrought,
whereby it appeareth, that they haue trade with some ciuill
people, or else are in deede themselues artificiall workemen."

The Thomas Ellis narrative of the expedition has it:

"The tentes were furnished with fleshe, fishe, skinnes, and other trifles: amongest the which was found a boxe of nailes: whereby we did coneicture, that they had either Artificers amongst them, or else a trafficke with some other nation."

Edward Sellman's version is:

"Some of our men that were with the Generall aland did see in their tente nayles like scupper nayles, and a tryvet of yron . . ."

It is agreed between ethnologists and archaeologists that Eskimos did not possess before European contact the art of securing iron from its ores, nor are they known to have had the custom of making up nails in quantity from any material. To keep a supply of nails in a box against future use is itself unlike Eskimos who have been little influenced by whites; but for Eskimos used to whites it is in character to keep nails in some quantity.

Regarding the "tryvet of yron," mentioned by Sellman, we may consider that among "Stone Age" Eskimos, as they were down to 1912 in Coronation Gulf, even a fairly massive thing of iron soon lost its identity. Gun barrels, for instance, traded from other groups and received without ammunition, were soon made up into various Eskimo-style implements. An iron trivet would be of no value to primitive Eskimos as a trivet, though priceless as material for cutting or piercing instruments. They would soon cut it up for indigenous purposes, unless they were keeping it against a time when other iron which they had was used up.

A case on how fast iron is used by Stone Age people is that of the Victoria Islanders and McClure's *Investigator* which he abandoned at the Bay of Mercy. Eskimos discovered it certainly not many years later, say around 1855. On several visits (during some ten or twenty years) they stripped it of all iron they could remove. The people actually engaged were not more than two or three hundred but they traded with a further six or eight hundred. By 1911, when scientists first visited them, there were probably not a dozen articles left that were of *Investigator* iron—knives, missile points, and needles.

Greenlanders would need iron more and use it faster than the Victoria people, who had plenty of native copper which they found satisfactory for many of their metal uses. It cannot, then, be that a trivet would have remained a trivet many years if derived from, say, a shipwreck. (In that case, what ship was wrecked?)

While Eskimos are never known to have smelted iron, smelting was practiced in Greenland by her European inhabitants, as we know from a study by Niels Nielsen, "Evidence on the Extraction of Iron in Greenland by the Norsemen," published in 1930. When commerce dwindled under the monopoly of Norway which followed 1261, scarcity of iron must have become, and must have remained, the severest handicap of the people. Then they resorted to smelting. If, as Nansen maintains, and as we are doing, there was a gradual Eskimoization of the culture and blood, a gradual turning from husbandry to the pursuit of game, the need of iron would still have continued. It may well be that smelting was one of those European arts which survived longest in Eskimoized Greenland.

Still speaking of the community of southern West Greenland who had the nails, Sellman tells that when Frobisher and his party went ashore, "they found people and tents, but the people fled from them, and they entered their tents, finding thereby by all things therein that they are a people like the people of Meta Incognita [Baffin Island] with like boates of all sortes, but the Generall doth take them to be a more delicat people in lodging and feeding then the other."

Thus in 1578 the inhabitants of southwestern Greenland were a little more like Europeans in their ways than those of Baffin Island. To Frobisher, who was in 1578 on his way home from his third summer at Meta Incognita and dealing with its Eskimos, this meant, in Best's phrasing, that they had "trade with some ciuill people." To us it means the same; but we add the suggestion that their being "more delicat in lodging and feeding" was perhaps because they were in part of European ancestry and had not yet lost all of the ways that were fashionable in medieval Europe.

That they fled from the English does not bear on either interpretation—the Orkney Islanders fled similarly when Frobisher landed there on his voyages, for they were used not only to trading ships but also used to pirates. As brought out elsewhere, the Greenlanders may have been used to similar pirates; they may even have been used to English pirates.

The application to Greenland of principles ordinary in the criticism of the history of religions would seem to show that the last definite observation of Christian Norse Greenlanders was made by John Davis. For it is generally agreed that when a religion is changing or dying there is more permanence about symbols than about anything else. The swastika, for instance, survives after its meaning has been lost, or sometimes among people with whom it has a new meaning. Significant is it, then, that near present Godthaab, in that northern district of the medieval colony which we know was most exposed to Eskimoization, John Davis found in 1586 graves of people about whom there was no European sign except that of the cross. He says: "This fourth of July the Maister of the *Mermaid* went to certaine Islands to store himselfe with wood, where he found a grave with divers buried in it, onely covered with seale skinnes, having a crosse laid over them."

John Davis found, then, just such a grave as might have been expected from Europeans who had been Eskimoized, from Eskimos who were Christian converts, or from a people who were a mixture of the two. A remaining possibility is that these dead had been survivors of some shipwrecked expedition. In that case, however, the presence of a cross, coupled with the absence of all other European signs, becomes a high improbability. Evidently that is how the Hakluyt Society's editor of the Davis journal, Admiral Sir Albert Hastings Markham, himself an explorer of the Greenland region, looked upon it: "It is possible that this spot was the last resting place of some of the old Norman colonists of South Greenland, those settlers in the East and West Bygd, whose fate, to this day, is involved in mystery."

The next description of these people, that of Baffin for 1612–16, is, as we have said, negative; he gives no indication that he saw any traits or articles which might have been attributed to European contact.

It has been said that the first extensive and carefully gathered information about the Eskimos of West Greenland resulted from the third expedition, 1654, of David Danell, a Hollander in Danish service, who kidnaped one Eskimo man and three women. He brought them to Denmark where Adam Olearius studied them and published a 100-word vocabulary, as well as their real or supposed answers to various questions which he asked through the help of a surgeon who had been in Greenland and who had some slight knowledge of the tongue.

The Olearius report is not really very enlightening; but we have available a source from only two years later, 1656, which is in its small compass a masterpiece among seventeenth-century descriptions of primitive man and which is, moreover, to a degree confirmatory of the Davis report as it was interpreted by Markham. This source has escaped until recently the attention of Greenland students, and even now it is unknown to all but a few specialists. The description remained unnoticed so long because it was about as well hidden as could be, in a book never widely known in any sphere and one that deals with a sphere remote from Greenland. For the narrative containing our description was concealed, of all places, in a "Natural and Moral History of the West Indies."

The *Histoire naturelle et morale des Iles Antilles de*

l'Amerique was printed anonymously. It was almost certainly written by Charles de Rochefort, but claims for the authorship have been made on behalf of César de Rochefort and also on behalf of Luis de Poincy. It first appeared in Rotterdam, 1658. There is a second edition, Rotterdam, 1665, and we have in English a translation by John Davies, London, 1666, *The History of the Caribby-Islands*.

The author of the "Natural and Moral History" digresses from his description of the West Indies to include the narrative of Nicolas Tunes, captain of a ship from Flushing, who had recently returned from a voyage to Davis Strait. As said, the entire narrative is a gem of accurate and detailed reporting of the appearance, clothing, equipment, and habits of a primitive people, and provides fascinating reading. We make our own translation here, from the Rotterdam edition of 1658, of the small portion which sheds light on the question of European contact, where Tunes describes the two types of people whom he found living together in Greenland at 72° N. Lat., therefore a little south of Upernivik:

"As for the people who inhabit this country, our travelers saw two sorts, who live together in good accord and perfect amity. One kind are of tall stature, well built physically, rather fair of complexion, and very fleet of foot. The others are very much smaller, olive-complexioned, fairly well proportioned save that their legs are short and thick."

We have, then, from old published records all the way down to and through recent archaeological finds, continuous support for the view that the gradually fading European culture overlapped by at least a century and a half the revival of westward enterprise which followed Cabot and Columbus. Thus physical traits of the ten thousand medieval Norse colonists never have disappeared from Greenland; they have merely been wrongly identified during the last two centuries when they have been considered wholly the result of modern intermarriage between Eskimos and Europeans.

CHAPTER XI

What Europe Knew about Greenland in the Middle Ages

WHILE THE CIVILIZATION of the Norse colony was dying out Greenland was not wholly without European contact, as we have already stated. Of that we keep discovering further bits of documentary proof. Then archaeology has shown, independently, that there was no complete isolation from European commerce down to 1500. Then Frobisher takes up the story and shows there was trade with Europe just before his 1578 visit.

In the fourteenth and early fifteenth centuries cartography developed and the fisheries and commerce of southern Europe reached farther into the North Atlantic. Greenland, which (along with the mainland of North America) had been introduced to the learned world by the *Historia Hammaburgensis Ecclesiae* of Adam of Bremen, about 1075, first appeared on the charts between 1424 and 1427, probably in 1424. This was through a Dane working in Italy, Claudius Claussön Swart, known as Claudius Clavus, Claudius Clavus Niger, Nicolaus Niger, and likely Nicolaus Gothus. That particular map had little, and perhaps no, influence on medieval geography, for the Nancy Codex containing it lay undiscovered till 1835. However, a second map made by Clavus, about 1430, did have great influence and is, indeed, so correct in shape, latitude, and in Greenland's relation to Iceland (though plac-

ing Greenland much too near Ireland), that we are inclined to
conclude it was based either upon a journey to Greenland
made by Clavus himself or else upon reports to him of men
who had been there. Still, it may be truly said that you would
expect from a Danish geographer, who had traveled in Norway, considerable fairly accurate knowledge of Greenland.
Clavus may have had Bardarson's sailing directions, from
which, and his personal knowledge as a Scandinavian con-
versant with the affairs of his day, the 1430 map can well
have been drawn.

The second (1430) Clavus map was printed in the Ulm
1482 edition of Ptolemy's geography and in later editions.
Greenland was, then, cartographically well known throughout
learned Europe after 1482, and more or less known to cartog-
raphers through fifty years before that.

The Gemma Frisius globe, engraved by Gerard Mercator
around 1536, is the earliest of surviving authorities for a
statement which always deals with Greenland or some region
west or northwest of it, but which appears in many variants
as to spelling of the name, nationality of the person, and precise location reached. This globe has on a polar continent to
the northwest of Greenland the legend: "Quij populi ad quos
Joes Scoluss danus peruenit circa annum 1476," which has
been translated by Björnbo as: "Quij, the people to whom the
Dane Johannes Scolvuss [Scolwssen?] penetrated about the
year 1476."

The nationalities assigned to this man, most frequently
spelled Scolvus, are Norwegian, Swedish, Danish, and Polish.
The expedition was Danish and one authority says that it was
"under the auspices of Christian I, King of the Danes." An
English state document, formulated about 1575 in connection
with the first voyage of Frobisher, has him "John Scolus,
pilot of Denmerke." The date here, as in the rest of the
Scolvus references, is 1476.

There is by now a substantial agreement among scholars

that Dietrich Pining, a high official in the Danish administration of Iceland, visited Greenland around 1476, the probabilities seeming to be that he spent three or four years there or revisited parts west of the North Atlantic several times.

Perhaps the first printed English reference to Pining and his comrade Hans Pothorst is the excerpt from Jacob Ziegler's *Schondia,* in Richard Eden's *Decades,* London, 1555. This runs: "On the toppe of a certeyne mountayne cauled Weyszarch, lyinge betwene Islande and Gruntland or Gronlande, is erected a shypmans quadrant of marueilous byggenesse, made by two pirates named Pinnigt and Pothorst in fauour of such as sayle by those coastes that they may therby auoyde the daungerous places lyinge towarde Gronlande."

The same knowledge was, no doubt, available to students of the period from many other sources—for instance, Hieronymus printed at Paris in 1548 a map showing an island to the northwest of Iceland with a legend which, translated, reads: "The lofty mountain called Witsarc, on the summit of which a sea-mark was set up by the two pirates, Pinnigt and Pothorst, to warn seamen against Greenland."

In 1909 Louis Bobé discovered at Copenhagen a letter dated March 3, 1551, from Carsten Grip, Burgomaster of Kiel, to King Christian III, which says: "The two sceppere (commodores, admirals) Pyningk and Poidthorsth who were sent out by your majesty's royal grandfather, King Christiern the First; at the request of his majesty of Portugal, with certain ships to explore new countries and islands in the north, have raised on the rock Wydthszerck, lying off Greenland and towards Sniefeldsiekel in Iceland on the sea, a great sea-mark on account of the Greenland pirates, who with many small ships without keels fall in large numbers upon other ships . . ."

According to this, the voyages of Pining were known at firsthand to at least two sovereigns, those of Portugal and Denmark. Conceivably the knowledge did not spread much in the Latin sector of Europe from secretive Portugal; but in the north the voyages must have been well known in view of Pining's prominence as a high official of the Danish navy, as a sort of governor of Iceland, and as a pirate or privateer.

According to the *Acta* of the Hansa, Pining was the most famous and infamous pirate of the time. For British knowledge of him we should remember that he had had much contact with the English and some trouble with them; moreover, this is just the period of which we have spoken when the Iceland trade was almost monopolized by English merchants who had extensive dealings with the Icelanders and with their Danish government officials.

It is generally accepted that the Pining-Pothorst voyage to (and beyond?) Greenland took place around the Scolvus period; so a debate arises whether Scolvus and Pining-Pothorst represent separate voyages or whether the former was a pilot with the latter. There are, after all, well-known cases in the history of exploration where one voyage sounds like two, as when the expedition commanded by Jacob Heemskerck is usually described as that of William Barents, who was Heemskerck's pilot. William Baffin, after whom the two great voyages of the *Discovery* are usually called, was in rank mate, and later pilot, to Captain Robert Bylot.

With Pining and Pothorst there enters the literature a feeling of dramatic change, a sense of things to come. There can have been motives of trade in these voyages; there probably were. There is likely to have been a freebooter's slant, for these leaders were pirates. There doubtless was curiosity to revisit the old scenes, re-establish contact with an Old World civilization in its New World setting. Those motives were old and are fundamental. Newness comes in that the Renaissance was now reaching north through the influence of one of the greatest geographers and pioneers of history, Prince Henry the Navigator, who, though dead for a quarter of a century, was still a power in the Mediterranean world and particularly with his nephews, the kings of Portugal. Men of affairs in the Iberian and Italian peninsulas were growing conscious of that doctrine to which scholars had held so tenaciously since the Greeks, that the earth is round and that the east can be reached from Europe by sailing west, north, or any course between. The overland highways to India were long, tedious, expensive, and were beginning to be obstructed by non-European powers. Portugal had not yet found the way around Africa and was inclined to try sailing west.

At this stage (1474) King Christian I of Denmark, Norway, and Sweden journeyed to Rome and may there have exchanged regrets with high officers of the Papacy. For, as a province, Greenland no longer paid him taxes or was remunerative to the tradesmen of the Scandinavian countries; as a bishopric, it no longer paid tithes to the Church or formed an intimate section of Christendom's broad community.

Since it is definitely stated that the Pining voyages, or at least some of them, were made on a suggestion from the King of Portugal to the King of Denmark, the probability is further increased that there was a triangular correspondence, by writing and through travelers, between the peninsulas of Italy, Iberia, and Scandinavia, concerning activities in the Greenland quarter and their results. This would explain the precise and fairly recent news of Greenland contained in the (hereinafter discussed) 1492 brief of Pope Alexander VI. That somebody must have known a lot about Greenland throughout the period 1450–90 has, in any case, been proved by the archaeologists through the finds at Herjolfsnes.

So this is perhaps a logical place to turn from our survey of what was known by somebody in Europe concerning Greenland during the Middle Ages and face the question: How generally spread was Europe's knowledge of the Greenland district before 1480?

As referred to already, Greenland under the name which has survived, and the American mainland as Vinland, were first presented to the learned world by one of the earliest and foremost of German historians, Adam, canon of Bremen and master of its cathedral school. His *Gesta* (*Historia Hammaburgensis Ecclesiae*) was finished about 1075. What he told of Scandinavian discoveries and relations was upon the authority of Danes, among them King Svein Esthridsson, in whose country he had resided. He explains his own interest, and that of the archbishopric which he represented, by saying that these islands (he considered Vinland, like Greenland and Iceland, to be insular), because of their relation to the Scandinavian countries, belonged to the archbishopric of Hamburg.

The *Gesta* is the first document on the Greenland–Labrador district which has as yet been unearthed—indeed, it needed no unearthing, for it circulated widely through the Middle Ages. But the Vatican must have had a good deal of information before the *Gesta*. Nor can their knowledge have been much of a secret, for it had to traverse Europe in getting to Rome and it was of a nature in which all concerned took pride, or at least a keen interest, so that there would be no tendency toward suppression. To begin with, the voyage of Leif the Lucky, which Christianized Greenland and discovered Vinland, was sponsored by one of the best publicized champions of the faith, King Olaf Tryggvason, an aggressive servant of the Church, not inclined to hide his light under a bushel. Nor would the Church be inclined to hide it. It was their light too.

When Greenland was constituted a separate bishopric, there must have been secured at least the assent of the Vatican. The news that Arnald had been consecrated at Lund as Bishop of Greenland in 1124, and that he had reached his seat at Gardar, Greenland, in 1126, would similarly cross Europe en route to the Vatican, again so free from secrecy in the nature of the case that a good many should have learned of it beyond those officially and directly concerned. Then, although the archbishops of northern Europe (Hamburg, Lund, Nidaros) were the immediate handlers of Greenland, the

Vatican cannot have been unaware of all those successive Greenland bishops who formed a line that remained unbroken at least down to 1530, perhaps to 1537.

Reasonably the popes would know about the Church in Greenland, if for no other reason than because it was the farthest outpost of Christianity. That most or all of them did know we have the more reason to believe because we can prove that the last pre-Columbian pope did know—Alexander VI who took office just before Columbus sailed and who held that supreme post of the religious world until 1503.

The later of the bishops had difficulty in reaching Greenland because of the breakdown in shipping which we have already discussed, and this was of itself a cause of Mediterranean and general European publicity—it worried the archbishops and even the popes, of which last we have direct proof in papal briefs, some of which we shall quote.

Through the community of medieval scholarship there must have been sprinkled over Europe a knowledge of that remarkable work of precept and information, *Konungsskuggsja* (*The King's Mirror*), most widely known by its Latin name, *Speculum Regale,* composed between 1220 and 1260, to which we have referred. Those who read its Greenland section would have had not only reasonably correct and full knowledge of the state of the country socially, politically, commercially, and in church matters, but would also have had geographical and climatological information which, though in spots fabulous, is in the main correct and on some points more rational and accurate than what ordinary English-language school texts have contained to our own time. For instance, readers of the *Mirror* learned that Greenland is suited to cattle and sheep, whereas the average person today is surprised when told that the Greenlanders cultivated these and other domestic animals through the last five centuries of the Middle Ages and that Eskimos now cultivate them in the same districts.

Not merely through *The King's Mirror* and chance hearsay,

not merely through these supplemented by formal reports from the bishops at Gardar, did the Vatican know the success of husbandry beyond the Atlantic. For the Church of Greenland paid tithes through several centuries and part of these in woolen cloth and hides of domestic animals, while butter and cheese were also known as possible, if not actual, Greenland exports. In addition to the regular Church taxes, Greenlanders contributed toward the expense of the Crusades. After 1261 they began to pay taxes also to the kingdom of Norway.

Through the very fact that the Greenland taxes were hard to collect they produced news. We can infer from the written complaints that there must have been a good deal of spoken complaint. The transport of the taxes, paid in kind, also bothered. As the regular ships from Bergen grew fewer during the third and fourth centuries of the colony's existence, the annoyances to the churchmen of Europe grew more numerous—it took years for the decrees to reach Greenland; it was difficult there for the tax gatherers to travel about and make the collections; the wares then had to be stored for years before a ship came to take them out where they could be sold.

Nor was it merely clerics who had firsthand opportunity for learning about the countries beyond the Atlantic. Sportsmen were also a class who knew of Greenland. For a great sport in medieval Europe, nearly or quite the most fashionable of all sports ever, was hawking, falconry. Many kings took active part; the rest were familiar with it. And so on down through the grades of nobility.

One of the best and most fashionable of the falcons came from Greenland. Their possessors, and those who envied them, knew (if perhaps vaguely) the land of their origin. At the minimum it was known that the Norwegians secured Greenland falcons by voyages to the west across the ocean past Iceland.

The incidental publicizing of Greenland through the Sport of Kings was not confined to talk. There were also books. For instance, the *De Arte Venandi cum Avibus* was composed by Frederick II, Holy Roman Emperor, King of Sicily and Jerusalem, between 1244 and 1250. This was an authoritative work, scientific for that time, and popular. It circulated widely before the days of printing and was a source for other works. In it Frederick does something more striking than to tell where Greenland is—he assumes Greenland to be well known and uses it as a point of reference for giving the location of other countries. For in placing Iceland he says that it "lies between Norway and Greenland" ("In Quadam insula que est inter Norvegiam et Gallandiam et vocatur theutonice Yslandia . . .").

Le Livre du Roy Modus, written toward the end of the fourteenth century and first printed in 1486, says, about certain falcons, that they come "from countries very far distant." In the Paris, 1931, edition of this work, the editor, Gunnar Tilander, comments: "These countries are Iceland and Greenland, as, among others, the Emperor Frederick II states in his famous treatise on falconry."

The sport of hunting with birds of prey grew to such a passion following the Crusades that not even the clergy were exempt from the fever, and a special dispensation was granted so that the spiritual princes might take part. There was, indeed, an edict that on occasion these prelates might celebrate mass booted, spurred, and otherwise prepared for the hunt, and that their special falcon might during the service perch on the corner of the altar. The favorite bird of these spiritual princes was a white one, and that was the Greenland falcon.

Singled out for spiritual as well as secular distinction, the Greenland falcons were probably, from the thirteenth to the sixteenth century, next after the writings of the popes in spreading and in keeping alive throughout Europe knowledge of the land from which they came and of the seafaring and other processes that were necessary to secure them.

The King's Mirror speaks of Greenland hawks in relation to European values of the thirteenth century: "There are in that country (Greenland) a multitude of large birds which in other countries would be considered precious, white falcons. They are found there in greater abundance than in any other land; even so, the inhabitants do not understand how to make use of them."

Probably in 1394 the Saracens, as a part of the Crusade struggle, captured a son of the Duke of Burgundy. Then we get proof that Greenland and its falcons were known even beyond the Mediterranean, for the Saracens asked for a ransom of twelve Greenland falcons. They received these from the Duke in 1396, which shows either that they had been secured in the meantime from Greenland or that a minimum of a dozen were on hand in Europe. But it is agreed by all students of falconry that they were never raised as domestic birds—that they were always captured in the wild. So, whether they were specially secured from Greenland or assembled in Europe, there is in either case proof of a brisk transatlantic traffic.

Prince Henry, destined to be called the Navigator, was two years old in 1396. His life came to be devoted mainly to struggles with the Saracen and to the extension of geographic knowledge by scholarship and voyaging. What is generally believed of his omnivorous and keen intellect would make it seem strange indeed if the sport of falconry, engrossing both to his associates and to his Saracen opponents, failed to convey to him, as a side light, that knowledge of Greenland which the Emperor Frederick II possessed. Strange, indeed, if the *De Arte Venandi cum Avibus* was not a part of Henry's famous library. It is known to have been at that time in various other libraries of Europe.

At the time when the prince was cultivating historical and theoretic geography at Sagres, his country was trading actively with Bristol, and Bristol was nearly monopolizing the trade of Iceland. It must have had particular meaning for the prince if he knew Iceland lay between Norway and Greenland. The probability of that knowledge gives further logic to what the documents say about its having been the King of Portugal who induced the King of Denmark to send, around 1470–80, the mentioned Pining-Pothorst expeditions for exploring the Greenland sector beyond the Atlantic.

Another thing which made royalty publicists for Greenland during the Middle Ages was that one of the rarest and most prized possessions of a king was a polar bear. These, also, were known to come from Greenland. Falcons, though costly, were articles of trade; but polar bears were so rare that they were not often sold—they were rather gifts to kings and perhaps occasionally to the higher temporal or spiritual nobility, intended to secure favor—a sort of recognized and proper form of bribery.

Then there must have been surreptitious publicity resulting from the surreptitious commerce with Greenland. As brought out already, treaties were made by which other nations promised the King of Norway that they would not trade in Iceland and Greenland. Historians tell us that this promise was not kept with regard to Iceland. Archaeology has now confirmed that it was not kept with regard to Greenland, for European fashions and goods continued to reach at least the Eastern Settlement up to 1500. Most of this trade, after 1410, was probably from Bristol. No matter how hard the merchants and seamen of that port may have tried to keep the voyages secret there must have been a certain leakage, some of it, as said, doubtless to Portugal.

In closing this subject we might consider whether it is possible that the voyages historically known or pretty definitely suggested by the records, the Pining-Pothorst-Scolvus enter-

prises around 1476–82, may sufficiently explain those archaeological findings by which we have strengthened the case for a
fairly extensive though unrecorded late fifteenth-century
Greenland trade.

The Pining group of voyages certainly might account for
much of what Nörlund found at Herjolfsnes showing contact
with Europe, for instance, the clothes of 1450–75 European
cut. The time for these in Greenland can be extended to, say,
1500, by admitting that a single trading vessel could well bring
in around 1480 garments, some of which would still be in use
after twenty years. Moreover, a particular fashion once introduced, the Greenlanders would follow it perhaps for decades
in cloth of their own weave.

But this and similar reasoning does not explain at least one
of Nörlund's findings. For, according to present theory, nothing except a long-continued, steady subordination of native to
imported foods can account for the heavy incidence of deficiency diseases shown by the Nörlund skeletons. Definitely,
such prevalence of rickets as these bones indicate is at present
found in the Arctic and sub-Arctic only among communities,
whether Eskimo or white, that depend in large part on imported foods.

Usually throughout the world, and so it was in Greenland,
these imported foods are chiefly cereals. Cereals (the sub-
stitution of which for meat would bring on the deficiency
troubles) come more logically from England, or from the
Hansa traders, than from Norwegian sources. Likely Pining
did bring some Danish cereals to Greenland, but, as said, he
could not have brought them for enough years to produce all
the deficiency-disease signs that have been reported. Other,
unrecorded, Danish voyages could have brought cereals, but
an unrecorded extensive Scandinavian commerce with Greenland during the second half of the fifteenth century is less likely
than such commerce from England or Germany.

After granting, then, that the clothing fashions of Herjolfsnes could have derived solely from the recorded Pining-Pothorst-Scolvus voyages, we still feel there is evidence for a further European trade which originated outside the Scandinavian countries.

Beyond everything as causes and effects of European interest in Greenland were the writings of the popes themselves. The intellectual world and the Church world were largely the same. What the Pope knew came to him in the main from the active servants of the Church, from the learned men affiliated with the Church, and from the kings and nobility with whom the Church was so nearly connected. What the Pope proclaimed was, conversely, thereby made known to considerable parts of the same circles. There can have been few monasteries, seats of the higher clergy, or communities of learned men that did not know something, and in some cases no doubt a good deal, about the farthest province of Christendom, the bishopric of Greenland.

We do not go into certain papal documents which refer to Greenland and Iceland as of a time earlier than that of their discovery—for which, and other, reasons they have been considered forgeries. Recently it has been argued that no intentional forgery was involved, but that in the course of recopying older documents which were badly faded scribes between the early tenth and the early twelfth centuries wrote in things which were true then, assuming them to have been true at the time of the documents.

If it be accepted, as argued, that the "forgeries" which inserted the names of Iceland and Greenland were done between 900 and 1132, we extend backward considerably the Latin sources on these regions. For apart from these the earliest (and isolated) Latin reference to Greenland (and North America) is, as said, in Adam of Bremen's *Gesta*, 1075.

The unquestioned Greenlandic communications of the popes, which have as yet been discovered in the Vatican archives and

published, were usually addressed to the head of that archbishopric which then included the bishopric of Greenland,
but in one important case a letter was addressed jointly to the
two bishops of Iceland. In the most important document of all,
the brief of 1492, we have a kind of circular to churchmen and
all of good will in northern Europe. Many of the communications were in reply to letters which had been written to the
Pope by the archbishops or others and which have not as yet
been found in the Vatican archives. Fortunately the Pope
usually summarizes the matter to which he is replying, so that
our loss in these instances may not be considerable.

Innocent III (1198–1216) is sometimes called the greatest
of all the popes. At any rate, his influence constructively per-
vaded Christendom. He was the mentor and guardian of Frederick II, whose elevation to the emperorship of the Holy
Roman Empire was due to Innocent. Frederick's knowledge
of Greenland, which we have already mentioned, was then
probably derived, at least in part, from Innocent and from
other Vatican associates. The Norse tradition in Sicily from
the time of Roger, and the interest in geography and Arabic
science which Frederick fostered at the Sicilian court, must
not be overlooked in this connection.

In a letter of February 13, 1206, addressed to the Archbishop of Nidaros, Innocent refers to the interest of the Popes
Nicholas II (1058–61) and Eugenius III (1145–53). Then
he says:

"Nicholas . . . decreed that the city of Nidrosi, committed
to your direction, be the permanent metropolis of the province,
and that . . . the bishoprics of Sutrhaia (Hebrides), Iceland, and Greenland be subject to it forever as their metropolis, and that their bishops obey both him (your predecessor)
and his successors as their metropolitans. Accordingly, that no
one may ever attempt to violate this ordinance, We, after the
example of the aforesaid Eugenius (III, 1145–53) of blessed
memory, and of Alexander (III, 1159–81), and Clement (III,

1187–91), Our predecessors in the Roman Pontificate, confirm the same by apostolic authority . . ."

Plans for the Crusades were still abroad during the brief tenure of John XXI (1276–77). He reached eastward for the spread of Church influence by messengers to the Grand Khan; he reached west across the Atlantic for sinews of the holy war —which sinews, we know from independent sources, were in part ropes of walrus leather. He wrote to the Archbishop of Nidaros on December 4, 1276:

"Your Fraternity has informed Us that, whereas in the Kingdom of Norway, the collection of the tithe for the Holy Land has been entrusted to you by Apostolic Letters, in which it is expressly declared that you shall personally visit all parts of the Kingdom for that purpose, this seems in a measure impossible, since the diocese of Garda, subject to your province and said Kingdom, is so far distant from the metropolitan church that, because of the difficulties of navigation, one can scarcely make the voyage, thither and return, in less than five years; so that you doubt that the apostolic command, or your own, can reach those parts within the time appointed for the payment of the tithe; you have therefore besought the Apostolic See to provide some solution of the difficulty. Desiring, then, that the gathering of the tithe be carried on with earnest zeal, We order and command your Fraternity by Apostolic Letters, that if the foregoing conditions are true, that you procure for those regions suitable and faithful persons, in regard to whom We purpose to bind your conscience, and who are to watch over and attend carefully to the collection of the tithe, and that you endeavour furthermore to provide other persons, accordingly as you will find it expedient for the tithe; nevertheless you should also apply yourself with diligent solicitude to the latter, that you may thereby prepare for yourself a reward from God, and merit more plentifully the favour of the Apostolic See."

Nicholas III (1277–80), tactful scion of the Orsini family,

On such a farm as this, in northern Greenland, early Norse settlers struggled to gain a foothold. From a painting by Emile Walters.

By courtesy of M. Clemmensen. Photo by C. Wagner, 1910

Ancient Norse church ruins near Kakortok; often such ruins show the influence of Irish church architecture.

had received a letter of complaint from the Archbishop of Nidaros. On January 31, 1279, he replied to the effect that, in view of what the archbishop said, perhaps it had been unwarranted to excommunicate the Greenlanders for being so slow in paying their tithes, the said slowness having resulted from the fact that "the island, on which stands the City of Garda, is seldom visited by ships, because of the dangers of the Ocean surrounding it . . ."

Greenland was now (after 1261) a province of Norway, and Martin IV (1281–85), a cosmopolitan and former Chancellor of France to Louis IX, wrote concerning the archbishop's double relation to Greenland and to the King of Norway. The letter is dated March 4, 1282, and says, among other things:

"Your Fraternity has informed Us that . . . the tithe of Greenland is received entirely in cattle-skins, the skins and tusks of seals, and whale-bone (?), which you assert, can hardly be sold at a fair price.* Wherefore you have asked to be instructed by the Apostolic See as to what you should do . . . We, therefore, commending your zeal, reply to your inquiry that you endeavour to convert into silver or gold the tithes . . . of Greenland . . . in as far as it will be possible to do so successfully and with benefit, and that you send this, together with the rest of the tithe collected in that Kingdom for the good of the Holy Land, to the Apostolic See as quickly as possible, faithfully specifying what and how much is sent. For the rest, We have directed to Our very dear son in Christ . . . the illustrious King of Norway, letters requesting that he neither hinder, nor permit any one to hinder, the free gathering of the tithe in his Kingdom, to be disposed of for the

*Except where otherwise stated, these translations are from the compilation *Norroena*. We were suspicious of this sentence and looked it up in the Latin. Our own translation is: "cattle-hides and seal-skins, and (walrus) tusks and ropes of whale-skin." If they were indeed whale-skin thongs they were probably from white whale hide (beluga). Eskimos consider them as good as walrus. These whales are numerous in Greenland waters today and an important source of food to the Eskimos.

benefit of the Holy Land according to the decision of the Apostolic See . . ."

After a long silence, represented no doubt in part at least by documents still existing in the Vatican, though not catalogued, we have in 1448 the already referred-to letter from Nicholas V, distinguished and active humanist, patron of learning, employer of hundreds of special scribes, founder of libraries. He wrote September 20, 1448:

". . . to Our venerable brothers, the Bishops of Shaoltensus and Olensus,* greeting . . . as regards our beloved sons, the natives and all the inhabitants of the Island of Greenland, which is said to lie in the province of Nidrosi, in the extremity of the Ocean, in the northern region of the Kingdom of Norway, We have heard with sad and anxious heart the doleful story of that same island, whose inhabitants and natives, for almost six hundred years, have kept the Faith of Christ, received under the preaching of their glorious evangelist, the blessed King Olaf,† firm and unspotted under the guidance of the Holy Roman Church and the Apostolic See, and where for all succeeding time the people inflamed with eager devotion, erected many temples of the Saints and a famous Cathedral, in which divine worship was sedulously carried on; but at length, thirty years ago . . . the barbarians gathering together in a fleet on the neighboring shores of the Pagans, attacked this entire people in a cruel invasion, devastating their fatherland and sacred temples by fire and sword, leaving in the island only nine parochial churches; these, it is said, extend into the farthest districts, where they could not

---

*The bishops of Skalholt and Holar, in Iceland. (Our source has some awkward translations and some misprints, but these do not alter the sense and we do not alter the text.)

†So the Papacy still remembered in 1448 how King Olaf Tryggvason sent Leif Eriksson on the voyage which Christianized Greenland—and discovered continental North America. But in speaking of "the blessed King Olaf" the Holy Father may have been a little confused—he seemingly thought of the great warrior and the Saint as if they were the same Olaf. In reality they were some twenty years apart.

approach conveniently because of the defiles of the mountains, and carrying away captive to their possessions the natives of both sexes, especially such as they deemed brave and fit to undergo the burden of perpetual slavery, just as if adjusted to their tyranny. As the same report subjoins, however, very many, after a time, returned to their own from said captivity, and, having thenceforth repaired the ruins of those places, desired to renew and extend the divine worship as much as possible after the pristine fashion but because, overwhelmed by the past calamities, and laboring under famine and want, they were unable to support priests and a bishop, they were deprived, for that entire period of thirty years, of the consolation of a bishop and the ministry of priests, except when anyone, in the desire of serving God, after traveling far and long, had succeeded in reaching those churches which the barbarian hand had passed unhurt; wherefore they have humbly petitioned Us to deign to meet their pious and salutary design with fatherly commiseration, and to supply their spiritual wants and impart Our benevolent approbation and that of the Apostolic See to the foregoing. We, therefore, favorably disposed toward the just and worthy prayers and desires of said natives and inhabitants of the aforesaid island of Greenland, but having no certain knowledge of the foregoing events and their circumstances, commit to and command your Fraternity, whom We understand to be one of the nearer bishops of the aforesaid island,* that you, or one of you (nearer bishops), ordain fit and exemplary priests, provide parishes, and establish rectors, who will govern the restored parishes and churches, and administer the Sacraments; and, furthermore, that, if it will finally appear to you or one of you as opportune and expedient, you will, with the advice of the metropolitan, provide the distance of the place permit, ordain and establish as their bishop some practical and able person, in communion with Us

---

*Here the Pope seems unaware that all Icelanders had been forbidden by the King of Norway to visit Greenland.

and the Apostolic See, and impart to him the grace of conse-
cration in Our name, according to the usual ecclesiastical
forms, and deliver to him the conduct both of spiritual and
temporal matters, having previously administered to him the
proper and usual oath of allegiance to Us and the Roman
Church . . ."

Studies by Icelandic scholars (summarized in *Kvaedasafn
eptir nafngreinda islenzka menn fra midoldum,* Reykjavik,
1922–27, pp. 169–74) have made it seem definite that the
adventures formerly assigned wholly to Björn Jorsalafari
(Björn the Pilgrim), who was driven by storms to Greenland
in 1385—when several other Icelandic ships were also driven
there—have been blended in the manuscripts with those of
another Björn, called the Rich, who was driven to Greenland
in 1446 and spent there the following winter. He was again in
Iceland by October, 1447, and may thus have brought out the
news and complaints which are found in this brief. Such an
Icelandic source for the matters which disturbed Pope Nicholas V would go toward explaining what has puzzled commentators, that this brief, and no other brief on Greenland,
is addressed to *bishops in Iceland* instead of (what was a logical as well as a uniform practice) to the Archbishop in Norway who had charge of the Greenland bishopric.

A man with grasp of world affairs was Rodrigo, of the
princely house of Borgia, who became Pope Alexander VI
(1492–1503) on August 10, 1492. He wrote, soon after his
ascension, a letter which is at once informative concerning
Greenland and dramatic in that it shows comprehensive
knowledge of things beyond the Atlantic on the very eve of
that period when there began an elaborate pretense that little,
and preferably nothing, had been known by Europe concerning the western world before Columbus.

The first paragraph of the letter has the marginal notation:
"Mandatum de expediendo gratis ecclesiam Gadensem, etiam
quoad minuta servitia." Then we quote in full translation:

"Since, as We have learned, the church of Garda is situated at the ends of the earth in Greenland, and the people dwelling there are accustomed to live on dried fish and milk for lack of bread, wine and oil; and since the shipping to that country is very infrequent because of the extensive freezing of the waters —no ship having put in to shore, it is believed, for eighty years —or, if voyages happened to be made, it could have been, it is thought, only in the month of August, when the ice had thawed; and since it is also said that no bishop or priest at all has been in charge of that church in personal residence for eighty years or thereabouts—a fact which, together with the absence of Catholic priests, has caused very many of that diocese, who were once Catholics, deplorably to renounce their sacred baptismal vows—and since the dwellers in that land have nothing as a relic of the Christian religion except a cer- tain corporal, which is shown once a year, and upon which a hundred years before the body of Christ had been consecrated by the last priest then residing there;* for these and other con- siderations, therefore, Pope Innocent VIII of blessed mem- ory, Our predecessor, wishing to provide a suitable pastor for that church, which was at that time deprived of the solace of such, upon the advice of his brethren, of whom We were then one, appointed bishop and pastor to it Our venerable brother Matthias, bishop-elect of Garda, a professed member of the holy order of St. Benedict, who, at Our instance, while We were yet in minor orders, had been announced as intending to sail there personally, fired by the greatest fervor of devotion to lead back to eternal salvation the souls of the strayed and apostate, and freely and of his own accord to expose his life to the greatest danger for the sake of wiping out such errors.

"We, therefore, commending very highly the pious and praiseworthy undertaking in the Lord of the said bishop-

*The bishops appointed for Gardar did not go to Greenland after 1385. They held their title and received their rewards in some northern country of Europe, frequently Norway.

elect, and wishing to succor him in the afore-mentioned circumstances on account of his poverty, by which, as We have
likewise learned, he is sorely pressed, do at Our own instance,
and with the certain knowledge of the consent and approval
of Our brethren, instruct and order, in a circular letter to Our
esteemed sons, the scribes, solicitors, keepers of the seal,
registrars, and all the rest of the officials of Our chancellery
and of Our vault, that, under pain of excommunication, *lata
sententia, ipso facto* incurred, they forward or cause to be
forwarded all and each of the Apostolic letters about and concerning the promotion of the said church at Garda, to the said
bishop-elect—this to apply in all and each of their offices
everywhere—gratis, for God, and without payment or levy of
any tax, and without gainsay; and We likewise instruct and
command the clerks and notaries of the Apostolic treasury, at
like instance and knowledge and under the aforesaid penalty,
to hand over and consign to the said bishop-elect the letters
and Bulls of this sort without payment or exaction of any tax
or even the tiniest fees, or any of the other fees usually paid
in such cases, anything whatever to the contrary notwithstand-
ing. Let this be done gratis everywhere because he is very
poor."

Thus we have a document written during or just after the
1492 voyage of Columbus by perhaps the worldliest of all the
popes, saying, among other things, that he had been actively
interested in Greenland since he was in minor orders (therefore since from around 1455), that he had helped to select
a bishop for Greenland during the papacy of Innocent VIII
(1485–92), and that he is now (1492) concerned that men
of good will in northern Europe shall help in the laudable
work of the Bishop of Greenland. This letter, written in Italy
sixty years after Clavus had placed Greenland with approximate correctness on Italian maps and ten years after the
Clavus map had been printed in the Ulm Ptolemy, would, even
if unsupported, be enough to show how little there is behind

the still-met-with assumption that learned Europe knew nothing of countries beyond the Atlantic till 1492.

The need to pretend, in the interests of the territorial claims of Spain, that Europe knew nothing of transatlantic countries was seemingly not realized till 1493. In that year Spain (as so staid a work as *Encyclopaedia Britannica* puts it) refused to join a coalition hostile to Alexander VI because she desired "to be on good terms with the Pope to obtain a title over the newly discovered continent of America." Spain's territorial claim, which Pope Alexander VI supported, was based in part on the assumption that before Columbus the existence of countries beyond the Atlantic had been unknown. Thereupon and thenceforth Pope Alexander VI, himself a Spaniard (Rodrigo Borgia, or Borja), refrained from proclaiming that he had long been interested in a diocese beyond the Atlantic, nor did his successors advertise for more than three centuries thereafter any pride of the Church in a transatlantic history of five hundred pre-Columbian years.

CHAPTER XII

The Revival of Greenland Sailings—Sixteenth and Seventeenth Centuries

THE DECADE BEFORE 1492 found the Italians, Columbus and Cabot, trying to organize voyages for crossing the Atlantic. During that period, according to the view of the majority of writers, Columbus visited Iceland. The dissenters usually admit that Columbus did visit Bristol, and it is agreed that Cabot lived in Bristol, a city which was cultivating the Iceland trade intensively at the time, as well as trade with Portugal; so that Bristolians were in touch both with the advanced geographic views and doings of the Portuguese and with the westward knowledge of the Icelanders.

Just before and around Cabot's arrival in England there occurred the historically documented expeditions to Greenland, and perhaps to Labrador, of Pining, Pothorst, and Scolvus, with Portugal and Denmark co-operating in one or more of these voyages—Portugal motivated by the theories which we associate with Prince Henry, Denmark motivated by the tradition and specific knowledge, some of it recent, that descended to her through Iceland and Norway.

There is continuity in the written record from Erik in 985 to Hudson in 1608. A still more intimate continuity is probable for verbal sharings of experience between the navigators of several nations, who cultivated shores and seas west of the Atlantic.

Somewhat as Columbus stirred up more interest than previous sailors to America, and Lindbergh more than previous flyers to Europe, so the voyages of Sir Martin Frobisher to Greenland waters, in 1576–7–8, and his landing there, created more interest than any preceding voyage to the same region, and he is frequently spoken of as the discoverer of Greenland. After him the whole of Europe shared more continuously than before the knowledge that came from westward sailings.

The Frobisher expedition was, in effect, commissioned by the government of England through Queen Elizabeth. It was for the discovery of a seaway to China around the north of America, and was at first believed to have been a success in that the vessels, at their farthest, still had open sailing waters ahead of them indefinitely.

Frobisher considered himself twice successful—he could have gone ahead to China; but he did not need to, for all he was in search of anyway was riches, and he found what he believed to be an unlimited supply of gold at approximately half the distance from England to China. Had he gone all the way he would have had to haggle and barter for the wealth of the Indies, and that in competition with the Portuguese and Spaniards; but here, not merely at a part of the distance but without competition, he was able to scoop the wealth up from the shore.

True, this was not as yet the view of Frobisher when he turned back from his first venture the autumn of 1576, after spending some time along the shores of what he thought was a strait. He sailed home merely satisfied that he had found the gate that led to the Southern Ocean, now called the Pacific. It was at home in England he was told by "goldsmiths" that some rock, which had been brought home as a curiosity, was gold ore.

From the goldsmiths' verdict developed a treasure-seeking voyage in 1577, with three ships, and a third expedition in 1578 with fifteen. Tons of what proved to be iron pyrites were eventually thrown overboard from the ships at their English docks, some of it to be recovered in the twentieth century during harbor dredgings.

The first sighting of Greenland by Frobisher was on the outward voyage in 1576, when he reached the coast of what he thought was "Frieseland"—the name of a mythical island foisted upon the world through an alleged narrative, really a hoax, which the Zeno family of Italy published in 1558. In reality this land was the east coast of Greenland, several leagues north of Cape Farewell. Frobisher attempted to row ashore in a small boat, with four men, but they failed to land, after many attempts, on account of the "monstrous great ilands of ice which lay dryving all alongst the coast thereof." In danger from the thick fog which had begun to envelop them, and from the drifting icebergs, they turned south and ran into a violent storm.

Weathering the gale, Frobisher rounded the south of Greenland and headed west. They identified the region they struck as Labrador, and may have been right. Coasting north, they entered a supposed strait which has since been named Frobisher Bay, for a bay it was.

The nearest thing to a contact with Greenland on the way back the autumn of 1576 was that they passed "Frieseland" on September 1, reaching the Orkneys the twenty-fifth. From the reference it would seem as if they merely glimpsed the southernmost parts of the country in passing.

On the second voyage, 1577, Frobisher again sighted Greenland. Two days to the west-northwest of the Orkneys the voyagers had met with a fleet of English fishermen on their return trip from Iceland, and sent letters home by them. For twenty-six days thereafter he sailed without sight of land, but on July 4 he "made the land perfect and knew it to be Freeseland." Again he tried to land in a boat, but on each attempt the fog was so heavy that he was afraid of losing contact with the ships, and finally gave up the idea. He sailed four days and nights along the shore and then headed westerly for the "straits" called by his name.

On August 23, after taking aboard some 200 tons of ore which "Jonas," whom they had with them for testing it, had found to be rich, the fleet put out to sea again. Though the three ships were separated during the return voyage, they all arrived safely in England shortly after the middle of September. The Queen received Frobisher at court with thanks and a gift of £100. To the newly discovered land she gave the name "Meta Incognita."

The fifteen vessels of the third voyage left England May 31, 1578, reached Greenland June 20, and for the first time landed there. Frobisher took possession in the name of the Queen and changed the name from "Frieseland" to "West England."

This was the occasion on which "they sawe certaine tents made of beasts skinnes," as we have told earlier, and "found a boxe of nailes: whereby we did coniecture, that they had either Artificers amongst them, or else a trafficke with some other nation." We have discussed this find elsewhere and remark here merely that our knowledge permits us to rule out artificers, or any aboriginal derivation. So the nails were really a sign that there was European trade with Greenland either contemporaneous with or just prior to the Frobisher voyages.

On this last voyage Frobisher entered Hudson Strait. He called it "Mistaken Strait" when it proved not to be the one he was seeking. There are indications that he would have liked to follow it deeper in and would have done so but for the controlling purpose of the voyage, mining.

After filling the ships with worthless "ore" the expedition returned to England.

The heavy financial loss that resulted from the vain search for gold on a fifteen-ship scale dampened Britain's ardor for northern sailing. But when the Greenland part of the Frobisher news reached Denmark it led to a series of Danish expeditions, most of them under command of, or guided by,

English or Scottish pilots. For the British Isles had taken over during the last two hundred years that primacy in Greenland voyaging which had earlier belonged first to the Icelanders and then to the Norwegians.

We can see from the courses sailed by these post-Frobisher navigators that the commanders and pilots were better informed on sealing and trading voyages than upon the old history of the relation between Iceland and the colonies in Greenland; for most of them steered north of Iceland, toward what is now the Scoresby region. This fits in with the Icelandic annals of the period, for they tell that the English were in the habit of sailing northwest from northwestern Iceland toward Greenland.

The object of the Danish expeditions was, as we have said, to find the Icelandic colonists and to convert them from Catholicism or from heathenism, as the case might be, to the doctrines of the Lutheran Church. Some of the expeditions penetrated almost to land on the east coast but were prevented from going ashore by the stream of southward-flowing ice in the Greenland Current, or by landfast ice.

Dr. Louis Bobé, Historiographer Royal of the Danish Orders of Knighthood, says that in 1582 the King of Denmark "had a favorable opportunity of discussing his Greenland projects with the greatest authority of those days, Frobisher, who came to Copenhagen with the English embassy, which was to present King Frederik II with the Order of the Garter. It is said that the King was so impressed by the accounts of the great Arctic traveler, his noble character and natural intelligence, that he applied for the consent of Queen Elizabeth to let Frobisher enter his service. The answer of the Queen is not known, but the hope of the King was at any rate not fulfilled."

Bobé says that Frederik II kept in touch with Frobisher at least until 1587 and that a letter from Frobisher of that year is still preserved in the Danish archives. The letter thanks the king for his constant favor and protests his readiness to serve him. However, there is nothing to indicate that Frobisher ever did anything for the Danish king, except perhaps to give advice.

After this, and before Davis, there was at least one further attempt by the government of Denmark to find Europeans in Greenland. The expedition was commanded by Olivier Brunel of Brussels who, according to Bobé, "for a long time had carried on contraband trading with Siberia and the land of the Samoyedes." This man and Arent Meier of Bergen, Norway, received the promise of a trade monopoly in Greenland if they were successful. However, it was stated that the chief object of the expedition was to preach the gospel. Bobé says that "nothing came of the plan any more than of the preceding ones."

The notable voyages of John Davis came in 1585–6–7. During these were explored the east Greenland shore from the latitude of Iceland south and the western shore up through the strait which bears the Davis name, far into what now is Baffin Bay.

Greenland was first sighted by Davis on July 20, 1585, probably just north of latitude 62° on the east coast. Janes, chronicler of the voyage, says it "was the most deformed, rocky, and mountainous land that ever we sawe." Davis wrote that, "The lothsome view of the shore and irksome noyse of the yce was such as that it bred strange conceites among us, so that we supposed the place to be wast, and voyd of any sensible or vegitable creatures, whereupon I called the same Desolation."

The Land of Desolation, as it came to be recognized, was approximately that part of Greenland, both east and west coasts, which lies south of 61° 30′ N. Lat.; it therefore included most of the land occupied by the Eastern Settlement of the Norsemen. The point of view shown by this naming of his first landfall was later modified by Davis, as when he reported that in one place he saw grasslands which were equal to fine English meadows. He apologizes for the naming when, in his book *The Seaman's Secrets,* he says, in a section entitled "Of the Frozen Zones":

". . . In the frozen zone I discouered a coast which I named Desolation at the first viewe thereof, supposing it by the loathsome shape to bee wast and desolate, but when I came to anker within the harbours thereof the people presently came vnto me without feare . . . ; thus by experience it is most manifest that those zones which haue beene esteemed desolate and waste, are habitable, inhabited and fruitfull."

Apart from the sighting of people at a distance and the inspection of their camp by Frobisher, the Davis expeditions were the first of record to come in touch with the natives of West Greenland; although, as concluded by Frobisher, there must have been unrecorded voyages around this time or just before it.

Because the Davis expeditions were the first in the new era of sailings to describe the people of Greenland, their findings are of great importance. Here we merely note that the group with whom Davis was most in contact appear to have been near the mouth of the present Godthaab Fjord, and that he portrays them as typical Eskimos in appearance and customs. There were, however, elements in their culture of seeming European origin, for instance the already mentioned placing of a cross upon a grave.

We have told of Frederik II of Denmark that he sought the company and advice of Frobisher, and that he promoted Greenland exploration, though with little result. The next monarch, Christian IV, after some futile gestures, saw to the organization of the first really important Danish expedition. As heretofore the Danes employed sailors from the British Isles as commanders or pilots—this time James Cunningham from Scotland and the Englishmen John Knight and James Hall.

It is said of Hall, the most important of these figures, that he had been "to Friesland and other neighboring lands toward

America." So far as the records as yet go it is anybody's guess what countries may have been these lands toward America which Hall knew; possibly he had been up in Davis Strait and Baffin Bay, visiting sections to the westward; perhaps he had been more southerly—in Labrador, to the southwest of Greenland.

The 1605 Danish expedition, which is usually known as Hall's first, left Copenhagen with three ships. They passed between the Orkneys and Shetlands, reached southern Greenland, and followed up the west coast at least as far as the present Fiskenaes, or to about 63° N. There was a sort of mutiny; and a Danish nobleman, Lindenow, sneaked off home with one of the ships, after trading for a good many furs with the natives. The other two ships did most of the expedition's discovery work, examining the coast to a probable most northerly point near Sarqardleq, 68° 35' N.

It has been considered absurd in the stories from the Middle Ages that Greenlanders in small boats would attack large European ships. Hall had an experience which proved that, however strange, this could happen; for his ship was attacked by the natives with a shower of arrows and stones.

Upon its return the expedition seems to have made a long report, but only a digest of this has been preserved. We have from this voyage a general map of the west coast between 66° and 68° 35' N., as well as special maps and plans.

The second of the Hall expeditions had five vessels. The same Danish nobleman, Lindenow, was along, this time formally in supreme command. They made a good navigation, avoiding "the west ice" of Greenland by passing north along the Labrador and Baffin Island coasts, and then turned in for a mountain they had discovered on the previous voyage which they believed to consist more or less of silver. The fjord is the present South Kangerdluarssuk, near 65° 30' N., and the ore may have been lead. As with Frobisher and his "gold," they loaded their vessels with "silver," which turned out worthless and annoyed the king so that he proposed to name Greenland "The Philosopher's Stone."

However, the Danish Government did organize a new expedition, called Hall's third. Of it Bobé says:

"In the letter of instruction given to the commanders of the expedition reference is made to a revised edition of Ivar Baardsön's description of Greenland, as far as the place-names are concerned with many corruptions, in respect of which they were to sail from Cape Lindesnaes by a W.N.W. course toward the southern extremity of Greenland in lat. 60°–61° N. 'albeit on the east side' that they might make an attempt to find Eriksfiord, where the best land and people of Greenland were to be found. They were to look for the localities mentioned by Ivar, and as no one entertained any doubt that the population of those parts were the descendants of the old Norse settlers, an Icelander and a Norwegian joined the expedition in order to be able to hold converse with them, while the sailors were earnestly requested to treat the Greenlanders with the greatest friendliness.

"This expedition, like so many others before and after that time sent out with the view of reaching the east coast and, furthermore, at an unfavorable season, seems to have returned without accomplishing its object."

For the next several years Hall lived in Denmark, apparently with great honor. But in 1612 he embarked a fourth time for the northwest, now financed by the "Merchant Adventurers of London." The object was partly to exploit the silver mine, in which Hall still believed, and partly to establish a trade with Greenland. From an historical standpoint the most notable thing about the enterprise was that it included William Baffin, destined to rank as one of the greatest figures in the entire history of northern exploration. He wrote an account of the voyage, which has been preserved.

It is supposed that Hall must have been a member of one of the Davis expeditions, for he tells certain things about the

Davis voyages, or rather mentions results of them, which are not found in known records left by Davis or by any other member of his parties. There may have been personal friction or envy between these two, both of whom are now such important figures, or it may have been simply that they had a different outlook. At any rate, the theory of personal friction has been called in to explain why the two explorers fixed such different sounding names on parts of the Greenland coast. As mentioned, Davis gave the name Land of Desolation to the section east and west of Farewell; for the coast line to the north, on the west coast, Hall chose the name Land of Comfort.

The most spectacular careers in Greenland exploration during the early part of the century were those of two Englishmen, Henry Hudson, known to have been a native of London, and William Baffin, thought to have been a Londoner.

The contribution of Hudson to the advance of geographic knowledge is high-lighted for us through the river which bears his name in the United States, the bay named for him in Canada, and his exploration of Spitsbergen which led directly to Britain's entry into that great northern "fishery." In Greenland waters his contribution was also notable. He did not follow the east coast to as great a latitude as the Dutch eventually reached, but he made on that shore the longest single forward stride in our knowledge during the period. For during the summer of 1607, on a voyage of commercial pioneering for the Muscovy Company of his home town, he sighted the east coast of Greenland now and again from southerly parts up to 73° 30′ where a name he gave, Hold with Hope, marks on our charts his approximate farthest. The Danes have recently given his name to the most northerly ice-free country seen by him before he swung northeasterly toward Spitsbergen, calling it Hudson Land.

William Baffin, more important for our knowledge of Greenland than Hudson, appears mysteriously in 1612 as chief pilot of Hall's fourth voyage. He is thought to have been born in 1584 and was, then, 28 when he joined Hall. That no trace can be found of him earlier has seemed baffling to all students, as to Sir Clements R. Markham, distinguished Arctic explorer and later president of the Royal Geographical Society of London, who said, as editor of *The Voyages of William Baffin,* published by the Hakluyt Society in 1881: "We are thus first introduced to William Baffin as an experienced seaman, in the prime of life, and I have been baffled in all my attempts to discover even a single fact respecting his former history."

Until some thirty years ago, when Rasmussen began to report Eskimo tradition that the Norsemen had been at Smith Sound in the Middle Ages, there was no evidence for doubting that Baffin had exceeded by three hundred miles in 1616 the farthest north of any previous European on the west coast of Greenland. For on his third journey to the Arctic he discovered all shores of what is fittingly named Baffin Bay, including the great westward straits, Lancaster and Jones Sounds, and Baffin Bay's northward extension which he called Smith Sound, all these named for commercial backers of his enterprise. And not until the summers of 1936 and 1937 were we really sure that Baffin's farthest north had been exceeded by the medieval Greenlanders, for it was during those seasons that the Danish archaeologist, Erik Holtved, first demonstrated that people of a blended Eskimo and Scandinavian culture had been living, at the time of Baffin's voyage or earlier, in Inglefield Land, some of them perhaps a hundred miles beyond Baffin's farthest.

Two things bring out dramatically the comparative magnitude of Baffin's work, as seen in relation to the history of Greenland exploration. The first is that no one equaled his highest latitude for 202 years; it was only in 1818 that John Ross attained the Smith Sound district and became the first of known modern Europeans to see the Cape York Eskimos. Even more dramatic is the corollary that during these two centuries Baffin's memory had faded and his reputation, what remained of it, had become so tarnished that there grew up a skepticism about the extent of his voyage and the truthfulness of his reports. We see the absurdity of this now, but at the time it seemed doubtful to the commentators that anyone's findings would remain unconfirmed for two hundred years if they had been genuine—the skeptical reasoners overlooking in Baffin's case, as similar skeptics had done for the northward voyage of Pytheas around 325 B.C. that you could not expect confirmatory evidence from a region which no successor had visited.

Sir John Ross had brought back from his voyage of 1818 preliminary confirmation of Baffin's results. It is considered, however, that not until the 1821 report of Sir Edward Parry on his first command in search of a Northwest Passage was Baffin's reputation firm on its supreme eminence. For the narratives and descriptions from the years 1819 and 1820 were then found to correspond so accurately with those of Baffin from 1612 to 1616 that the parallels are customarily referred to as remarkable or startling.

It is usually considered that Baffin's most important contribution to our knowledge of Greenland and of Greenland waters is in his charting of them and his reports on ice and other navigation conditions. He also has many and informative comments on vegetation and animals, but such things remain in the twentieth century as they were in the seventeenth.

It is human things like culture patterns which change most readily; and this third in the line of discoverers from England —Frobisher, Davis, Baffin—was the first of the three to give us no indication that there had been previous commerce by the Greenlanders with Europe.

Frobisher had inferred from examining a deserted camp site that the people were either themselves civilized or in trade relations with a civilized country; Davis had reported a cross upon a grave. Baffin tells nothing that would not fit with his having been among people whose only previous relations with white men had been through the Davis and Hall expeditions.

This may have been, however, a result of his reasoning that any European articles or traits which he observed were due to the various contacts with Davis and Hall.

Shortly following Hall and Hudson there arose between England, the Netherlands, Denmark, and Norway a quarrel over sealing and whaling rights that has for us pertinent historical implications.

The medieval Norse had held a theory that there was a land connection, apparently in a rainbow curve, from Greenland somewhere north of Scoresby Sound, to the Russian mainland east of the White and Kara Seas. Accordingly, when Spitsbergen came to the knowledge of Europe, through the efforts of the Dutch toward the end of the sixteenth century, it was at first supposed to be a part of Greenland and was indeed called Greenland for upward of two centuries.

Also there was the circumstance, apparently not much dwelt upon in European discussions but certainly familiar to the Icelanders of the time, that land to the north had been discovered from Iceland in 1194, which discovery they named Svalbard. This was probably a further section of the east coast of Greenland, but the Norwegians have maintained (especially since 1918 and no doubt somewhat for political reasons) that what the Icelanders discovered in 1194 was Spitsbergen.

In the period we now deal with the King of Denmark was able to crystallize into a doctrine the idea that all lands were part of Greenland if they lay to the north of Iceland or to the north of Norway. The view got such a hold that it became an international custom to say those ships were whaling in Greenland waters that were up around Spitsbergen; while ships that plied the true west coast of Greenland were not spoken of as Greenland whalers but as operating in Davis Strait. In this nomenclature the east coast of Greenland was called "Old Greenland," on the theory that the Eastern Settlement lay there.

Norway, and Denmark because of rule over Norway, re-

newed after Frobisher that claim for Greenland which Norway had asserted following the amalgamation of 1261. This
Norwegian claim never died down at home, but we are not
clear that it was much recognized abroad until the eighteenth
century. However, about the middle of the seventeenth the
Danish king took steps to formalize the claim. Of one of them
Bobé says:

"As an outward sign of the suzerainty over Greenland as
part of the Danish-Norwegian crown, King Frederik III,
probably in consequence of the voyages of Danell, incorporated its coat of arms—a polar bear (as a rule couchant,
more rarely upright) in azure—with the stockfish (Iceland)
and the sheep (the Faeroes) as is seen in the seal under Lex
Regia."

The first half of the seventeenth century was, on the whole,
a Dutch period in the cultivation of Greenland.

Along the west coast the sailors of Holland do not seem to
have gone farther than 73° N. Lat., where now is the Danish
colony Upernivik, but much of the coast south of there was so
well known to them that their maps and sailing directions, especially for the section around and south of Disko, were not
superseded till after the middle of the nineteenth century.
Some of the names which they gave to seaways and landmarks
have been preserved and are their memorials. In the main,
however, Dutch names have been replaced. Part of that is
right, for the names put in their stead are Eskimo and therefore have an even longer history. Some of the Eskimo words
are, no doubt, the first names that man ever applied to features
of the Greenland coast.

Dutch work on the eastern coast was more extensive though
less intensive. By 1670 their voyages had reached 78° 30', the
present Lambert Land. This was the farthest north of the
Dutch in Greenland and was at that time a long way beyond
any other nationality.

Around the turn of the century came a number of trading

voyages by Danes and Norwegians. Some were in a pioneering spirit, but most of them were trying to wrest from the Dutch a share of their Greenland commerce. Some of these attempts were tragic through shipwreck; they were all commercial failures in the long run, although some prospered temporarily. No individual or company maintained continuous operations through more than a few years.

CHAPTER XIII

Resettlement of Greenland
and Exploration of the East Coast

IN 1721, FOR THE FIRST TIME in 300 years, Europeans came to Greenland with a desire to spend the winter. It was a combined mission and trading venture from Bergen, Norway. The promoter of the expedition and its leader was Hans Povelsen Egede, a Norwegian who had received his higher education in Denmark. For at this time Norway was subordinate to Denmark, both kingdoms ruled from Copenhagen.

Egede was born in 1686 at Sengen in the Nordland section of Norway. The reading of Peder Claussen's description of Greenland, 1632, is said to have fired him with the ambition to go there and preach the gospel to the descendants of the Norsemen. Another view is that the interest did not start from Claussen's book but developed gradually during Egede's training for the ministry, 1704–05.

At any rate, it was about 1707 that Egede began trying to promote a missionary enterprise in Greenland. As we have said, it had been in the air of Scandinavia since the Reformation that the European Greenlanders must need one of two things, rescue from heathenism or from Romanism. Egede's main purpose, then, was to preach Lutheranism to the European Greenlanders, whether they should prove to be heretics or heathen. But more than any of those who had previously advanced this program he appreciated that what was then considered the Western Settlement was now occupied by Eskimos. It was in part for the conversion of these non-European heathen that he planned his mission.

Egede's campaign made little headway at first. There was a great pestilence in northern Europe during 1711 which crippled enterprise and brought the thoughts of people into other channels. And then came war.

Egede did not lose interest, though he failed to stir much of it in others. He decided finally that the best chance was to go to Bergen where the medieval commerce with Greenland still lived in memory. During a Bergen residence of three years he gradually converted people to his views and plans until a group of leading merchants was formed to revive the trade that had lapsed in the fifteenth century. They provided three ships, and forty people altogether sailed with Egede, including his wife and four children.

Guided by the reports of friends and of relatives who had been in Greenland, Egede planned the colony for about 64° 10′ N. Lat., where the first winter was spent on what Egede named the Island of Hope. Seven years later the colony was moved to the present Godthaab (Good Hope).

During the fifteen years spent in Greenland Egede came into personal touch with some four hundred miles of the coast, from a southern limit near Nanortalik, about 60° N., to beyond present Sukkertoppen, near 66°. His most important journeys of investigation were made in 1723 and 1724.

In 1723 Egede traveled south in boats and was guided by the Eskimos to a number of the most conspicuous ruins of Norse churches, including the best preserved of all, Kakortok. He found the remains of churches and homes as far south as near the turning point, at Ivigtut.

The news of the 1724 journey was an eye opener to those in Europe who had believed that everything was frozen solid along the Greenland shore in winter. February is there the coldest month, as in many other northerly countries; and it

was on February 22 that the party started northward in two
boats with twenty men. They were not much hampered by ice
directly but were retarded by northerly winds and finally
turned back at 66° because of protracted and strong norther-
lies.

On this voyage they learned, as the medieval Norsemen had
learned before them, that the hunting improved as you went
farther north along the coast. This included whaling, and one
result of the journey was the establishment of a whaling station at Nipisat, near 67° N. Lat.

Commenting on this journey, and upon the results of other
years, Bobé says:

"The old Norse ruins in which Egede, on this voyage as
everywhere else, took a great interest, and which he found on
the whole of the distance lat. 60°–66° N., led him to the conclusion that he had traversed the 'Vesterbygd' [Western Set-
tlement] throughout its extent. His voyages in a southern direction strengthened him in the view already set forth in
February 1723, as to the destruction of the original settlements, whether, as substantiated by native traditions, the
settlers had succumbed to privation and hunger, or they had
been slain by the savages. That some of the old Norsemen
might have mixed with the natives he concluded from the Norwegian words which he thought he found in the Greenland
language, and the natives did not gainsay him when he called
them the 'children of the Norwegians.' On the other hand, he
still believed in the existence of the Österbygd [Eastern Settle-
ment] on the other side of Hukken [i.e., on the east coast beyond Cape Farewell], with a population of purely Norwegian
extraction."

The belief of Egede that only the Western Settlement had
been on the west coast, and that the Europeans of the Eastern
probably still survived beyond Cape Farewell, led to action
from Norway by his supporters who, in 1724, sent two ships
with instructions to search the coast, one of them from abreast

of Iceland to Cape Farewell and the other to begin searching
on the west coast and to proceed east through Greenland by
way of "Frobisher Strait," which was then supposed to cut
the land in such a way as to leave Cape Farewell as the southern tip of a considerable island. The captains and crews seem
to have known only the current Danish and Norwegian languages; they were furnished with vocabularies of everyday
Icelandic words to use in dealing with the Greenland colonists
if they should be able to get ashore on the east coast.

The expedition detailed to search the eastern shore cruised
back and forth all summer between latitudes 60½° and 66½°.
They were frequently near the coast, and once only a mile from
it, but were never able to land. The vessel sent to the west
coast for navigating "Frobisher Strait" was seen by Dutch
fishermen, after which there was no news of her.

By this time the failure of large sailing vessels to negotiate
the ice stream and get ashore, where the European colony was
supposed to be, on the east coast of Greenland southwest of
Iceland, had so impressed the Danes and Norwegians at home,
and Egede in Greenland, that he and most others were urging
one or both of two plans—to cross the icecap from West
Greenland afoot or with horses, and to attempt using small
boats for rounding southern Greenland and working up along
the east coast. For these purposes Egede wanted a new colony
planted on the west coast far enough south so that Greenland
would there be narrow for the overland crossing and so that
the distance south around the country for the boat voyage
would not be too great. Accordingly, Frederikshaab was established near latitude 62° in 1742.

Meantime, efforts had already been made to cross overland.
Claus Enevold Paars became governor of Greenland in 1728
and the following April he started with seven companions,
planning to cross the icecap. He penetrated some distance
from Godthaab into Ameralik Fjord and then climbed a little
way up an ice slope, finding crevasses two or three fathoms

wide which intimidated him. This was just about where Nansen descended from the Inland Ice after the first crossing of
Greenland 161 years later, in 1890.

A second attempt to cross overland was made by a Norwegian, Matthias Jochimsen, who had lived some years in
Iceland and who was familiar with the use of reindeer in Norway as pack and sledge animals. He got the idea of capturing
some Greenland reindeer (caribou), taming them and using
them instead of horses for traversing the icecap. He may have
developed the plan from learning that Greenlandic caribou
hunters sometimes pursued their game up on the icecap—not
often, for hunters who did this occasionally broke through the
snow-crust roofing of a crevasse and were never heard from
again.

Since Jochimsen was a Norwegian familiar with mountain-
eering, as the Danes were not, and since he did have the idea
of using skis as well as pack reindeer, it has been considered
that he might have succeeded had he secured proper support.
His original plan was that the expedition should consist in part
of Icelanders who would not only be good men for the job, he
thought, but would also return to Iceland when the expedition
was over and recommend Greenland as a place to which their
countrymen might emigrate. Conditions were particularly bad
in Iceland at this time, and it seems not unlikely that Jochimsen would have succeeded with both the colonization plans and
the crossing. But the Danish Government made the mistake of
first accepting his program and then cuttting him down in equipment, resources, and personnel to a point where success was
scarcely possible.

In the spring of 1733 Jochimsen went south from Godthaab
by ship to about latitude 61°. There he was unable to do more
than barely approach the ice, for the Danes who had been
furnished him as companions refused to go farther. They
really or pretendedly believed that a vessel was being sent
from Denmark this year to evacuate the Danes of the Green-

land colony, and these particular Danes were anxious to get back home.

Seemingly Paars had done no more than scramble a few hundred yards up onto a glacier slope, and the honor of being the rightful pioneer of the Inland Ice is given to Lars Dalager, the first merchant appointed to the new trading station at Frederikshaab.

A Greenlander had told Dalager in 1751 that while hunting he had gone so far up on the Inland Ice that he had seen the mountaintops of the east coast which, in conformity with the usual belief, he referred to as the mountains of the Eastern Settlement. So, accompanied by five Greenlandic natives, four men and a woman, he entered the northern arm of Tiningnertok Fjord near 62° 30′ N. Lat., crossed Lake Taserssuaq by kayak, and climbed the slope of the Inland Ice, which he found as smooth as a city street. On the second day he reached what he considered the highest west-coast nunataks and believed, like the Eskimos, that he was able to see toward the east the tops of the east-coast mountains. He was, of course, really seeing other west-coast nunataks somewhat farther inland. These now bear his name.

Peary and some other Greenland explorers of a later time built the success of their overland journeys to a considerable extent upon the ideas and methods of the natives; but Egede and the Danes who followed him failed consistently in their attempts upon the Inland Ice although they habitually associated with the local people, spoke their language, were sympathetic with them, and had them for traveling companions. This has appeared to some a curious if not an insoluble discrepancy. The key is in the difference between southern and northern Greenland.

In North Greenland the sledge is the chief vehicle; in south Greenland it is the skin boat—umiak or kayak. The northern Eskimos use dogs and sledges a great deal; they understand travel over snow and ice and had been led naturally, centuries before Peary, to the gradual acquisition of a technique that proved suitable to the Inland Ice, or at least adaptable to it. The southern Greenlanders had no knowledge and no technique that would serve for the overland ventures of the Danes. They could teach Europeans how to live comfortably in the Godthaab and Frederikshaab districts and how to be self-supporting there. The early Danes, especially the very earliest, made a use of this knowledge which increased their safety and promoted their comfort and success; it was of no value to them for reaching the east coast by crossing the land ice.

But the seamanship of the Eskimos of Frederikshaab and Godthaab furnished the best possible technique for reaching East Greenland coastwise. However, the Danish missionaries and traders did not at first emancipate themselves sufficiently from European ideas. The rediscovery of the east coast awaited thirty years a man of the necessary training and experience.

Peder Olsen Wallöe, a Dane, began sailing to Greenland in 1737 and was trade assistant and trader at Christianshaab and Godthaab from 1743–50. In the latter year he started on an exploring expedition south toward Frederikshaab and is considered to have been the first man who explored thoroughly what is now the Julianehaab District, wintering there the first season.

In the large Eskimo boat, the umiak, with two white companions and some natives, Wallöe made his way south gradually from fjord to fjord during the summer 1751. Then he traversed the passage that separates Statenhuk Island on its north and was the first known European since the Middle Ages both to navigate a strait connecting the east and west coasts and to set foot on an east-coast beach.

Wallöe now met three families of east-coast natives who gave him information about the northeastward trending coast line, including the names of villages up in the district now called Angmagssalik. The farthest he himself was able to penetrate, however, was just north beyond the present Lindenow Fjord. The farthest land seen by him was named Cape Wallöe in 1829 by Graah, the first to surpass Wallöe, who had remained unequaled for seventy-seven years.

A number of things make the Wallöe journey notable, among them his thorough way of examining the country; his careful gathering of information from and about natives, for he spoke their language; his full use of Eskimo boats and Eskimo technique; and his willingness and ability to live on local food secured in the local way. The journey involved three winterings and occupied the whole period from August 1751 to February 1753, when he reached Frederikshaab.

Bobé comments that not only did Wallöe use the right methods but that they continued to be the only methods which gave important results for knowledge of East Greenland during one hundred years. It was through a similar plan and the use of the same Eskimo technique that Graah was able to beat Wallöe's record in 1829–30 and that Holm was able to beat Graah's in 1883–85.

We come now to Povl Egede and must explain his unique position.

It may be an understatement that it is harder for a European, say a Dane or an Englishman, to learn Eskimo than to learn in succession Latin, Greek, Russian, and Hebrew. There seems to be no record that a European has acquired even a moderate conversational use of the tongue, with bad accent and frequent blunders in structure and idiom, by less than four years of intense application when surrounded by Eskimos and seldom or never hearing a word of another language. We have testimony that some white men have remained married to the same Eskimo wife for ten, fifteen, or twenty years, and have raised large families, without ever being able to understand fully what their own wives were saying to the children. This means that a perfect command is thinkable only for children who grow up with Eskimo housemates and playmates.

That is how Egede's children grew up, speaking both Danish and Eskimo at home; speaking Eskimo in the homes of their playmates and when at play out of doors.

Through this sort of bringing up one of the children, Povl, was enabled to become the first man to publish a book on the natives of Greenland and on their country that was written by one who knew the language, people, and country from the inside. True, his point of view could not be identical with theirs, for he was brought up within the rather narrow intellectual boundaries of an eighteenth-century religious home and without shedding completely the naïve superiority feeling which, basic in human nature, has had a special development since Europe attained that dominance which rests on pioneer use of explosives for killing purposes. Within such limitations, the writings of Povl Egede give us a unique light on the country and people.

This homily is a digression here, where we are dealing chiefly with the expanding geographic horizon. Strictly pertinent is no more than to say that in his *Efterretninger om Grönland,* 1788, Povl Egede tells us it had been his constant thought for fifty years to rediscover the Eastern Settlement of the medieval Greenlanders. During that time he was one of the chief forces in keeping alive Europe's interest in the Eastern Settlement and in promoting journeys of investigation and studies of the medieval literature as well as of the medieval ruins.

Povl Egede secured various types of support. His scholarly backing came to an extent from Iceland; and an Icelander, Jon Erichsen (Eiriksson), was particularly identified with the plans for exploration. One of the things which he did in connection with advancing the program was editing and publishing extracts from the traveling journals of Danell.

By 1785 Povl Egede had been able to interest Danish royalty and the government voted him twelve thousand Danish dollars, a coin with a theoretical value about half that of the American dollar but no doubt purchasing in those days a great deal more than ours do now.

With the twelve thousand dollars, and no doubt a good deal of other financial support, Egede promoted a series of attempts during 1785 and 1786 for reaching the east coast of Greenland by ship, thus by a method at least partly disavowed by his father who believed in overland crossings from the west and in boat voyages around the south. The coast was sighted by these expeditions at various points, chiefly between 64° and 66° N., with little geographic result except that fjords and other landmarks were determined by triangulation as they could be seen from the open water east of the Greenland Current's stream of floe ice.

Anders Olsen, a man who rates higher as a pioneer of commerce and of animal husbandry than as an explorer, has a place, too, in the history of South Greenland exploration. He established the trading stations of Fiskenaeset, Sukker-toppen (the old one—Kangagmiut), and Julianehaab. Olsen was not merely the first stock farmer in modern Greenland; he was the first man since the period of the Norsemen to be recognized as the owner of farm land. In fact, he is considered to have been the first modern private owner of real estate of any kind in Greenland. Other land ownerships, if any, had been those of missions or of trading stations and were more in the nature of city lots or port facilities than of farms.

Olsen re-established in Greenland the Icelandic way of life, a dependence upon European types of livestock, with hunting and fishing as contributory food sources. Incidentally he and his successors confirmed, after eight centuries, the judgment of Erik the Red who, after spending three years exploring the country from Farewell to Disko, had finally decided to settle at what is now the Igaliko neighborhood; and it was just here that Olsen, upon the best knowledge anyone in his time had of southwest Greenland, decided to re-establish stock farming.

The Olsen venture for the discovery of the imaginary

The young: mother and child.

The old: two old women of Greenland sit smoking their pipes.

Eastern Settlement was launched from the very heart of that settlement, the Erik the Red neighborhood, in 1783, when he was aged sixty-four. The results may be covered in a sentence; his brief report may be still more briefly summarized in that he passed Statenhuk and penetrated fifteen or twenty miles northeastward before he had to turn back.

Between Wallöe, who just passed Lindenow Fjord, on the east coast, and Graah, the first to excel him, there were many journeys of exploration, none of them particularly notable in geographic discovery. Most interesting, perhaps, were the studies made between 1777 and 1779 by Andreas Bruun and Aron Arctander. For they furnished descriptions and explanations which justify and clarify the farming enterprise of Anders Olsen, reports which were indeed far ahead of their time in visualizing what might be done with animal husbandry.

There were also sporadic whaling operations, chiefly by the Dutch but also by ships of other flags which kept prowling the east coast, seldom reaching land but often seeing it. They reported the coast line northward well past 78°.

Bobé says that by the end of the century all the settlements of West Greenland which now exist south of 72° N. Lat. had been founded. In addition to Godthaab colony, first on Hope Island, 1721, later at Godthaab, both just north of 64° N. Lat., the places, locations, and dates are:

Christianshaab	Lat. 68°	49′ N.	1734
Jacobshavn	Lat. 69°	13′ N.	1741
Frederikshaab	Lat. 61°	59′ N.	1742
Ritenbenk	Lat. 69°	45′ N.	1755
Holsteinsborg	Lat. 66°	55′ N.	1760
Sukkertoppen	Lat. 65°	24′ N.	1761
Egedesminde	Lat. 68°	42′ N.	1763
Umanak	Lat. 70°	40′ N.	1763
Upernivik	Lat. 72°	47′ N.	1772
Julianehaab	Lat. 60°	42′ N.	1775

In eastern Greenland no post had yet been established and there was no trade by the Danes except with an occasional small party of easterners who visited the southern west coast, one or several families who traveled by umiak with accompanying hunters in kayaks.

The first years of the nineteenth century were like the concluding decades of the eighteenth with a gradual but slight increase of knowledge for the whole east coast, resulting in the main from whaling voyages, few of which were able to approach the shore closely. Then came the notable expedition of Vilhelm Augustus Graah.

Graah also was searching for the lost colony. Without realizing that he was then at his goal, he spent the winter 1828–29 in the Julianehaab District, examining the ruins of the very settlement which he thought he might discover if he were able to round the south of Greenland and penetrate north along the east coast. He did have geographic success. With his supplies in umiaks, and with kayakers along for doing the sea hunting, he rounded Cape Farewell and made as he traveled northeastward the first good map of the coast between Farewell and Cape Dan. His farthest was Dannebrog Island, near 65° 15′ N. Lat.

From Egede's time all voyages to the east coast had been guided by native information, for there had been even from pre-Dane times a certain amount of trade and some slight intermarriage between west-coast and east-coast natives. What they told the Danes was partly misleading, the deceptiveness a result of several factors, among them that the whites misunderstood the west-coast natives through combined difficulties of language and ways of thought. Then the west-coast people did not quite understand those of the east coast because they blended their own beliefs, as to what the eastern people and conditions would be like, with the information which they received.

In a sense the ethnological results of Graah are meager when compared with those of Holm fifty years later; but they were important and unique in that Graah lived with Eskimos some of whom had never seen a European before. He gave of them a truthful though not a very comprehensive report.

One result of the Graah expedition was that Eskimos from the southeast coast began to move around and join those of the southwest. It has been alleged that this migration was due to better climate and country in the west; but the chief reasons were probably commerce and religion. The easterners wanted to trade with Europeans, and neither the Danes nor any others had as yet found it possible to establish shipping connections direct; and then the natives got the idea that Christianity was a good thing and wanted to live where they could have its benefits.

The 1883–85 expedition of Gustav Frederik Holm is usually considered the most important that has to date explored the southern half of Greenland's east coast, but this more because of its ethnographic than geographic work. They came from the west coast by umiak and kayak. According to G. C. Amdrup their farthest was just beyond 67° 47′ N.

In Lindenow Fjord, the most northerly district of East Greenland where ruins of Scandinavian farms of the Middle Ages have been found, Holm was impressed with impenetrable willow groves and a general abundance of vegetation. On the whole that was his tendency; he had an eye for the redeeming side of things and did much to counteract the reports of those who had dwelt exclusively on barrenness and desolation. He was sympathetic, too, with the natives; and portrays them not solely through emphasizing their differences from us but also through balancing similarities and dissimilarities against each other.

Holm reported that during the years 1883–85 he had been associating on the southern east coast of Greenland with people who appeared to have in them so much European blood that all of it could not possibly have resulted from mixture with whalers who might have survived from the wreck of their ships. He felt the main source of the white racial traits would have to be the medieval Norse colony. We translate from his *Den Östgrönlandske Expedition, udfört i Aarene 1883–85,* Copenhagen, 1888:

"The East Greenlanders are typically a slender and well-formed people, with oval heads; many of them are tall and have regular features with large and attractive teeth, prominent noses and beards. These are not Eskimo traits; but they do have other traits which are distinctly Eskimo, as heavy and coarse black hair and eyes which are black, although not usually slanting. They have the remarkably small hands and feet which are typical of Eskimos.

"Many inhabitants of the southern west coast have also physical traits which are not Eskimo; for it is not rare among them to find tall, slender, powerfully built individuals with oval heads. This would be a natural result from settlement there by people from the east coast.

"It seems probable that the inhabitants of the east coast are a race mixture between Eskimos and Europeans. It has been suggested that these may be the descendants of Eskimo intermarriage with shipwrecked sailors from the whaling fleet destroyed there in 1777. This I consider most improbable. . . ."

Holm points out that his own observations about the European-like traits of East Greenlanders are not the first of the kind. He quotes Giesecke who had seen the most southerly easterners during 1806: "The Greenlanders who inhabit the southern part of the west coast have in their physical appearance little in common with true Eskimos, such as are found on Disko Bay and in northern West Greenland; the East Greenlanders appear to me still less Eskimo-like."

Following this quotation from Giesecke, Holm continues with his own view:

"It is clear that the southern West Greenlanders had these traits in common with the East Greenlanders earlier than there could have been any possibility the foreign blood reached them from this particular source [wrecked whalers]. For even if some shipwrecked sailors did reach the coast before 1777 it seems incredible that they were in such numbers that the entire population was changed in appearance as a result, especially when one considers that the numerous intermarriages known [in times after Hans Egede] on the west coast have left most of the population still with numerous Eskimo traits.

"It is more reasonable to believe that the East Greenlanders are a mixture of Old Norse and Eskimos. Even though the Eastern Settlement of the Norsemen was in the Julianehaab District [southern West Greenland] it seems fair to assume that the last of the Old Norse settlers there had to begin living as Eskimos when active commerce with the mother country ceased, and that they intermarried with the Eskimos. Thereafter they would have made their way to the excellent fishing grounds of the east coast; or it may be they were driven in that direction by Eskimos coming from the north.

"That the Norsemen should go over completely to the Eskimo culture must have been a case of life and death for them. The same conclusion follows if you look at it the other way; they had to find a new means of livelihood [i.e., hunting instead of husbandry] and from this would result that they would adopt manners and customs like those of the Eskimos."

The writers who have opposed the conclusion of Holm, that there certainly was a great deal of European blood and that it probably came from the Old Norse, fall back chiefly upon osteology, particularly craniology. These claim they know what the bony structure would have been like had the people been pure Eskimo or with various degrees of European blending. These shapes and sizes they say they do not find. A recognized spokesmen for this school is Sören Hansen who concluded from studying the bones that "the East Greenlanders must be regarded as a pure and unmixed Eskimo tribe without any ostensible traces of foreign element."

Holm continued active in Greenland matters throughout a long and distinguished naval career. As to one of his big jobs there we may still agree in 1942 with what General Greely said in 1910:

"The last and most important work on the East Greenland coast has been the establishment by the Danish government of a missionary, trade, and meteorological station at Angmagsalik, and the closing of that coast to other nations. This ensures the future welfare of these natives, under the same beneficial methods that have marked Danish sway in western Greenland. Captain G. F. Holm landed at Angmagsalik fiord 26th August 1894, and constructed for these purposes two buildings on the shores of King Oscar Harbor."

Still there has been a deal of good exploratory work between Farewell and Scoresby since 1894. Several oceanographic expeditions have studied the shore waters; the land has been surveyed by others. Danish enterprise has generally taken the lead, but a number of other nationalities have also done significant work. There were, for instance, the two expeditions led by H. G. Watkins in 1930–31 and 1932–33, the first to study aviation conditions with British financing and the second for the continuation of the same work under American auspices, those of Pan American Airways.

The first Watkins expedition did much sound work but nothing more sound than the spectacular enterprise of August Courtauld who contributed to the study of Greenland climate by spending five months, from December 6, 1930, to May 5, 1931, alone on top of the Greenland Icecap at about Lat. 67° 03' N., Long. 41° 49' W., eight thousand feet above sea level. To this we shall refer hereafter.

The work of the second Watkins expedition was carried on after his death under the direction of John Rymill, whose ability and success in Greenland led to the organization of the successful British Graham Land Expedition to the Antarctic which he commanded through 1934–37.

As in nearly every other part of Greenland, valuable knowledge concerning the southeast coast was gathered by Knud

Rasmussen who directed toward this region two of his expeditions, in 1931 and 1932.

The sketch of southern coastal exploration brought down to the present, we turn to the northern section.

It may have been the Scoresby region, or the Blosseville coast just south of it, that was first in all Greenland to be approached by Europeans, among them the Greek Pytheas of the fourth century B.C. Many believe it was these parts to which the Annals of Iceland refer when they say that in 1194 Svalbard was discovered; but there is the difficulty about this that one would think from the record that there must have been several earlier visits from Iceland to this neighborhood. We have mentioned how it has been a game through nearly or quite all the centuries of Icelandic history since 900 for children to look at the Blosseville-Scoresby mountains through a hole in a flat stone erected on a mountaintop in the Isafjord neighborhood, and how the Icelanders in early modern times recorded their visits to the Scoresby locality, sometimes as passengers on one or another of the English ships that watchers from shore reported so frequently sailing toward and disappearing below the horizon northwestward from northwestern Iceland.

But with all this, and the numerous other reports of the coast which we have mentioned, like those of Hudson, we may still say that our detailed knowledge of eastern Greenland north of 69° N. Lat. begins with the Yorkshiremen, William Scoresby and his son William Scoresby, Jr., in the second and third decades of the nineteenth century.

With the father in command, they had been together on the whaler *Resolution* at 81° 30′ N. Lat., to the north of Spitsbergen, in 1806. In 1811 the son became commander of the *Resolution* and thereafter they had different ships. Before the main explorations Greenland had been sighted by them at least twice, in 1819 and 1821.

In 1822, from the ship *Baffin,* young Scoresby made sketches and a chart of the coast from Hudson's Hold With Hope near 73° 30' to beyond 75° N. Lat. The mapping of the summer continued from June to August and excelled that of previous observers in the care of astronomical observations and the accuracy of the triangulations.

It was the elder Scoresby, in the ship *Fame,* who sketched and explored what is now Scoresby Sound. With its ramification, this has turned out to be the greatest fjord system in the world. The neighborhood has also proved to have the most extensive grasslands of the east coast, if not of all Greenland; and here is found the greatest distance from sea to Inland Ice, about 185 statute miles.

The extensive reaches of the Scoresby district that are snow-free during every summer are to this day pasture for herds of musk oxen; but two species which were there in Scoresby's time have since disappeared, the caribou and the Eskimo.

Nobody knows why the caribou became extinct, but likely what destroyed them was a combination of two or more winters with heavy soft snow that enabled the wolves to overtake and devour the last survivors. Man, when armed with only bow and arrow, has never been known to exterminate this animal from any region.

The disappearance of the people is also a mystery. It cannot have been solely because the wolves killed off the last caribou, but this may have been a contributing factor. The main factor can have been a European disease, such as measles or influenza, that was somehow carried to them by the only group of whites who ever saw them; for there are records from other parts of the world that measles do sometimes kill as much as ninety per cent in their first attack upon communities whose ancestry has never previously been attacked, the death rate being about equally heavy with South Sea Islanders and Eskimos. Influenza has been known to be almost as deadly. With most of a group dead from an epidemic, the rest may die from a famine. From other Eskimo lands there are many reports of famines that have resulted from epidemics.

Nobody knows how these now-gone Eskimos reached northern East Greenland, but likely they came around the north coast; for remains of Eskimo dwellings have been found in Peary Land at the very northern extreme of Greenland. They may have come from the south but, if so, a long time ago.

There were 431 Eskimos at Angmagssalik when Holm wintered there in 1883–84, and a total of 548 on the whole coast south of 69°. But only twelve natives have ever been reported since the period of Icelandic voyages from north of 69°. They were seen on Clavering Island, near 74° N., by Captain Douglas Charles Clavering and his distinguished colleague, Sir Edward Sabine, leading mathematician and physicist who was making the famous pendulum experiments for gravity measurement that gave their name to Pendulum Island, as Sabine's and Clavering's names have been given to features of the neighborhood.

Both Sabine and Clavering published accounts of their observations, and both accounts are now hard to come by. Neither, so far as we know, has ever been reprinted, and there are few libraries in America which possess either document. So we have decided to print one of them here and have chosen Clavering's, which appeared after his death in *The New Edinburgh Journal,* for April–June 1830.

On September 16, 1823, the ship *Griper* found herself near 74° N. Lat. We quote Clavering with no additions; but we omit things not relevant to the natives and show the omissions with dots.

"[August 16] At this station, which was named Cape Borlase Warren, we found traces of the natives, and also several graves, and hoards of blubber, which are piled up all along the shores, and are marked by heaps of stones being placed over them, and which also keep the birds of prey from devouring them. Their graves did not remain free from our curiosity; we opened some of them, but nothing but a few mouldering bones was discovered. . . .

"[August 17] On the yawl's coming up, which had been left much behind, I was informed the natives had been seen about a mile from our present situation. I immediately proceeded to the spot, and found a small tent, made up of seal-skin, pitched upon the beach, within a few yards of the high water. There was nobody in it; the inhabitants, having become alarmed on seeing us, had retreated to some high rocks at a short distance. We observed two of them watching our motions. Accompanied by one of my officers, I advanced towards them, making such signs of good-will and friendship as occurred to us. They allowed us to approach the base of the rocks, which were about fifteen feet high. We deposited a looking-glass and pair of worsted mittens, and retired a few steps, upon which they immediately came down and took them up, withdrawing immediately to the top of the rock. After allowing them a few minutes to examine them, we again approached, when they permitted us to come close to them and shake hands,—a ceremony they by no means seemed to comprehend, trembling violently the whole time, in spite of our best endeavours to inspire them with confidence. We now led them to their tent, which we examined more minutely, and which we gave them to understand we greatly admired.

"The tent was small, occupying a space about twelve feet in circumference, and about five in the highest point in the middle; the frame-work was composed of wood and whalebone; the former they must have picked up along the shore.

"There was a small canoe, capable of containing but one person at a time, which was also of seal-skin, and in no respect different from those described by Crantz or Egede. Their harpoons and spear were lying at the side of it; the handles were of wood, the points tipped with bone, and some of them with iron, which had all the appearance of being of meteoric origin. We now shewed them our boat, which they were unwilling to get into from fear. Leaving them for the present, we returned to our tents for the night.

"19th.—Next morning we were very anxious to renew our intercourse with our Esquimaux friends, and were happy to find that we had been successful in inspiring them with confidence. In the course of the day, men, women, and children found their way to our tent. They brought with them large pieces of blubber, being the flesh of the seal and the walrus, which they offered for our acceptance, tearing off large pieces with their hands and teeth in the most disgusting manner. We gave them in return biscuit and salt meat: the latter they immediately spat out. They were much surprised at my ordering one of the children to be washed, for they were so stained with dirt and oil, it was impossible, without this proceeding, to know what was their real colour, which now exhibited a tawny coppery appearance. They had black hair and round visages; their hands and feet very fleshy, and much swelled. The expression of their countenances was extremely stupid and unmeaning; but this was in all probability much increased by their astonishment at every thing they saw. They were clothed in seal-skin, with the hair inwards.

"Knowing that we should again meet them on our return, and being desirous not to lose farther time, which, from the lateness of the season, was now becoming valuable, we left them about 4 in the afternoon. . . .

"August 23 and 24. These two days were spent with the natives, whom we found to consist of twelve in number, including women and children. We were well received by them, but our attempts at making ourselves understood were very unsuccessful. They are evidently the same race as the Esquimaux in the other parts of Greenland and the northern parts of America. Our intercourse was of too short duration to acquire any of their language; but the descriptions given by Captains Parry and Lyons of the natives at Igluleik in many particulars resembled those of our friends. I observed particularly the same superstitious ceremony of sprinkling water over a seal or walrus before they commence skinning it.

"Their amazement at seeing one of the seamen shoot a seal was quite unbounded. They heard for the first time the report of a musket, and turning round in the direction in which the animal was killed, and floating on the water, one of them was desired to go in his canoe and fetch it. Before landing it he turned it round and round, till he observed where the ball had penetrated, and, putting his finger into the hole, set up a most extraordinary shout of astonishment, dancing and capering in the most absurd manner. He was afterwards desired to skin it, which he did expeditiously and well.

"Wishing to give them further proofs of our skill in shooting, several muskets were fired at a mark, but without permitting them to see us load. A pistol was afterwards put into their hands, and one of them fired into the water; the recoil startled him so much, that he immediately slunk away into his tent. The following morning we found they had all left us, leaving their tents and every thing behind, which I have no doubt was occasioned by their alarm at the firing."

The twelve human beings described by Clavering and Sabine were never again reported by Europeans, but the belief that they or their relatives and descendants would be found somewhere in northern East Greenland persisted into the twentieth century.

There were many things to foster the belief, among them ruins of a considerable habitation which were found here and there. Then the country seemed the more habitable the more it was explored; for Europeans associate habitability with grasslands, seldom quite realizing that the Eskimo staff of life in Greenland is never the vegetation itself and seldom even the grazing animals which depend upon the vegetation. The chief food of carnivorous man in Greenland is the carnivorous sea mammals, the clam-eating walrus, the shrimp-eating seal, and the seal-eating bear.

The important geographic discoveries of the Scoresbys and the sensational human discovery of Clavering were followed by small contributions from many sources. In 1833 the Frenchman Lieutenant Jules de Blosseville skirted the shore from 66½° almost to 69° N. Lat., what is now the Blosseville coast. In 1868 a Scotch whaler, David Gray, found Scott's Inlet at 73½°. In 1879 the Danish Captain C. F. Wandel made a survey between 66° and 69°, but seldom from a distance of less than six miles; he was never able to reach shore. These were no more than nibbles at the coast line; and while they added to our knowledge they do not seem of high rank as pioneer work, especially when we remember that Clavering and Sabine had made a fairly good sketch map from 72° to 75° N. Lat., with land visible as far north as 76°, and indeed that 78° had been reached in a previous century.

Meantime there had come along, in 1869, the first of northeast Greenland's wintering expeditions. It was German and in two vessels, the *Germania* commanded by Karl Koldewey, the *Hansa* by Paul F. A. Hegemann.

It was the *Germania* that made for the undertaking its reputation as one of the greatest of scientific polar expeditions. The *Hansa* contributed within a narrower field but did add much to our knowledge of what can happen when ships and men drift in the northern pack. She also gave to polar exploration one of its great adventure stories.

Through a mistake and misunderstanding the *Hansa* got herself blocked in the pack September 5 and froze completely into the ice of the Greenland Current on September 14, 1869, near 73½° N. Lat. She was crushed by the floes October 19 and sank two days later, about six miles from the coast near latitude 70° 50'. The interval of two days between crushing and sinking gave plenty of time to unload supplies upon the ice. Therefore her people took up their residence on the drifting floes reasonably provisioned and fairly well equipped, so that no great hardships resulted.

There may have been the hardship of mental strain, for the drift of the *Hansa* was a new sort of experience to explorers, though whalers had faced the like a number of times on the Greenland coast, especially during the great wreck season of 1777. Some of those wrecked whalers just possibly got ashore on the east coast, as we have considered when discussing the European-seeming traits of the eastern Eskimos reported by Holm; but the few we know to have escaped were those who drifted around Farewell and reached the Dane-occupied section of southern West Greenland.

During fall and winter the *Hansa* party had had a good many thrilling experiences, with the floes breaking up on which they were camped so that they had to reassemble on other floes and erect new habitations. Spring was more difficult. By late April they had drifted 600 miles and were in danger through a scattering and melting of the floes. There was now too little ice for safety, too much open water, with resulting waves and teetering and tipping action of the floes. So, on May 7, they had to take to their boats at a point just north of 62° N. Lat. In the boats they were able to round the south of Greenland. They reached the Danish Frederikshaab colony June 13, 1871, after 244 days on moving floes and 24 in open boats.

Except for the case of the Hall survivors, under Tyson, mentioned in the next chapter, the *Hansa* drift is usually looked upon as the most remarkable in the history of polar exploration. They had, for one thing, a hundred-per-cent safety record, which would seem hard to beat; the Hall expedition were able to improve on it only because they had a woman in the party who bore a child that survived. The Tyson average of well-being was also higher; for the Germans, although they used admirable common sense and were resourceful, had not the advantage in comfort and safety which Tyson derived from the use of Eskimo hunting and camping methods.

The *Germania* wintered at Sabine's Pendulum Island. They

looked for the people reported from the district by their predecessors and did not find them, but they found the evidences of long habitation.

This expedition did the first exploratory sledging ever done on the east coast of Greenland, but without dogs, the men pulling in harness. This was when Koldewey and Julius Payer, who later distinguished himself through the discovery of Franz Josef Archipelago, traveled the spring of 1870 from Lat. 74° 32' at Pendulum Island to 77° N. Lat., a northing which was not excelled for thirty-seven years—not until 1907 by Erichsen and Koch.

The summer of 1870 the *Germania* entered the magnificent Franz Josef Fjord, one of the two or three greatest known fjords, which lies just north of 73°. It contains some of the most startling scenery in the world. By their determination, one cliff rises precipitously 5600 feet from the sea, and there was a view of Petermann Peak which they took to be about 12,000 feet; it is now rated at 9662.

The Koldewey expedition made history in the voluminous and excellent scientific reports that continued to appear for many years. For there is a difference between polar expeditions which is all-important to the scientist, though not usually suspected by the public, that some are widely heralded as scientific and do produce scientific results, extensive and of high quality; while others, no less publicized as being scientific, leave behind them information of small quantity and negligible scientific value.

Around the turn of the century came a series of notable journeys. Between 1898 and 1900 G. C. Amdrup made thorough scientific studies, chiefly in the region between 65° 30' and 70° 15'. His work emphasized magnetism and meteorology, but he made substantial contributions to other sciences. During the years 1899 to 1905 there were expeditions of value by the Swede Nathorst, chiefly in the Franz Josef Fjord vicinity; by the Norwegian Naero, around 75° N. Lat.; and by the French Duke d'Orléans who reached 78° 16' and was the first to give us some description of a coast which had been sighted in 1670—a "rediscovery" that shows how slow was the progress of our knowledge, when both the eighteenth and nineteenth centuries had failed here to match an achievement of the seventeenth.

The Danish explorer, Ludvig Mylius-Erichsen, who had already distinguished himself in northwest Greenland, commanded a successful but tragic expedition to the northeast. The fall of 1906 his *Danmark* was able to reach for wintering purposes a harbor at Cape Bismarck, 77° N. Lat., which is called after her Danmarkshavn (Denmark Harbor). It was believed then, and had been for some time, that Greenland would trend northwesterly thence toward Peary Land. But on a sledge journey in 1907 Erichsen discovered that instead the coast ran to the northeast, so much so that Nordöstrundingen (Northeast Foreland) is about two degrees of longitude farther east than any point in Iceland—at about West Longitude 11½°.

From Northeast Foreland, Erichsen gave J. P. Koch the job of northwestward exploration, which set on his brow the laurel of having finished Greenland's coast line, for he was able to meet Peary's work at Cape Bridgman. He turned back from 83° 30' N. Lat. and got home to the ship without mishap.

Accompanied by the Dane N. P. Höeg-Hagen and the Greenlander Jörgen Brönlund, Erichsen headed west and southwest into Peary's Independence Fjord and reached Navy Cliff, whence Peary had discovered, in 1892, what we now call Peary Land.

The return journey was much hindered by open water. At one time they were on drifting ice sixteen days. This and other delays used up the summer and the daylight, so that it was in darkness or by the moon that they made their crossings of the Inland Ice southeast toward Lambert Land. They had been more than 550 miles from home when they first ran completely out of food. They kept securing game now and then while they were still on the grasslands; high on the Inland Ice there was no chance of discovering food and they were in danger from crevasses.

It is nearly or quite the most remarkable story in polar travel that they made the 160 miles of the glacier crossing in 26 days and all reached Lambert Land. There Hagen died. Erichsen's death followed when he was practically in sight of the food depot.

Brönlund reached the depot with frozen feet. He used his last strength to write down in the Eskimo language a sober account of where they had been and what they had done. He had brought with him Erichsen's most important documents, which he placed in a box to preserve them. The map of their extensive discoveries he put in a bottle tied by a string around his neck. That was how Koch found him the next spring.

Since Erichsen's time there has been detailed work by several nationalities in northern East Greenland. Perhaps the Danes have led, for they had notable expeditions, particularly those commanded by Ejnar Mikkelsen and Lauge Koch. Mikkelsen was in search of Erichsen but covered new ground and made valuable contributions. Koch's work included exploratory flying over northern East Greenland from a base in Spitsbergen, through which he demonstrated, for one thing, that Peary's results, which had been disputed by some, were essentially correct.

An element new to Greenland's modern history was brought in by Norwegians who "flocked" (in restricted numbers) to the northern east coast during the second and third decades of the twentieth century, for this was partly a colonization movement.

The medieval colonists who followed Erik the Red were of Icelandic citizenship but largely no doubt of Norwegian blood. As we have shown elsewhere, that active period of westward movement, which began from Iceland in 985, ceased as far as the records show with a group who sailed from Norway, and were therefore outright Norwegians, in 1124. It was fitting that the eight hundredth anniversary of the last known ship-load of colonists, 1924, should fall within the revival, and that the colonists were again arriving from Norway.

Danes had been living in Greenland for two centuries, but they were usually not of the colonizing type or outlook. They were instead missionaries who came in a spirit of self-sacrifice and for the good of mankind, doctors who served with a like purpose, teachers who were socially minded. There was also the larger official class who did the trading and governing and were of civil-servant status—a high type but not true colonists, even if it did happen frequently that they lived in Greenland several decades, some dying there at a high age.

True, many of the Norwegians who came to the northern east coast around and after 1924 were technical men on brief assignment. But there were also men with scientific training, and successful in that work, who had nevertheless come to make a living in Greenland as hunters and trappers and who might have proved the nucleus of a modern parallel to the Erik colonization. One of many indications of this plan was that they named an East Greenland district Land of Erik the Red.

The colonization had a political background. There were motives of patriotism and territorial aggrandizement, for this region was to be an extension of Norway, the rights based upon discovery, exploration, colonization, and development. That explorers were botanists, zoologists, archaeologists, and competent in many other sciences, did not change the fact that they were also hunters and trappers, prepared to make a living and to stay as permanent inhabitants. The plan was that Norway would place a territorial claim before the International Court at The Hague.

Norway did submit her claims, but the court ruled against her, deciding in effect that the flag of Denmark covered the whole of the island continent. This dampened the ardor of the Norwegians somewhat, but many nevertheless continued to work in Greenland under a compromise arrangement made between the Danish and Norwegian governments.

During the late nineteenth century, and since, the Greenland explorations of the Danes have been made through support by foundations like those with which we are familiar under the names of Carnegie and Rockefeller. Some expeditions have had partial government support; there has been exploration wholly at the public expense. The results have usually been published by foundations and through government support. There is many a notable series of these; but overshadowing the rest is *Meddelelser om Grönland,* of which there has been at least one volume per year, except for one or two missed years, since 1879. At first the articles were mainly in Danish, but gradually they increased the use of the more widespread languages, German, French, and English. Of late years more than half and perhaps two thirds of this serial has been in English.

For her expeditions following 1918 Norway used chiefly the method of direct support by the taxpayers. Her government set up Norges Svalbard og Ishavs-Undersökelser (Norway's Foundation for Research in Svalbard and the Polar Sea). Publication of the results was also usually by this government bureau.

The most notable single enterprise since the time of Mylius-Erichsen was the German expedition of 1929 and 1930–31 commanded by Alfred Wegener. This was only in part East Greenlandic. The work which was central in the program was also central geographically—operating for a year a research station at Eismitte (Ice Center) on the Inland Ice, at Lat. 70° 53′ 8″ N., Long. 40° 42′ 1″ W., 9800 feet above sea level. One of the shore stations was on the west coast at Nordost Bay, another on the east coast in Scoresby Sound. Really there were two stations on the east coast, both in

Scoresby District, one at the village and another, the "East Station," farther west in the interior of the fjord. We deal with this expedition in a later chapter.

During the twentieth century the French have been more active in polar work than at any other time in their history. Of notable consequence for Greenland was a series of expeditions by Jean Charcot, in his ship the *Pourquoi Pas?*. This famous son of an equally famous father is usually thought of as an Antarctic explorer, but he made numerous voyages to Greenland, usually to the east coast and always accompanied by a staff of scientists. Their published results are notable but do not compare with what was about to be published at the time of Charcot's tragic death, when in September 1936 everything on the *Pourquoi Pas?* was lost, and all lives but one, when the vessel mistook a danger beacon for the harbor light of Reykjavik, Iceland, and sailed straight upon the rocks in Breidafjordur. Charcot had converted his ship into a combination library and laboratory and had aboard most of the diaries and original records of his many voyages, as well as his unequaled technical library. He planned this for his last voyage, though not last in the sense it proved to be. What he intended was ten or twenty years of study, writing, and publication based upon the records he had assembled aboard the *Pourquoi Pas?*.

CHAPTER XIV

Exploration of the North and West Coasts

BETWEEN EGEDE'S PIONEERING of 1721 and the end of his century Denmark had established a series of nine main trading stations along the west coast from just north of Cape Farewell to just south of 72° N. Lat., which means they had explored to the head of Baffin Bay and to the mouth of its northward extension, Smith Sound.

The exploratory work of the early nineteenth century, north from Baffin Bay, was rediscovery. We have mentioned the Eskimo traditions collected by Rasmussen which confirm the medieval accounts of voyages by the Europeans from southern West Greenland to the Cape York neighborhood; we have mentioned the archaeological proof that these Europeans went still farther north. Even the modern explorers had anticipated the Danes by attaining the Cape York neighborhood in 1616, on Baffin's remarkable voyage.

It remained for a British expedition, which did not penetrate quite as far north as Baffin, to become the first in modern times to see the people of northern West Greenland. For Captain Sir John Ross discovered the Cape York Eskimos in 1818, calling them Arctic Highlanders.

The Cape York or Smith Sound people were apparently two or three hundred in number when discovered, and they have fluctuated around those figures ever since. They are of

typical northern culture. The first of them must have come
from the Canadian islands originally; some of them came so
recently from Baffin Island that Rasmussen, the first student
of the region who spoke the language, was able to gather a
fairly circumstantial account of their immigration, not omit-
ting a statement of several cultural elements which they
brought in with them—which had either never existed on
Smith Sound or had been forgotten.

As previously indicated in a number of places, there has
been dispute as to how much evidence of European blood there
is in the appearance of the Greenlanders farther south along
the west coast. No one, apparently, has suggested that the
Arctic Highlanders were other than typically Eskimo—stiff
dark hair, sparse beards, "Chinese" complexion, brown eyes
that are straight or slanting, high cheekbones, a generally
"Mongol" appearance. This fits in with the conclusion of
Rasmussen that a considerable part of the Smith Sound blood
came recently from Baffin Island or farther west. It would not
seem unlikely that all of it came in from the west subsequent
to the flourishing of that culture in Inglefield Land which the
Danish archaeologists have recently described as being either
Scandinavianized Eskimo or Eskimoized Scandinavian.

The proper geographic exploration of Smith Sound, and of
the waters north, began in 1852 when Commander E. A.
Inglefield, as part of the Franklin Search, investigated the
coast of what is now Inglefield Land, to about 78° 28′ N. Lat.
and 74° W. Long. Thereafter the exploration of these narrow
waters between Greenland and Ellesmere Island was a continuation of the Franklin Search; for next after Captain Inglefield was Dr. Elisha Kent Kane, an American participant in
the quest for the lost British expedition. He reached that en-
largement of the narrow waters which appears rightly on our
maps as Kane Basin, and he discovered its northeastward out-
let which he named Kennedy Channel. He wintered in 1853–55
at Rensselaer Harbor, 78° 37′ N., 71° W. His farthest north

was attained by sledge in June 1854, at 80° 10′ N. Lat., 67° W. Long.

Kane's associate, Dr. Isaac I. Hayes, was in the same region the years 1860–61. But while he added to our general knowledge he did not extend his travels along Greenland beyond Kane's farthest point.

Third in the chain of these Greenland explorers was still another American, Charles Francis Hall, whose tragic expedition reached 82° 11′ N. Lat., two hundred miles beyond Kane. That was by ship. On a sledging journey, Sergeant Frederick Meyer, of Hall's party, reached 82° 07′ in 59° W. Long.

The tragedy of Hall differs from most in northen exploration because there was a widely circulated, although never officially studied, charge of murder.

Hall's third expedition, during which he died on November 8, 1871, was wholly financed and controlled by the U.S. Government and had a staff of scientists who were able, some of them distinguished. The commander himself was a religious enthusiast of limited education and no scientific training who had gone north originally because what he took for a spiritual voice told him that some of the Franklin expedition still survived and needed rescue.

We understand now what fewer understood in Hall's day, that an honest man who is a close observer and diligent reporter can bring home results of high value, especially in the fields of geography and oceanography. For instance, the few travelers who have been in Frobisher Bay since Hall's time have nearly or quite all returned with great admiration for Hall's work in that district on his first expedition. Undeniably his point of view, however, was very different from that of a typical scientist, and we can sympathize with both sides in the quarrels which developed; to an extent we can condone the insubordination of the scientists. Some think this led to arsenic poisoning, others that Hall died from "acute indigestion."

In a generally brief sketch of nineteenth-century Greenland exploration we pause for these remarks because of a circumstance fascinating to the mystery fan, that Hall may have been buried deep enough so that his body has not since then thawed. It is likely, then, that if you were to open his grave you would find him as if he had died yesterday. For men buried a good deal longer than Hall yet has been have shown, when exhumed, no indication that their last breath was drawn more than a few hours ago. It might be possible, no doubt, if Hall had been buried in his native Cincinnati to ascertain this year whether his death was the result of arsenic; but it would not be feasible to determine precisely a natural cause of death, as, for instance, "acute indigestion." But a post mortem on Hall today would be no more complicated than if he had died yesterday.

We have, then, the fascinating possibility that a problem of murder unique in the history of exploration could be solved this year or a hundred years from now. Many have suggested this verbally but have refrained from publishing their views because of the sensibilities of those who might be accused, or of their descendants. However, a study of the evidence would indicate that any one of several men could have administered the poison, if there was poisoning, and that a number might be considered to have had a sufficient motive. We need not worry about sensibilities, for no one open to suspicion can now have a relative closer than a grandchild; and no one could say which grandchild ought to worry, since the number of suspects is considerable.

Not only in the murder suspicion was the Hall expedition remarkable. There was also the drift which is described in one of the most sensational and fascinating books in polar literature, *Arctic Experiences: Containing Capt. George E. Tyson's Wonderful Drift on the Ice-Floe,* New York, 1874.

On October 15, 1872, the people aboard Hall's ship the *Polaris* felt sure she was being crushed by the ice and that she was about to sink. They dumped tons and tons of miscellaneous supplies and equipment on the floes and dragged her boats away from the ship's side, together with the supplies. But the *Polaris* was not crushed, nor did she sink; she wintered safely, together with most of her people.

But ten white men, two Eskimo men, their wives, and five children found themselves the next morning drifting on a loose floe within sight of the *Polaris*. Apparently no one saw them drifting off. They had with them on their piece of ice far more of certain things than they could possibly find any use for, but others were wanting which they desperately needed.

In the judgment of those on the floe it was not feasible to reach either the ship or the shore at this time. They hoped for a later chance, but none ever came. From 79° 35', a latitude so northerly that in December there is only the barest trace of daylight in the southern sky at noon, they continued moving south in the West Greenland current. Through Eskimo methods of camping and housekeeping they were comfortable; through the success of the Eskimo hunting they had plenty of fresh meat not merely for ordinary nourishment but to prevent the development of what nowadays we call a dietetic deficiency. For scurvy and its cousins of the deficiency-disease group never afflict those who have a considerable amount of fresh animal tissue in their diet. The beasts Tyson's party secured were chiefly seals, which gave them not merely the fat they needed dietetically along with their protein but also the fuel they required for heat and light as well as for cooking.

There was no scarcity of game and little discomfort or danger so long as the cold was intense and their latitude far enough north. Gradually, however, when the days lengthened and the cold slackened, with a drop in latitude and an advance of the season, their troubles grew from day to day. The floes began to scatter enough so that the wind, when it blew, was able to create wave action that split up the ice. When the piece on which they were camped got too small they would have to load themselves and their supplies and equipment into the boat and move to a larger floe.

By the beginning of April the floe camp was off Labrador and the situation was growing desperate; for there was now so little ice and so much open water that even a breeze would kick up a sea dangerous to their floe and dangerous as well to their boat, which was of necessity overloaded as they moved camp to a more promising site.

On April 30 the drifters were picked up, every one in perfect health, and the party more numerous than it had been at the start. For one of the Eskimo women had borne a child which thrived, as Eskimo children usually do, on mother's milk and chunks of meat to suck. They had been on the floe more than six months (193 days) and had drifted more than 1300 miles.

The next expedition in our present sector of Greenland was commanded by George Nares, later Admiral and Sir, with the later Admiral Sir A. H. Markham as second-in-command. Their work was chiefly by sledging, their main purpose to reach the North Pole over the drifting pack to the north of Ellesmere Island. Their chief handicap was disease, for their health was not protected by seal and polar-bear meat, as Tyson's had been. Several of them died of scurvy; the sledging expeditions were foiled by the bodily weakness and mental sluggishness which are early manifestations of that disease. Even so, they did excel Hall's record along the Greenland shore; for a sledge journey by Lieutenant Louis A. Beaumont, later one more of the admirals and sirs, reached latitude 82° 20′ at Long. 51°, thus a bit north and a good deal east beyond Sergeant Meyer of the Hall expedition.

Since we have been paying special attention to the interrelation between Europeans and Eskimos, we mention here in its place what we have discussed elsewhere, that a monument and an eider-duck-nest shelter were discovered by this expedition. Nares, Markham, and the surgeon of the expedition, Dr. Edward L. Moss, have each in his own separate book said that in their opinion neither monument nor eider-duck shelter could have been either of Eskimo or recent European origin and that therefore they must have been from the days of the old Norsemen. The duck shelter was on Norman Lockyer Island at 79° 22′ Lat., 75½° Long., and the monument on Washington Irving Island, 79° 34′ N. Lat., 73° 5′ W. Long., both localities thus opposite that section of the Greenland coast from which, again as discussed elsewhere, the Danish archaeologists of the last ten years have reported, from the medieval ruins excavated, a blending of Norse or of Eskimo cultures.

Following the short interregnum of the British Nares expedition, the exploratory work of northwest Greenland passed back into the hands of Americans. Adolphus W. Greely, later Major General of the U.S. Army and Chief of its Signal Corps, commanded one of the two American expeditions which participated in the International Polar Year studies of 1881–83 (the other expedition was under Lieutenant P. H. Ray and was sent to Point Barrow, Alaska).

When Greely's work was over and a vessel should have arrived to bring his party home, there was a series of misadventures, nearly or quite all due to human frailty, some of the frailty in Washington and the rest aboard the various ships which had orders to supply or evacuate Greely. It is easy to see now that Greely's party could have saved itself by staying at their base, Fort Conger, for an additional winter (1883–84), and also that better use could have been made of the local game supply. It is equally true, however, that a careful study of the Greely records shows many traits of courage, ability, and foresight which offset the criticisms.

The expedition kept scurvy away throughout the first and second years by an adequate use of fresh meat. The published evidence gives suspicion rather than proof that during the third year scurvy may have contributed to a result which in the main was plain starvation. The supplies on hand in the fall were less than a third of a proper ration.

On January 18, 1884, the first man died of hunger; one after another they died, in spite of the remarkable achievements of a number of the hunters—remarkable because the hunting did not start until the men were so weak that three or four miles were probably as difficult for them as thirty or forty would have been for well men; and thirty or forty miles of walking on a single hunt is not an unusual record among those who live by Arctic hunting.

It is perhaps invidious to single out one man where several did well, but it happens that the one who contributed most to the survival of the seven out of twenty-five is also the only one still living. He is Brigadier General David L. Brainard, author of two books on the Greely expedition which are at once revealing and reticent. If we select for distinction one of those who died it should perhaps be the Eskimo, Jens. Almost up to the time of his death he was a mainstay of the expedition.

The American story was carried forward after Greely by Robert E. Peary, later Admiral, who had begun his apprenticeship with a journey, far more successful than any before him, from the coast line of middle West Greenland up on the Inland Ice. That was in 1886.

From 1891 Peary's work was in northwest Greenland and, although notable in many years, was perhaps especially distinguished in 1892 when he stood on Navy Cliff on July 4 and looked northward over what has proved not only the most northerly land in the world but nearly or quite the largest ice-free section of Greenland, a land that resembles Montana or Dakota in having snow in winter and no snow in summer.

In 1900 Peary came from Greely's Fort Conger on Grant Land and passed the farthest attained by the Greely expedition, on which Lieutenant J. B. Lockwood and David L. Brainard had reached 83° 24′ N., at Long. 41° W. In May

1900 Peary reached Cape Morris Jesup, which has proved to be the most northerly cape on earth, and rounded it to the almost as northerly Capes Bridgman and Wycoff, about 150 miles beyond Lockwood's farthest.

It is usually considered that on this expedition Peary demonstrated the insularity of Greenland. There had always been some who guessed it would be an island; but the theory most in favor around 1900 was that of a great Arctic continent reaching from Cape Farewell across the full width of the Arctic Sea to where Wrangel Island, north of northeastern Siberia, had been sighted and was believed to be another corner.

In his earlier expeditions Peary occupied himself with the exploration of Greenland and Ellesmere Island, and contributed sufficiently to our knowledge of them so that he would have been a foremost polar explorer even had he not discovered the North Pole. That achievement unquestionably was his chief passport to fame, if there be a distinction between fame and greatness. But likely enough Peary's reputation as a great explorer will in the long run rest more on what he did ashore than on what he accomplished by sledging over the deep sea. Also material to his claims of greatness is that he developed Arctic methods of life and travel that were in most respects superior to any used by explorers before him.

Peary attained three farthest norths offshore from Greenland, 83° 54′ N. at 30° W. in 1900, 84° 17′ N. at 70° W. in 1902, and 86° 06′ N. at 70° W. in 1906. He reached the ultimate farthest north, 90°, on April 6, 1909. However, on that journey he did not start from or return to Greenland but used Cape Columbia, Ellesmere Island. But the North Pole *is* north from Greenland, and Greenland is the nearest land; and so it is pertinent that he showed the ocean there to be deep, for he took a sounding which gave a 9000-foot depth. His line was not equal to reaching bottom; but Peary's finding of a deep sea at the earth's axis was confirmed in 1937 by the Soviet explorers under Ivan Papanin who got bottom at 11,483 feet.

The late winter of 1928 Sir Hubert Wilkins sighted the north coast of Greenland when flying from Alaska to Spitsbergen on the first airplane crossing of the Polar Sea. If he had found islands they would have belonged to the Greenland complex, but he did not see any. Some weeks later Captain Umberto Nobile flew the dirigible *Italia* from Spitsbergen to northeastern Greenland and thence to the North Pole, also without discovering islands. Dr. Lauge Koch, as we have mentioned, searched for land by airplane between Spitsbergen and Northeast Foreland in 1938, without success. The verdicts of all three flyers being negative, it would seem that no islands can be found that belong with Greenland.

We may say, then, that the story of Greenland's exploration which began with Erik the Red in 982 was closed by Peary's determination of great oceanic depths at the Pole in 1909.

CHAPTER XV

Administration and Development of Greenland

IN EARLIER CHAPTERS we have discussed in considerable detail the Eskimos of Greenland with whom the early Norse colonists came in contact. We summarize here the extent to which the island continent is now inhabited by Eskimos, or Greenlanders, as they are commonly and more correctly called. For, as said, the admixture of European blood has been so great that there are today probably few individuals in Greenland whose ancestry is exclusively Eskimo. If there are any full-blooded Eskimos they are probably to be found on Smith Sound.

In this first half of the twentieth century the whole of the west coast of Greenland is inhabited, from Cape Farewell northward to Melville Bay. Then comes a break, for the coast of Melville Bay is uninhabited from Holm Island to the most southerly dwelling place of the Polar Eskimos, who live in the Thule District of West Greenland. Even this uninhabited gap is so narrow that it can be covered in two or three days of travel by dog sledge, and the two groups are, moreover, drawing closer together—the West Greenlanders extending their hunting operations, and therefore their settlements, farther and farther north, while the Polar Eskimos are extending theirs to the south, without, however, abandoning their traditional areas.

Frederik VI Coast of southern East Greenland, once occupied by Eskimos, was later abandoned, and it is only since 1925 that a trickle of settlers is beginning to return. It is probable that the coast was inhabited in the Middle Ages. The first definite testimony is from Hans Egede, who in 1728 heard of natives living in the southern part of the east coast and in 1733 met a woman who had been well to the north in this region. In 1829–30 W. A. Graah estimated that southeast Greenland had a population of 600 persons, but the more southerly of these had already begun to migrate to the mission posts on the west coast, so that by 1832 Graah placed the number of those remaining at 480.

In 1884 Gustav Holm found only 135 people on Frederik VI Coast; by 1900 most, if not all, of these had moved away— the majority of them to the west coast, but a few going northeast to Angmagssalik after the establishment of a trading station there in 1894.

With the encouragement of the Danes a settlement was reestablished the summer of 1925 in Lindenow Fjord; about the same time some of the Angmagssalik Eskimos began to move southward.

After the depopulation of Frederik VI Coast, and until the recent establishment of new settlements at Scoresby Sound to the north, the Angmagssalik District was the only inhabited place on the east coast of Greenland.

According to the tradition of the Angmagssalik people, the coast northward of Angmagssalik had, until comparatively recent times, been populated as far as about 68° N. Lat. Then there was a gap where the inhospitable Blosseville coast intervened. Farther north frequent remains of Eskimo habitation (but no people, except as noted hereafter) have been found at Scoresby Sound, King Oscar Fjord, and Franz Josef Fjord, on the coast between Clavering and Shannon islands, and at Dove Bay. The most northerly place at which the ruins indicated a fairly large settlement was found by the

Danmark expedition of 1906–08 a little north of Dove Bay, therefore just north of 76° 30'. From this point northward signs of habitation are more and more scattered; still they occur at rare intervals all the way to Independence Fjord, which may be considered as marking the boundary between the east and the north coasts, from the anthropological and historical points of view. Here the First Thule Expedition found tent rings and other indications of at least temporary habitation.

The only place at which living people have been seen by European explorers is Clavering Island, where Clavering landed on August 18, 1823. As more fully described by us already, he met here a group of twelve whose clothing and weapons were similar to those of the West Greenlanders. Since that time no natives have been seen in northeast Greenland.

There are two main reasons why a more serious attempt at recolonization has been made northward of Angmagssalik than in the more southerly districts of East Greenland. The hunting is better at and north of Scoresby Sound, for reasons which have been sufficiently developed already, and there was a rivalry between Denmark and Norway as to territorial sovereignty over East Greenland.

The uncertainty regarding the Scoresby Sound region prior to April 1933 (at which time the Hague Tribunal decided in favor or Denmark) led to a Danish scheme for settling Eskimo colonists in Scoresby Sound, for the purpose of insuring sovereignty by occupation and in order "to protect the economic interests of the more southerly Greenlanders"—this latter was considered urgent in view of the numerous permanent hunting stations that had been established by the Norwegians on the coast farther north, those stations being only in part true commercial ventures, the purpose being also to bolster Norwegian claims of sovereignty.

Foremost in promoting the Danish scheme was Ejnar Mikkelsen who, with the aid of an influential Danish newspaper and of large public subscriptions, was able to carry out the project. In the summer of 1924 he led a small expedition to Scoresby Sound to build houses for the settlers and to prepare for their arrival. A site for headquarters was selected on Rosenvinge Bay, near the spot where William Scoresby a century earlier had first set foot on East Greenland soil. Locations for other dwellings were chosen at scattered points near by, and a small party was left to winter and to build houses.

In September 1925 Mikkelsen returned, bringing with him ninety Eskimo colonists from West Greenland and from Angmagssalik.

During the first year there was an influenza epidemic and four of the settlers died. There have been other reverses, but on the whole the colony has proved a success. An abundant supply of seals, narwhal, walrus, etc., has been found in the waters of Scoresby Sound and of land game on the shores. Charcot, the French explorer, who visited the colony on several occasions, reported that in 1932 there were three principal settlements—the headquarters at Rosenvinge Bay and smaller establishments at Cape Tobin and Cape Hope, all on the southern end of Liverpool Land; there was also a small settlement at Cape Stewart on Jameson Land.

The 1936 census, the most recent figures available, showed the combined population of the settlements to be 170 Greenlanders and 6 Europeans.

The north coast of Greenland, from Polaris Bay to Independence Fjord, has yielded traces of human habitation at only one place, at Frankfield Bay, where remains of a meat cache show that Eskimo hunters had been in this vicinity. That no further remains have been found does not necessarily mean that the north coast has not been visited elsewhere and perhaps frequently, for there are many localities where both land and game hunting is good. Perhaps the people who came here (if they did come) used snowhouses as dwellings, in which case no telltale ruins would survive.

It appears, then, that past settlements and migrations rounded the full circumference of Greenland; at present the settlements are strung along about three quarters of the total coast line. The communities are small. In 1940 the total population of Greenland was given as 17,500 of whom 500 were Europeans.

The attitude of the Danes toward the Greenlanders has been one of benevolent paternalism, as will appear from our brief description of the administrative setup of the country.

Until the invasion of Denmark, in April 1940, the affairs of Greenland were administered by a government board, known as Grönlands Styrelse, Greenland Administration, a special department of the Ministry of the Interior, at the head of which there was a director, resident in Denmark. All affairs relating to administration were subject to this department, except that questions relating to ritual, etc., were subject to the Ministry for Ecclesiastical and Educational Affairs of Denmark. Under the director, who in 1940 was Mr. Knud Oldendow, of Copenhagen, was a manager of the trade department who arranged for the sale of merchandise exported from Greenland and for the purchase of commodities to be sent there.

The trade and administration of Greenland were bound up with one another in their manner of development, the trade officials having at the same time administrative and judiciary powers, while the costs of administration, as well as of churches and schools, were defrayed from the profits of the trade. It has, however, been estimated that the administration of Greenland cost the Danish Government about $50,000 a year, over and above the income from the country's exports.

On the western side Greenland was divided into two inspectorates, the boundary between lying at about 67° 40′ N. Lat., with the capital of the northern inspectorate at Godhavn and that of the southern at Godthaab. These inspectorates were ruled by two Danish governors, who were responsible to the Director of the Greenland Administration in Copenhagen. Also responsible to Copenhagen was the archdeacon, the highest local authority in all ecclesiastical and educational matters, residing at Godthaab; a deputy archdeacon supervised the parishes of the northern inspectorate.

We tell later of the changes that have resulted from the German occupation of Denmark, cutting her off from her colony, and of how as a result Greenland has turned, both economically and politically, to the Western Hemisphere, of which she is geographically a part. But, in spite of this reorientation, the internal affairs of the country follow much the same pattern as before, so that we shall in the main be accurate in describing the former political subdivisions and internal administrative processes as in effect today, modified by wartime conditions.

Each of the west coast inspectorates is divided into districts, of which there are a total of thirteen. In each district the chief settlement is presided over by a Danish factor; the several outposts and hunting stations within the district are supervised by Greenlanders who are responsible to the chief factor of the district.

In 1940 there were about sixty-nine Greenland trading stations, taking those of the west and east coasts together.

The thirteen west coast districts have each its own council, with a number of district officials. The main tribunal, consisting of the chairman of the district council with two Danish and two Greenlander justices, makes a circuit of each district as required. Criminal cases are passed upon, but endorsement of the judgment has to be secured from the governor of the inspectorate. By the acts of 1908 and 1925 a distinction was made between persons coming under the Greenland law and those coming under Danish law.

Within the districts of West Greenland there are sixty-four communes, or municipalities, each having a local council elected by the adults of the community. The council administers all funds belonging to the community, expending them on their own responsibility, for necessary relief—for every Greenlander of fifty-five years of age and over, if unable to provide for himself, is entitled to relief.

The east coast has no inspectorate of its own, nor does it come under the administration of one of those of the west coast; since there were only two real settlements, at Angmagssalik and at Scoresby Sound, no attempt was made to set up local governmental machinery. Instead at each place the head of the trading station acted as the representative of the Greenland Administration. His position, owing to the more isolated situation of these communities, was much more independent than that of officials on the west coast. When the natives suffered want they applied directly to the trader for assistance, and he was authorized to grant government supplies. Affairs relating to church and school were under direction of the local clergyman.

With the occupation of Denmark on April 9, 1940, both the officials resident in Greenland and the United States Government felt that the Danish Government in Copenhagen was no longer able to exercise its full sovereignty.

As a result, on July 1, 1940, the governors of the West Greenland inspectorates issued an edict setting up the "Greenland Administration," with a Greenland flag which is the Danish flag with the addition of crossed harpoons. The legal basis for this action was Article 10 of the law of 1925 which states that the governors may "in special cases make such arrangements as the welfare of the population may render necessary." Citing this authority, Governor Aksel Svane (South Greenland) and Governor Eske Brun (North Greenland) issued a decree in which they stated that during Governor Brun's absence in the United States in the summer of 1940 he would be empowered to act for Greenland there, while Governor Svane would carry on the administration of the whole country at home. Tentative plans called for the two governors exchanging places from time to time.

On June 27, 1940, announcement was made of the organization of the American-Greenland Commission, with offices in New York, to act in an advisory capacity to the Greenland Administration. During August of the same year there was set up as a separate entity the Greenland Delegation, also with offices in New York, which would act as a clearinghouse for Greenlandic exports and imports.

Canada and the United States were prompt in cementing relations with the new Greenland Administration, and early in the summer of 1940 consulates were established by both countries at Godthaab.

On April 10, 1941, Greenland was formally taken under the protection of the United States. On that date an agreement was signed in Washington with the Danish Minister, Henrik de Kauffman, "on behalf of the King of Denmark," it being assumed that the Danish sovereign could not exercise his powers so long as Denmark remained under German occupation. Besides giving the United States the right to establish air bases and other naval and military facilities in Greenland, the agreement provided for free entry of American supplies and assured sympathetic consideration for the needs of the Eskimos. While technically Denmark would retain sovereignty over the area, the United States, so long as the agreement was in force, would have full jurisdiction, except that Danes and Eskimos would be turned over to the local authorities if they were to commit an offense. It was further stated that the agreement should "remain in force until it is agreed that the present dangers to the peace and security of the American continent have passed."

The shift from economic dependence upon Denmark to commercial relations with the United States has resulted in some changes in the manner in which trade is carried on within the country. Nevertheless we sketch the trading customs which prevailed prior to 1940, for many elements of this procedure still hold true; its chief interest, however, will be in the illustration which it affords of the Danish paternalism toward the Greenlanders and of the economic circumstances to which these people of our wartime protectorate have been accustomed.

Greenland is commercially the least developed of the circumpolar countries, but in social progress it is more advanced than either northern Canada or Alaska. The prime concern of the Danish Government was to keep its seventeen thousand Eskimos alive and in good health, and from this sprang the policy of keeping Greenland a "closed" country. Foreigners, including Danish individuals or companies, were prohibited from establishing commercial relations anywhere within the country, and tourists, scientific investigators, visitors of every kind were barred from entering without having secured first the consent of the Greenland Administration in Copenhagen. Such permits were issued sparingly and only for good reasons.

Except for transactions between Greenlanders, and between Greenlanders and Danish officials, all trade was handled for the Danish Government by the Royal Greenland Board of Trade, which, although a government department, was run much along the lines of the Hudson's Bay Company.

The government reserved the right to purchase all native produce and fixed the price to be paid, which prices were adjusted each year to conditions then prevailing in Greenland. Some goods, for instance, blue-fox skins, usually brought a price far below the current world market, while others, such as fish, were bought at prices higher than any private concern would pay. Out of the payment for goods five sixths went to the seller and one sixth to the Greenland Public Fund, for charity, public works, and emergency purposes.

In general the prices paid for Greenland products were low. In part this was because losses were sustained in the sale of practically all imported articles. Perhaps the chief reason was that it was considered dangerous to raise the prices paid for blubber and sealskins, as these are of vital importance to the economic life of the natives who might be tempted to sell more than they could well spare.

With regard to imported commodities, a distinction was made between articles which were considered necessary for the Greenlanders (for instance, ammunition, hunting and fishing implements, building materials, etc.) and those which were considered luxuries (e.g., coffee and tobacco). Those articles which were classified as necessities were sold at a very small profit, sometimes even at a loss; the luxuries were charged for at a higher rate which, however, was hardly sufficient to cover original cost plus the high transport charges. All government stores other than Angmagssalik sold bread, flour, sugar, salted butter, tobacco, and coffee, also dried figs, chocolate, and candy. Natives were also permitted to order goods, other than prohibited articles, direct from private dealers abroad, by paying freight at stated rates.

In spite of the high prices which were intended to discourage their use, coffee and tobacco, of which the Greenlanders are very fond, formed a large proportion of all purchases. Harold Lindow, writing on trade, remarks that "These articles [coffee and tobacco] play such a very great part in the lives of the Greenlanders that they would rather dispense with everything else than have to go without them." It has been estimated that the South Greenlanders of the west coast spend 76% to 80% of their income from native products on the purchase of coffee, sugar, and tobacco.

Import of spirits was prohibited, except in small quantities for the use of the Danes. At Angmagssalik coffee and bread were also prohibited, to prevent the Eskimos in that vicinity from becoming used to these scarcely obtainable luxuries. Importation of gasoline was prohibited everywhere in Greenland, but kerosene was permitted.

In 1914 imports to Greenland amounted to $145,000; in 1937 they came to around $535,000; 1939 imports, including cereals and other food products, textiles, wood products,

Port of the mining village of Ivigtut on the Arsukfjord; here cryolite for America's aluminum industry is loaded onto ships.

Greenlandic miners at work.

petroleum products, iron and steel and machinery, were between $1,000,000 and $1,500,000.

Formerly each of the chief settlements was visited annually by one or two Danish Government vessels. Blubber, the chief article received from the hunting and fishing stations, was forwarded to the settlement, or "colony," in casks; here it was turned into oil and sent to Copenhagen. Other items of export were salted codfish, blue- and white-fox skins, eider down, walrus skins, sealskins, feathers, salted salmon, salted halibut, and salted mutton.

The principal source of revenue, however, has been royalty from cryolite. For Ivigtut, in the Frederikshaab District of the west coast, seems to be the only place in the world so far known where cryolite, an ingredient used in the manufacture of aluminum, is found in sufficient quantity for commercial exploitation. Greenland Eskimos were familiar with cryolite—they knew it would melt in a candle flame, like ice. Apparently the Danes became aware of the mineral and of the Ivigtut supply in 1794. Commercial mining began around the middle of last century and has yielded the Danish Government more than $15,000,-000 in taxes.

Ivigtut is a company town, everything being owned and operated by the cryolite company, an American corporation, the Pennsylvania Salt Company of Philadelphia. With the employees of the mine and their families there was in 1940 a population of around three hundred. It is a modern village, with electric light, modern residences, and up-to-date facilities.

By a decree of June 3, 1940, Governors Svane and Brun assumed control of the cryolite mine and appointed a board of directors to supervise its operation.

In line with its policy of keeping Greenland a "closed" country for the benefit of the natives the Danish Government formerly placed rigid restrictions on the use of Greenland waters by non-Eskimo fishermen. During recent years, however, with the tendency for fishing craft of all nations to ply more northerly waters, the restrictions were eased in certain areas in the interest of Danish and Faeroese fishermen. Permission to fish was granted for designated areas, and access to certain harbors on the west coast was granted to these fishermen. Chief of these was Faeringerhavn (Harbor of the Faeroese), fifty or sixty miles south of Godthaab.

While hunting, sealing, and fishing remain the chief occupations of the Greenlanders, some of them have in recent years, under the direction and encouragement of the Danish Government, turned to the raising of sheep. Although this was initiated within the last thirty years, the raising of domestic animals was no innovation for Greenland. During the Middle Ages the European colonists of West Greenland were so largely pastoral that they paid their tithes to the Church of Rome partly in milk products, wool, and the hides of domestic animals, and there appears to have been some further export.

In 1913 A. L. Walsöe was sent by the Danish Government to investigate whether pastoral communities might be reestablished, with particular reference to sheep farming. After a study he gave a moderately favorable report on the Julianehaab District, in southern West Greenland.

On the strength of this investigation the Greenland Administration decided to make the experiment, and Walsöe returned to Greenland in 1915 with 170 sheep from Iceland. They weathered the first winter, and an experimental breeding station was established at Julianehaab to provide initial stock for willing and able Greenlanders and to instruct those wishing to make sheep raising their chief occupation.

The sheep were distributed to selected households; for each sheep received as breeding stock one ewe was to be returned eventually to the government station, which also retained general control over the undertaking. Products could be sold to the station at fixed prices.

The results of the experiment were encouraging. Sheep farmers made good money and requests for breeding stock came from other families. These were met where the grazing conditions were considered favorable and the applicant dependable.

Greenlandic apprentices were sent to Iceland for a period of five years, three years of schooling and two of practical work. Upon their return to Greenland they were sent as pioneers to new districts.

In 1924 the first pioneer left Julianehaab to extend sheep farming to Kagssiarssuk, in the interior of Tunugdliarfik Fjord, the Eriksfjord of old—thus near the location of Erik the Red's farm. This modern Greenlander had 145 sheep and was supported by a loan of about $750. In six years he had returned ewes for the sheep furnished him and had paid back the cash loan. He then had four hundred sheep, six horses, and two cows, a large and well-built house, and four barns. Year after year more families have settled here, so that in 1935 fifteen trained farmers with their families were living at Kagssiarssuk, forming a pastoral community of 125 people.

By 1935 sheep farming extended from Frederiksdal, in the Julianehaab District, northward to Godthaab. From its beginning in 1915 with one hundred and seventy imported animals and an additional sixty animals privately owned in Frederiksdal, there were at the end of twenty years a total of seven thousand sheep, divided between two hundred farmers, forty-five of whom make sheep farming their main occupation.

Winter fodder was the great problem and it was necessary to experiment. Students visited Norway, the Faeroes, Shetlands, and the Orkneys to observe how these districts had solved the problem of winter feeding. There was no country, however, really comparable to Greenland, and compromise methods were developed. There is mowing of hay to a certain extent, and this is supplemented by gathering types of seaweed that are abundant on the beach in some districts. Although not used by itself, seaweed does very well when used with hay.

It has been found that, as in Iceland, sheep can feed out

during the winter to a far greater extent than cattle. However, it appears that Greenland sheep are being stall-fed to an extent recognized as not quite necessary if you have had experience with sheep in the Rocky Mountains of the United States and Canada, where ranges have colder weather than found even in the northern part of the west coast of Greenland, let alone the southern portion.

The Church of Greenland forms part of the national Danish Evangelical Church, under the supervision of the Bishop of (Danish) Zealand. For the two inspectorates or provinces of West Greenland there is an archdeacon (Provst), who is the highest local authority in all ecclesiastical and educational matters, being at the same time head of the Greenland clergy and (formerly) the intermediary, in ecclesiastical questions, between them and the authorities in Denmark. The archdeacon maintains his residence at Godthaab and actively supervises the southern inspectorate, while a deputy archdeacon is in charge of the northern province. The mission for the east coast was under the immediate supervision of the government in Copenhagen.

The 161 settlements and outposts in West Greenland are divided into ten parishes and four districts, served by seven Danish and ten native clergy. In the course of the year these visit every settlement in their respective parishes two or three times.

In addition to the ordained clergy there are about two hundred native catechists (Kateket) who assist in church and school work. About a third of these have received training at the schools and seminary at Godthaab for a period of six years, while most of the others have attended for three years. Some have received private instruction from a parson; a small number have no training at all.

About seventy-five per cent of the Greenlanders are communicants of the Church. There are in all 108 churches, chapels

The settlement of Marmorilik; ninety of the two hundred inhabitants work in the marble quarry.

Slabs of marble, ready for the first leg of the journey to the outer world.

or rooms set aside for divine service, which is held at least once every Sunday.

On the west coast there are 109 schools, with an enrollment in 1936 of 3125 pupils. Two Danish schoolteachers serve the entire school system in a consultant and supervisory capacity.

Since the schools of Greenland have been developed under the tutelage of the Church, religion has always been stressed and enters into the presentation of many of the subjects. Legally the schools are required to teach arithmetic, elementary history, and geography, in addition to reading and writing in both Eskimo and Danish. Drawing, nature study, singing, and gymnastics are supplementary subjects. In most of the schools this program is adhered to; but when it comes to the outlying districts one often encounters catechists who themselves have only a slight knowledge of the subjects they teach.

There are four continuation schools, two for northern West Greenland, both in Egedesminde, and two for southern West Greenland, one in Godthaab and the other in Julianehaab. Each boarding school has twenty pupils; one of those in Egedesminde is limited to girls. The aim of these schools is to give Greenlanders a further general education and to prepare them for the high school proper.

The high school, at Godthaab, has two departments. One offers a practical curriculum to prepare students for positions with the local administration; the other is cultural, to prepare students for the seminary.

The seminary at Godthaab trains its students for positions as teachers or clergy. The course is two years and gives the graduate the title of catechist. Some of the catechists are sent to Denmark for a further two years' course of study.

In Canadian and United States territories, Eskimos learn in the schools only through a language foreign to them, English or French. Taking the reverse approach long ago, the Danes have followed a course (since adopted by the Soviet Union) of educating the natives in their own language. As a result, knowledge spreads more or less automatically from community to community. A further result has been the development of a native literature. Whether this literature would command respect among the professors of remote countries the admirers of this system maintain is of secondary importance. The main thing, they contend, is that the people are getting a means of self-expression which enables them to develop normally and to use the art of reading and writing for constant enjoyment and daily convenience.

The idea of a newspaper in the Eskimo language, edited and printed by Eskimos, originated with Henry Rink, who felt the need for this means of spreading education among the natives; entertainment was of only secondary importance. The first number of the newspaper *Atuagagdliutit* was dated January 1, 1861. In the beginning the issues were sporadic; only after 1874 were twelve numbers printed regularly each year. In the beginning the articles were chiefly narratives and translations from the Danish, aimed at forming the reading habits of the population. As time passed there was a change in content, from serial stories, etc., to questions vital to the Greenlanders themselves. The newspaper is, as the name implies, distributed free, the publication being financed by the South Greenland Community Fund.

In January 1913 the *Avangnamick* was started, owned and published by the community treasury of northern West Greenland. Its twelve issues a year are distributed every month throughout this province and once a year to the rest of Greenland. There are two privately owned periodicals, one for Julianehaab District and one for the northern districts of southern West Greenland. Mimeographed and typewritten newssheets also make their appearance from time to time.

The Greenland Literary Society was formed in 1909 by Danes who were anxious to provide interested Greenlanders with a wider range of reading matter. Up to this time the

Bible and religious tracts, schoolbooks, and the newspapers had been the only reading available. The society published about half a dozen books, accepting interested Greenlanders as paying members.

The Society for the Advancement of Knowledge in Greenland was formed in Godthaab in 1930. This time Greenlanders and Danes jointly put the idea across. The original plan was to publish from four to five books annually, financed by membership fees, but for lack of funds the output to 1936 had been only nine books.

The paternalistic attitude of the Danish Government toward its Greenlandic wards was most strongly expressed in the field of public health, and here the results have been perhaps the most significant.

The regulations provide that everyone in Greenland shall receive free medical care, hospitalization, and medicines. Public funds defrayed all expenses in connection with the health of the people, and the physicians were paid a fixed salary by the state.

The entire country is divided into medical districts which, generally, have the same boundaries as the administrative districts and receive their name from the principal "colony" in each district. Each medical district has a hospital located in the chief settlement, supervised by a resident Danish doctor and Danish nurse; an exception is Angmagssalik, which has no resident doctor but is in charge of a Danish nurse. All outlying settlements and outposts within the district are visited at least once a year by the doctor in charge. For this purpose the doctor is furnished a single-masted auxiliary motorboat equipped with bunks for the medical staff. This craft is also used to transfer to the district hospital patients who are seriously ill.

The hospitals are in most cases large wooden buildings of two stories, well constructed and adequately maintained, each having a surgery and laboratory, as well as a solarium for tuberculosis victims. Each doctor is, of necessity, a general surgeon and is confronted by a wide variety of cases.

In addition to the nurse and doctor in each hospital there are generally several young native girls who act as ward helpers. These girls serve four years in the hospitals, during which time they receive training as practical nurses and midwives. At the end of the four-year training they go to the various small settlements and outposts to serve as midwives and nurses in the interim between visits from the Danish doctor.

The Greenland Eskimos have comparatively good health along with their population growth. Tuberculosis of various types is far the most prevalent disease, it being estimated that from ten to fifteen per cent of the population has clinically demonstrable tuberculosis. However, the Greenlanders are still practically free from certain diseases that have begun to afflict Eskimos who have "advanced" by adopting white men's food. As mentioned earlier, rickets is an example. Dr. Alfred Bertelsen points out that in Greenland the Danes, who live largely on Danish food, have about the same percentage of rickets in their families as they would in Denmark, or perhaps somewhat higher; that the Greenlanders who work for these Danes, and who live in part on Danish food, have an intermediate percentage of rickets, and that those numerous Greenlanders who still live away from the trading centers and eat mainly their native diet (from which vegetable elements are nearly or quite absent) have no rickets.

Tooth decay, which afflicts all Eskimos who use white men's foods extensively, is still absent from the same large Greenland percentage who are free from rickets—in fact, the whole group of deficiency diseases seems to have been kept at bay from most of Greenland's people by the Danish encouragement of the native way of life.

The policy of keeping Greenland a "closed" country and the trade monopoly have been used as means of preventing disease from entering, and every arrival, Danish or alien, must pass a strict medical examination. That the Danes have benefited their Eskimo wards by quarantining the whole island perpetually against epidemics, by establishing a medical service, and by requiring the natives to be self-supporting (retaining native habits and native foods) will be generally admitted to give these Eskimos an advantage above those of Canada and Alaska, since it is not disputed that these are the things which have enabled them to increase in numbers while others have decreased.

CHAPTER XVI

Strategic Importance

THE STRATEGIC VALUE of Greenland, as now recognized, was understood in practically the same terms at least as long ago as the presidency of Abraham Lincoln. For his Secretary of State, William Henry Seward, used to argue with his fellow Cabinet members and with the rest of his colleagues that we needed Greenland to dominate the North Atlantic. This was part of his general argument that we should dominate the northern sectors of both oceans, Atlantic and Pacific. For the Pacific he wanted Alaska and was finally successful in getting it purchased from Russia; for the Atlantic he wanted Iceland and Greenland but apparently failed ever to get that idea to the point where our government approached the Danes formally.

The strategic value of places so remote from Washington as western Alaska, which lies farther west than the Hawaiian Islands, and easternmost Greenland, which lies farther east than Iceland, farther than any land west of the Atlantic, farther east, indeed, than the west coast of Africa—the strategic value of such remote places can be grasped by the average legislator only in time of war. When the war is over he soon forgets about strategic values.

Seward's strategic concept of Greenland was based upon a navy of sailing ships and of primitive ironclads like the

Monitor and the *Merrimac;* in communications it was based on the possibility that a submarine telegraph cable would be laid touching both at Greenland and at Iceland. Today we think of Greenland's strategy in terms not merely of battleships, cruisers, and destroyers but of submarines, flying boats, land planes, and radio.

One of Greenland's chief values is in the forecasting of weather, and that conception also was at best rather vague in the mind of Seward. Yet the fact appears to remain that, with the arguments far more numerous than they used to be, our conclusion is the same as his. We need Greenland for the domination of the North Atlantic.

As said, part of our need for that domination is in our need to forecast the weather of the North Atlantic and of the countries immediately to the east. Thus, with Greenland to help us, we ought to be able to bomb Germany with foreknowledge; without Greenland to help her Germany should be flying to England by guesswork, or by foreknowledge less precise than ours. For it is a true saying, if understood with its proper limitations, that "weather comes from the west." Those who have today's information about meteorological conditions along the eastern coast of North America, among the Canadian Arctic islands, in Greenland, Iceland, and Jan Mayen, know tomorrow's weather for northwestern Europe.

The broadness of Greenland upon the horizon of western Europe is well seen if you place your mind's eye at Scapa Flow, the great British naval base just north of Scotland. Looking thence, Greenland's Cape Farewell is practically straight west, her Northeast Foreland is practically straight north. If "weather comes from the west" is even a half-truth, then it is bound to mean a great deal to northwestern Europe that the island continent can supply weather news from so wide an arc of the western and northwestern horizon.

Perhaps the most dramatic illustration we have ever had of the value of western weather was from the 1921 establishment of the meteorological observatory on Jan Mayen Island by the American engineer, of Norwegian descent, Hagbard Ekerold. He had not been sending out his radio bulletins for more than a few months before his warnings of approaching storm had saved so many lives and ships in Norway alone that it was unthinkable for them to let the island station lapse into silence. The Norwegian government took it over, therefore, and have maintained it ever since. But even so, the value of Jan Mayen by itself is meteorologically a small fraction of the value of the Greenland coast back of it.

In 1939, just as the war was starting with the German invasion of Poland, there were on the east coast of Greenland six weather stations reporting by radio. There were Norwegian stations at three points and Danish ones at three other points. On the west coast there were also several Danish stations.

To know from hour to hour the sea-level weather of Greenland, east and west coasts, is important, but it is not the whole story. It should be supplemented by radio reports from stations on the Inland Ice, eight thousand to ten thousand feet above sea level. In that, pioneering was done in 1930–31 by two expeditions—the British Arctic Air Route expedition to the Angmagssalik vicinity, commanded by H. G. (Gino) Watkins, and by the German Wegener expedition, commanded by Alfred Wegener.

For the British the Inland Ice work was done through the midwinter period by Augustine Courtauld; for the Germans through the whole year by a staff of three, Johannes Georgi, Fritz Loewe, and Ernst Sorge.

The work of Courtauld was the more dramatic and in a sense the more significant; for, in addition to learning about the weather, he demonstrated that a single competent man was able to maintain a valuable scientific post on the Inland Ice through the coldest period and therefore during all seasons. This is particularly important in time of war; for an outfit much better than Courtauld's, including radio-sending apparatus and power plant capable of functioning a whole year, can be dropped by parachute from a single transport plane. To do so would be child's play for us, who control the coasts of Greenland. The Germans also could do it, from Norway or elsewhere, by methods which they could borrow from the Soviet North Polar expedition of 1937, from the Danish flights to Greenland in 1938, and from the experience of the Watkins and Wegener expeditions, which we now sketch.

On August 11, 1930, five members of the British expedition, E. W. Bingham, Martin Lindsay, Quintin Riley, J. R. Rymill, and J. M. Scott, led by Scott, started up the glacier at the head of the fjord Suportup-Kangerdlua, where the expedition's main base was located, about thirty miles southwest of Angmagssalik. They were to establish an observation station halfway across and at the highest part of the Inland Ice, on the line of a proposed air route from Angmagssalik to Disko Island, which would have been at an altitude of between nine thousand and ten thousand feet. The journey, however, was so much slower than expected that they were only 140 miles west from the eastern margin, only one third of the way across and at only 8200 feet when they were unable to go farther because so much food had been consumed that even from this point the dogs would have only half rations on the return journey.

Here, at 67° 03′ N., 41° 49′ W., the camp was pitched on August 27. The next day Bingham, Rymill, and Scott started for the coast, leaving Lindsay and Riley to begin the work of the Icecap Station. During the autumn, trips were made to them for relieving and changing personnel. On November 1 a final relief party started westward, this time with the intention of leaving Augustine Courtauld and Captain P. Lemon at the observatory. Again the journey took longer than expected and the base was not reached until December 3. Then Courtauld volunteered to stay alone, for they had eaten so much food on their way to the station that there would not be enough supplies for two people; moreover, bad weather might continue till February or even March, preventing a sledge party or an airplane from bringing in supplies. Even for him alone the rations would be small, but he argued that by spending most of his time inside of a comfortably warm camp he could get along on what would be half rations for a man who was constantly active and much exposed to cold. These methods would stretch his supplies to the end of April.

Leaving Courtauld there alone on top of the ice dome was perhaps the most sensational thing that has been done in the long history of polar exploration. However, at least one of the sensational elements, that of loneliness, has overimpressed the public. For it is commonplace with trappers in Alaska, Canadian trappers of the Far North, Norwegian trappers of northeast Greenland and Soviet trappers at various northerly places in Siberia, to go for many months without the sight of a human being. True, there is a difference in their favor, for they are constantly traveling about, setting traps, hunting, and the rest. Courtauld would have been tied to his post with a routine of observations.

During the first weeks of his stay Courtauld had gone outside to read his instruments six times a day, but following March 22 all outside meteorological observations were discontinued because he could no longer dig his way out. However, buried as he was, he did keep records of wind-force, estimated from the noise outside, and he kept pressure readings from the barometer.

Although his comrades had full confidence in Courtauld's ability to take care of himself, and in the adequacy of his provisions, two attempts were made in February to fly over the camp and drop letters and luxuries. Due to head winds and adverse weather conditions both flights came short of the Inland Ice station.

By March 1 friends and relatives of Courtauld in England were beginning to agitate that relief should be sent. In consequence of this a sledge party was started somewhat earlier than otherwise; they would have preferred to wait for the early spring gales to abate. Had the base camp been in a different location, the early stages of their trip would no doubt have been less difficult. For the meteorological observations of the expedition showed that, due to the configuration of the fjord, Suportup-Kangerdlua was subject to violent and frequent local gales, gales which exceeded in frequency and intensity those at Angmagssalik only thirty miles away—as they might have anticipated from the name of the fjord, for *suporut* means the blower, the bellows, the blowhole.

On March 9 a sledge party left the base, headed by Scott. They returned on April 18 to report that, although they had spent nearly three weeks in the vicinity of the observation station, they had been unable to discover the camp where Courtauld must now be buried. Scott could have stayed out for several more weeks, finally killing the dogs and hauling the sledges back by hand, but he sensibly decided to return while his party still had plenty of food, so as to get a fresh search started before Courtauld's supplies ran out.

Restocked, Scott's party set out again and this time they found Courtauld, on May 5, though with difficulty and only because the weather was now good.

During the latter part of his stay Courtauld's rations had come down so low that, after March 15, he knew his only chance of living through was practically to hibernate, to lie still in the warmth of his nest with the least possible physical exertion and to sleep as much as he could, for during sleep the physiological processes are slowed down more than in any other way—sleep is next to hibernation for conserving energy, with a decreased necessity for eating. This, Courtauld says, was deliberate—that by putting himself on a strict ration at the beginning he could have spread the supplies to last him at that rate until the latest possible date of relief. He preferred, however, not to limit himself at the start and to be as active as necessary during the early months of his weather studies, then resorting to practical hibernation when that course became necessary.

During the hibernation period Courtauld's only connection with the upper world was a two-inch ventilator pipe in his tent house, through which he was able to get fresh air— through this and through the porous snow which at the last was a foot or two deep near the ventilator. He had no phonograph or radio, nor had he felt their lack.

Read Courtauld's own story in F. Spencer Chapman's *Northern Lights* and you will find it does not occur to him even to be modest. To him the job had been so simple, so easy, so without incident that it never struck him he had need in telling the story for that diffidence and shyness which we find so charming in our heroes.

While Courtauld had been spending the midwinter eighty-two hundred feet above sea level and about forty miles north of the Arctic Circle, the mentioned staff of three German scientists had been spending the winter nearly three hundred miles north of the Circle in what they figured was the center of the Greenland Inland Ice and which was approximately that. They called it Eismitte. It was at 70° 54′ N. Lat., 40° 42′ W. Long., about ten thousand feet above the level of the sea and just over three hundred miles north of the Arctic margin.

Because he was alone and the British expedition not sumptuously equipped, Courtauld was able to bring back only weather information, chiefly thermometer and barometer readings, directions of winds, and measurements of wind-force. The Wegener expedition did much more than that.

In the German staff, Johannes Georgi, of the Naval Observatory, was meteorologist, Fritz Loewe, of the Aviation Weather Bureau, assisted Alfred Wegener, the commander, with glaciological studies, and Ernst Sorge, a secondary-school teacher, did glaciological work and measured the thickness of the Inland Ice by the echo method. The expedition also had a large staff of scientists at its stations on both coasts, east and west. Their results were voluminous in a number of sciences and have been published in a series of volumes. There are five of them on my own shelf, and I may not have them all. Almost certainly I do not have the full results; for, although the outfitting and planning were under the German Republic, the printing and publishing were under the Nazi regime, when the plan for world conquest was already taking shape.

The work of the English and German expeditions of 1930–31 was supplemented two years later by an expedition financed jointly by the University of Michigan and Pan American Airways. They had a base at Peary Lodge, on Nugssuaq Peninsula, Upernivik District, on the west coast. In late June 1933 Dr. Ralph Belknap, now professor at the University of Michigan, made a journey 180 miles eastward from the western edge of the ice to 74° 70′ N. Lat., 47° 30′ W. Long., some 560 miles north of the Arctic Circle and at about 8840 feet above sea level. There he made for seven weeks a complete daily cycle of observations which have been published in the *Reports of the Greenland Expeditions of the University of Michigan*.

In time of war it is reasonable to consider how the United Nations and how the Germans may be taking advantage of such pioneer work as that of Courtauld, the Wegener group, and Belknap.

Whether we talk of our side or that of the enemy we are in the field of conjecture, for in both cases we are discussing military secrets. If the Germans are on the Inland Ice then they are keeping it a secret; if our side has discovered the Germans up there then we have not as yet been told of it. If our side has ice stations the news has not leaked out. If the Germans have found our stations upon the Inland Ice they have said not a word either. So we are discussing pure theory.

For the argument, we suppose that the Germans wanted to cash in on the studies of Wegener. They were not merely familiar with his work but had also the Greenland experience of a number of their best flyers. Their stunting ace, Ernst Udet, a general in the Nazi army up to his death in 1941, had spent several months of 1932–33 flying in West Greenland with a motion-picture expedition, the one that made *S O S Iceberg*. Another flyer of theirs, nearly as famous, Wolfgang von Gronau, had crossed Greenland coming from Iceland and bound for Canada on three different occasions, in 1930, 1931, and 1932, at points as far north as Scoresby Sound.

Besides the plane, there is another transport which many consider favorable for the Inland Ice, that of sledges with airplane motors and airplane propellers. Wegener had used such sledges.

The Germans are scholars; there is little that has been published in any country that has not been analyzed and digested by them, particularly if it has a military application. They are supposed to have a good intelligence system and no doubt already possess much knowledge from other lands that has never been printed. But, quite apart from this, they had in their own experience everything needed for making the fullest use of that weather information which is obtainable by Inland Ice stations such as those of Wegener and Courtauld.

So put yourself in Hitler's place and what might you have done?

Even without knowing, as the Germans did know, that the Danish explorer Lauge Koch had flown two nonstop round trips in 1938 from a base in Spitsbergen to Peary Land— indeed, on at least one of the trips a German pilot alternated at the controls with a Danish pilot—even without paying attention to that, you would see instantly by looking at a globe that it is easy to fly from Norway to Spitsbergen and easy to fly from Spitsbergen to Peary Land. For that matter, it is even easy to fly from northern Norway direct to Peary Land.

And Peary Land is a marvelous hiding place. It is not ice-covered nor even properly mountainous, but a country of rugged hills, with much broken rock, with many deep ravines, with a varied topography of several colors. Masters as they are in camouflage, few things would be easier for the Germans than to establish a base of practically any size in Peary Land and have it practically indistinguishable from the rest of the scenery to a pilot flying over.

In 1937 the Soviet airplanes had each brought two and a half tons of pay loads more than five hundred miles from the Franz Josef Islands to the sea ice at the geographic North Pole, where all four made safe ski landings, followed by safe take-offs. The distance is less from Spitsbergen to Peary Land, and the German planes of 1941 were presumably better than the Soviet planes of four years earlier. A three-ton pay load for each plane should not have been difficult. Landing would be simple also, for it could be on one of the lakes or on one of the lagoons. Certainly the conditions would not have been worse than they were on the drifting pack when the Soviet flyers established the Papanin expedition.

Now the four Soviet planes gave the Papanin expedition of four men a dwelling house, an observatory, a windmill to generate power for electric light and for radio transmission, gasoline for heat and for power if the windmill did not supply enough, provisions for a full year, and a great deal of heavy and cumbersome scientific equipment for much of which a meteorological expedition to Greenland would have little use —cables for lowering dredges two and a half miles down into the ocean, traps for capturing animals and plants at various depths, and things of that sort. It would be, in fact, much easier to establish a meteorological station in Peary Land, with radio of the desired power and with all necessary meteorological instruments, than to establish a group of research biologists, magneticians, and meteorologists at sea near the North Pole.

With a control station established in Peary Land, they could run a series of minor stations directly south. They might make it three stations in addition to the main one, each three hundred miles south of the other. Or they might run only six hundred miles, deciding not to have a station too near the south tip of Greenland for fear their radio messages might be detected— they might then leave the reporting around Cape Farewell to the prowling submarines that could come to the surface at synchronizd times, take the weather, and relay it to Germany; or they could get the Farewell weather by airplane.

If unfamiliar with the history of polar exploration you might think it would be easy to discover a station upon the level and literally snow-white surface of the Inland Ice. But, quite apart from the trouble his comrades had to find the buried Courtauld, read such stories as that of Nobile and you will begin to have your doubts.

In 1928 Nobile and five companions were dwelling in a red tent on white sea ice twenty or thirty miles northeast of the most northeasterly Spitsbergen island. They had a radio and were able to report their position. They told the airplane searchers that the color of their tent was red, that they were spreading dark-colored rags over the snow to make a large patch that would presumably be easy to see from above, and that they were burning animal fat to make smudges. Yet the Nobile party saw several airplanes on several different days before any airplane saw them.

A German station spying for weather certainly would not have as many men as Nobile, at the most three. They would be living in a snowhouse or in a white tent over which they would shovel snow. All their equipment would be buried in the snow. They would see to it that nothing stuck up to cast a shadow, which would be the easiest thing to discover. If they needed the use of a radio mast, which might cast a shadow, they would erect it temporarily and pull it down after use. Certainly they would be specially keen on the watch for airplanes whenever the mast was erect. Their camp would study to hide itself as Courtauld's involuntarily did. They would not hibernate, like Courtauld, but they would pop back into their under-snow burrows whenever each job of work was done.

There would seem to be only two ways of discovering such a chain of stations if it exists in Greenland.

One detection method would be the long-continued, systematic, and watchful swarming of airplanes, like a bomber patrol spying for periscopes at sea. No doubt if you kept this up long enough you would sometime catch one of the stations unawares—you would see the shadow of a mast or the dark shadow of a white-clad man standing erect on the snow.

The other chance would be radio detection. It is said to be possible to beam a short-wave transmitter within an angle of fifteen degrees, but the waves will spread when they go far. Accordingly, as we have suggested, the Germans might not attempt a very southerly Greenland station. Let us say the most southerly would be abreast of Iceland, sending two or three hundred miles to the next station north of it, using a radio as weak as possible to limit the spread of the waves. The second station would send north to the third station, and this one to the control station in Peary Land.

From Peary Land the message could be beamed east to Spitsbergen and from a station there south to Norway. Or it could be beamed direct from Peary Land to northernmost Norway.

We took the enemy angle first because they need ice cap reports more than we do, since we have the coastal reports, and also because that angle is the more dramatic. Less dramatic, but equally probable because it would be much easier, is the establishment by our side of a chain of stations such as we have just described. We could readily fly them from the Greenland coast to the median line of the Inland Ice; we could fly them in from Labrador or from Iceland. In doing so we would use just such methods as the Germans would use, except that we might perhaps take less pains with concealment, thinking it unlikely that the Germans would want to waste the time of their bombers flying so far in search of a target so difficult to hit and with the numerous and obvious risks involved.

With our side in control of the shores of Greenland and of the seas roundabout, there leaps to the mind an additional use we could make of the central Inland Ice which does not fit into any probable German category. Presumably we are now ferrying to Europe not merely bombers and other long-range planes but also short-range fighters. Then why not have a relay station for the fighters somewhere near the center of Greenland? They are wheeled planes and could not land on the unprepared soft snow of the middle Inland Ice zone as ski planes do. We would need for them a field that was level, packed hard, and strong enough so that the surface would not give way under an even slightly awkward landing. This hardness, flatness, and strength could be attained by rolling the snow, just as snow is normally rolled for like purposes during winter on certain Alaska airports and on others in Canada and in Siberia.

The gasoline supplies needed for these power rollers, as well as for refueling the fighters, would be brought to the central station by transport planes.

To people whose thinking is based mainly on temperate zone or tropical experience, the strategic values of the rest of Greenland are more obvious than those of the Inland Ice.

When you are supposed to have knowledge of Greenland you are asked most frequently, and wherever you go, a practically routine series of questions. We take them in the usual order.

An anxious mother or a budding military strategist wants to know how cold it is in Greenland, fearing no military use can be made of the country's location and qualities because of the cold, at any rate in winter.

The first reply is that up on the Icecap it does get chilly in

winter. But the theoreticians debate whether the Cold Pole
of the northern hemisphere is in Greenland, just north of
where the Wegener expedition had their base, or whether (as
hitherto supposed) it is in the forested mixed-farming country
of Yakutia in the vicinity of the town Oimekon, which is well
within the "temperate zone," about two hundred miles south
of the Arctic Circle. The decision may go either way, but the
thing to remember is that Oimekon is an ordinary small town;
that the country is inhabited not merely by "natives" of Mon-
golian type but also by blond European Russians; that they
raise cattle and horses; that they have cereal crops; that the
temperatures go above 90° in the shade during summer; and
that children play outdoors freely even during the coldest
spells.

Of course we do not mean to say that the coldest spot in
Greenland, up on the Inland Ice, is a cereal country or that
midsummer temperatures go to 90° in the shade. We merely
want to bring out that midwinter temperatures, whether at
the Cold Pole of Greenland or Siberia, are nothing to which
men of your race, whether you are a Mongol or Nordic, are
unaccustomed; that temperature is nothing to prevent children
from playing their normal games, if suitably clad.

At the Greenland cold spot, with the sun shining on the
Fourth of July, you could probably read a freezing temperature if your thermometer were in the shade; but if you yourself are in the sun, and especially if you wear dark clothes, you
will be uncomfortably warm. Indeed, it is common when
people are traveling afoot across the Inland Ice to take off
all garments above the waist except a flimsy one of some sort
which is there to guard against sunburn. For it was a painful
and nearly tragic experience of some of the early travelers in
interior Greenland that they stripped naked to the waist and
walked that way for hours, whereupon they had the type of
sunburn which was not merely excrutiatingly painful but which
could even have been fatal, especially to a blond whose skin

thus gave less protection than otherwise to the tissues beneath which are subject to injury by the penetration of sunlight. Then, of course, there was the danger of septic poisoning from the blisters.

On the coasts of Greenland winter temperatures are, generally speaking, those with which we are familiar in nearly half of the states of the Union and in literally every province of Canada. Take, for instance, the case of the Donald B. MacMillan expedition which spent the years 1914–17 in northwestern Greenland, more than eight hundred miles north of the Arctic Circle. The lowest temperature they observed at any time during the three years was 42° below zero. But, according to the 1942 Yearbook of the Department of Agriculture, there are twenty of our forty-eight states which have that record or a colder one. There are, in fact, ten of our states that have records 10° or more colder than MacMillan's three-year minimum in northwest Greenland. They are: New York at −52°; Colorado, Oregon, and Wisconsin at −54°; South Dakota at −58°; North Dakota at −60°; Montana at −63°; Wyoming at −66°. All these records are from towns or villages, most of them standing on low ground.

However, if you spend three years at Cape Morris Jesup, the north tip of Greenland and the most northerly land in the world, you will probably drop sometime as low as −60°, the minimum of my own home state of North Dakota. You might go as low as the −63° of Montana. It is even conceivable that you might reach the minimum record of Yellowstone National Park, Wyoming, because the sea that ordinarily modifies coastal climates is pretty heavily iced over at the northern tip of Greenland. It is likely enough that the lowest temperature which can be recorded at Cape Morris Jesup is at least 10° colder than the lowest you would ever observe if you camped on the floating pack at the geographical pole about four hundred miles farther north; for the ice at the pole is comparatively thin, is mobile and frequently broken to form leads of open water, but ice near shore may lie hard aground, thick, immobile and uncracked.

The next question asked by the amateur strategist is usually whether the Greenland harbors are frozen. There is no simple answer, but we begin by saying that some of the harbors never freeze. For instance, Pan American Airways, the season 1935–36, maintained an aeronautical observer at Godthaab, West Greenland, near N. Lat. 64° 11′. This was the Danish Naval Flight Lieutenant Kurt Rudolf Ramberg. He reported that there had not been one day during the entire winter when a flying boat could not have come down on Godthaab Fjord. There were certain sheltered coves which, with the wind from certain directions, would form a skin of ice temporarily, but this always broke when the wind changed; and what you had to do, if you came in for a boat landing, was either to look around before you descended or else get a report from the ground as to which of several spots you had better choose.

Most of the harbors that you can count on entering with a ship at any time of year are on the southern third of the west coast of Greenland. Other harbors are either frozen over or made unsuitable by calving icebergs or drifting sea ice.

But we must not fall in with the elementary misconception that steamers are unable to land their freight in a northern country unless they can enter a harbor. If that were so many of the best-known polar expeditions, and some of the most successful, would never have been able to get their supplies ashore. We take a special case to illustrate.

It used to be believed that the northern east coast of Greenland, between latitudes 75° and 80°, was inaccessible to ships except in summer, extreme views having it that the coast was accessible only in late summer. But apparently in 1932 the Danish naturalist J. G. Jennov published the statement that likely this coast would be easiest to approach in winter. Seemingly without having heard of this Danish view, the great French polar explorer, Jean Charcot, on the basis of numerous

voyages to Greenland (though none of them in winter) and
his study of the literature, came to a conclusion which he expressed to me in Reykjavik in September 1936, that almost
certainly the best month of the whole year for reaching the
northern coast of East Greenland would be either March or
April.

Charcot's reasoning was that the steadily increasing cold
of winter made stiffer and stiffer, less and less mobile, the polar
ice that is crowding south through the gap between Spitsbergen
and Northeast Foreland. The more trouble the floes had in
squeezing through, the more scattered they would be later as
they drifted south along the coast in the East Greenland Current; and the more scattered they were the easier for a ship
to worm its way to the coast. He thought it likely that in
March or April there would be wide gaps between floes. To
illustrate, he mentioned a summer experience when there had
been no floes on a coastal stretch perhaps one hundred miles
long. That, he said, was a most extraordinary thing in summer; he thought it might be less uncommon in winter.

During the last few years a number of Norwegians have
wintered at a number of different points between the Foreland
and Scoresby Sound. The general opinion of these, that late
winter is the best time for reaching this coast by ship, has been
expressed by that one of them who is perhaps the very best
informed, John Giaever; for he was depending not merely on
what he had seen but also on a knowledge of the records of
Norges Svalbard og Ishavs-Undersökelser, that research body,
now in the hands of the Norwegian Quislings, which for many
years before the war conducted studies for the Spitsbergen and
Greenland region.

Those familiar with northern navigation, including the unloading of cargoes, agree on procedure. The ship would pass
northward through the Atlantic, either just west or (preferably) just east of Jan Mayen Island, and would keep on until
a little farther north than abreast of the destination point in

Greenland. Then you turn an approximate right angle and head toward the coast. If you find ice you work your way in among the floes, partly drifting with them southward and partly using your chances to dodge westward when the openings come to view. If you find ice in the Greenland Current you will enter it only when the wind is off the land—most winds are offshore in this region. When you get to the vicinity of the beach you will find a line of open water, because the wind is offshore.

In front of the land will be the shore ice, the landfast ice. In some places this may not be more than half a mile wide; in others it might be several miles. Whatever the width, you will lay your ship broadside as if the ice were a dock; you will fasten it to snags in the ice and start unloading. With things on a military scale you will have trains of sledges drawn by tractors; or, as in the old days, you could use man-drawn sledges and dog teams. If the ice is rough the start of the unloading is delayed a few hours, even a day or two, while a gang of men goes out with miners' pickaxes and smooths down a road. This is quickly done and with an ease that will seem incredible to you if you are used to working with picks in a coal mine or at an overland road-making job. A medium-sized pickax, when dealing with ice, will accomplish what may seem to you a marvel.

For good or ill, for offense or defense, it is then possible for us, or for our enemies, to land supplies and men from a steamer on the shores of half the entire circumference of Greenland at any time of year. In many parts this is more easily done in summer; in at least some it is more easily done in winter.

It is difficult for most of us to be rational about dangers of a strange type. In statistical fact, you are as likely to be injured by taxis when you are crossing a New York street as by polar bears when you are crossing a pack-ice belt of the northern ocean. A European, familiar with taxis, scarcely gives them a thought but dreads a polar bear; an Eskimo used to polar bears does not worry about them yet might be scared stiff by a taxi. You have to be equally used to cabs and bears if you are to take them both at their statistical danger value.

This is not saying, of course, that northern and southern dangers are necessarily equal. There is, for instance, no northern wind that is as dangerous as a hurricane; there may be northern dangers which are greater, of their kind, than southern ones, but I do not seem to be able to think what they would be.

To use Greenland as a base for surface ships and submarines, however, we are largely confined to the southern third of the west coast, particularly if we want a 12-months-in-the-year operation, for only on that stretch are there many good harbors free both from local ice formation and from drift ice which comes from afar.

Submarines can use the bases that are suited for surface vessels. They may not be quite so strong, if they come in touch with the ice, but they have a greater maneuverability and can avoid the ice more easily. They can, for instance, dive beneath and come up on the other side. This is a safe practice where only sea ice is involved, for it never reaches more than at most one hundred and fifty feet below sea level, while submarines can cruise at three hundred feet and deeper.

Around Greenland, however, in square contradiction to every other part of the interior polar basin, there are icebergs; and these may be of a far greater depth than permissible for a submarine dive. So if you are going to dive below ice and come up on the other side of a belt of it, you would do well to have information from an airplane, or some other reliable source, that the strip ahead of you is free of bergs all the way up to the open water in which you are going to reappear.

We mention here in passing the conclusion reached by Sir Hubert Wilkins, and by his second-in-command, the oceanographer Dr. Harald U. Sverdrup, on the voyage of the *Nautilus* to the pack north of Spitsbergen, that when you are beneath the surface in a submarine you can tell by looking up whether there is ice above you or water. If water, there will be a shimmering, mildly comparable to diamonds; if ice, a steady appearance somewhat darker than water, of a slightly different color, and without the shimmer.

The harbors which are available to surface vessels and submarines all the year are available all, or at least most, of the year to flying boats, as suggested above when we quoted the Pan American Airways verdict on Godthaab Fjord.

And, naturally, you can use wheeled planes in Greenland. Much of the topography is extremely rough, but here and there you find places suitable for airfields, with the necessary length of runway and with a topography not too unfavorable for planes that are coming in or taking off.

A special situation for planes is that of the Inland Ice.

The violent gales along the shores of Greenland, like those of the Antarctic shores, are local and produced essentially by the force of gravity. In front of the land during winter is either unfrozen water or ice so warmed by the liquid waters beneath that it is not nearly so cold as the land. Because the land is cold, the air on it is cold also; and because cold air is heavy it starts sliding down the incline toward the sea, crowding out the somewhat lighter air that has been warmed by the sea water or the sea ice. Accordingly, you find when you climb the slopes of Greenland, whether eastern or western, that there is usually a wind in your face, blowing with a strength that changes from time to time—there are occasional calms and even an occasional reversal of the local wind in obedience to a widespread meterological condition.

As a result of the violent coastal gales, the slopes of the Inland Ice are what the name implies—they are in effect ice, for the snow that makes up the surface covering has been wind-pounded until it is glare. The snow surface has also been carved and shoved into a wavelike form, reminding of a sea when there is a moderate breeze. It is difficult for a plane to land in this marginal zone; but still the very first airplane landing ever made on the Greenland ice, that of Bert Hassell and Parker Cramer, was in this difficult marginal zone, among not only the corrugations which result from the wind but also among the crevasses that are likewise peculiar to the ice margin. They came down because they were out of gas and chose an Inland Ice descent because they knew that if they tried it on the snow-free coastal land they could not avoid a smash. They left their plane, scrambled down the ice slopes, and eventually found, or were found by, the University of Michigan party of Professor Hobbs. That was in the Holsteinsborg District of the west coast.

Once inside the crevassed and heavily corrugated seaward margins of the ice, you come into a wide belt of proper snow —snow not beaten into glare ice. The waves in this snow, technically called sastrugi, become less pronounced as you proceed toward the interior, and the drifts get softer.

Approaching the center of Greenland, eastbound or westbound, you come to the north-south median zone. You find the winds gentle because you are now remote from either of the margins where the niagaras of chilled air pour westward toward Davis Strait or eastward toward Denmark Strait. The sastrugi are gentle in curvature; they are in fact likely to be camouflaged by newly fallen, perfectly soft snow during most of the year, the drifts showing only after a cyclone of wide scope has swept over Greenland, neutralizing temporarily the local system of circulation.

This central zone is of course much longer from north to south than it is wide from east to west—perhaps one thousand or twelve hundred miles long, tapering to the south, with a maximum width in the middle and north somewhere between one hundred and two hundred miles. In this area you have the finest natural landing field in the world for airplanes mounted on skis. A good pilot can make a blind descent anywhere.

This level inner zone, however, has two difficulties for

taking off. First there is the soft snow, into which you sink three to five or even six inches at a step. And then the altitude will be something between nine thousand and ten thousand feet, according to whether you are on one of the gentle ridges or in one of the slight valleys, which perhaps conform to the underlying topography of Greenland—echo soundings have shown that the ice near central Greenland may be as much as eighty-eight hundred feet deep, which seems to indicate that our half-size continent is a bowl, with mountain ranges at east and west coasts and a low interior basin.

For taking off with skis from soft snow at ten thousand feet your plane must of course be fairly light. If you are alone you taxi back and forth in rapid succession along a track as long as you think you are going to need, say five miles. If you have trouble taxiing straight you mark out a line by placing dark objects, like socks or mittens, at intervals of several hundred yards, lining them up with each other.

The take-off strip evenly pressed down by your skis, you wait for the snow to harden; for it is a principle that when soft snow has been compressed mechanically it is at first no harder than what you expect from the greater compactness, but that if you give it time it will "set" practically like concrete, so that in an hour or two, or better still the next morning, you will have a solid track, permitting you to attain high speed.

But if you have a base in the interior of Greenland then, of course, you will service it as bases in snowy lands are serviced normally, part of this being that you press down the surface with a heavy power roller. If that is done after every fall of snow for a few weeks you will surely have a surface not merely hard but also thick enough and strong enough to take bumps from the wheels of even the heaviest bombing planes.

In the final analysis the strategic value of Greenland is no doubt in its size and in its geographic position. It reaches farther east than Iceland; it reaches as far south as Oslo, Norway, practically as far south as the north tip of Scotland. Together with Iceland it dominates the middle of the North Atlantic, for Iceland is about as far northwest from Scotland as Greenland is northeast from Labrador; and the two, Iceland and Greenland, are so close together that a ship near the middle of the strait between them can see both from one location, without benefit of mirage.

From these two well-placed lands our planes and ships can swarm forth in an emergency. From them are conveniently maintained patrols that close the whole gap between Newfoundland and Labrador on the west, Norway and Scotland on the east. And these lands do not merely harbor our planes and ships; they give us also the largest single contribution to that knowledge of weather which we need for the proper operation of our fleets of air and sea in the combat areas in and east of the North Atlantic.

Acknowledgments

APART from specific acknowledgments contained within the text, the bibliography of this volume lists the main sources on which the author has relied.

Through the courtesy of The Macmillan Company we are able to reproduce the photograph of an Eskimo umiak, furnished by Rear Admiral E. D. Jones, whose permission is also gratefully acknowledged. This photograph is from the book *Ultima Thule*, by Vilhjalmur Stefansson, published by The Macmillan Company, New York, 1940.

The illustrations of fifteenth-century clothing found at Herjolfsnes are from photographs by S. Bengtsson, staff photographer of the National Museum, Copenhagen. They first appeared in *Meddelelser om Grönland*, Volume LXVII, Köbenhavn, 1924, which contains the paper "Buried Norsemen at Herjolfsnes," by Dr. Poul Nörlund.

The picture showing ruins of a church at Kakortok is from *The Voyages of the Norsemen to America*, by William Hovgaard, published by The American-Scandinavian Foundation, New York, 1914.

The author wishes to express gratitude also to Commander Donald B. MacMillan for the photograph showing an Eskimo mother and child, and to Ferdinand Vogel for the view of a fleet of Eskimo kayaks. He also appreciates the privilege of using the photograph of the painting by Emile Walters, show-ing an Icelandic farm.

Thanks are due also to the following publishers for permis-sion to reprint the selections indicated:

Longmans, Green & Co., Limited, for a quotation from *New Land,* by Otto Sverdrup.

Cambridge University Press, for a quotation from *Icelandic Sagas,* by William Craigie.

Brown & Nolan, for a quotation from *Brendaniana: St. Brendan the Voyager in Story and Legend,* by Rev. Denis O'Donoghue.

Bibliography

Adam of Bremen: *Adami Gesta Hammaburgensis Ecclesiae Pontificum* . . . Edited by Georgius Henricus Pertz, Hanover, 1846.

Adamnan, Abbot of Iona: *Vita S. Columbae,* edited from Dr. Reeves's Text with an Introduction on Early Irish Church History, Notes, and Glossary by J. T. Fowler, Oxford, 1894.

[redacted], G. C.: "Carlsbergsfondets Expedition til Öst-Grönland, udfört i Aarene 1898–1900 under Ledelse af G. Amdrup," *Meddelelser om Grönland,* Vols. XXVII and XXVIII, Kjöbenhavn, 1902, 1909.

"Den östgrönlandske Kystekspedition," *Geografisk Tidsskrift,* Vol. 16, Kjöbenhavn, 1902.

Baffin, William: See Markham, Sir C. R.

Balle, Knud: "The Church of Greenland of the Present Day," *Greenland,* Vol. III, Copenhagen and London, 1929.

Bardarson, Ivar: *Det Gamle Grönlands Beskrivelse.* Udgiven efter Haandskrifterne af Finnur Jonsson, Köbenhavn, 1930.

Bede, The Venerable: *Bedae Opuscula Complura de Temporum Ratione diligenter castigata,* Coloniae, 1537.

Belknap, R. L.: "Meteorological Report of the University of Michigan-Pan American Airways Greenland Expedition, August 1, 1932–July 31, 1933," *Reports of the Greenland Expeditions of the University of Michigan,* Part II, Ann Arbor, 1941.

"The Michigan-Pan American Airways Greenland Expedition," *Geographical Review,* New York, April 1934.

Beretninger vedrörende Grönlands Styrelse, Köbenhavn, 1934–38.

Bertelsen, Alfr.: "Sanitation and Health Conditions in Greenland," *Greenland,* Vol. III, Copenhagen and London, 1929.

Best, George: *A True Discourse of the late voyages . . . of Martin Frobisher,* London, 1578. (See also Stefansson: *The Three Voyages of Martin Frobisher.*)

Birket-Smith, Kaj: "The Greenlanders of the Present Day," *Greenland,* Vol. II, Copenhagen and London, 1928.

Björnbo, Axel: "Cartographia Groenlandica," *Meddelelser om Grönland,* Vol. XLVIII, Köbenhavn, 1912.

Bobé, Louis: "Early Explorations in Greenland," *Greenland,* Vol. I, Copenhagen and London, 1928.

"History of the Trade and Colonization until 1870," *Greenland,* Vol. III, Copenhagen and London, 1929.

(with Bendixen and Ostermann): "Beskrivelse af Distrikterne i Sydgrönland," *Grönland,* Vol. II, Köbenhavn, 1921.

Böggild, O. B.: "Mining in Greenland," *Greenland,* Vol. III, Copenhagen and London, 1929.

Boyd, Louise A.: *The Fiord Region of East Greenland* (Am~~erican~~ Geographical Society, Spec. Pub. No. 18), New York, 1935.

Brainard, David L.: *The Outpost of the Lost, An Arctic Adventure,* Indianapolis, 1929.

Six Came Back, Indianapolis, 1940.

Broche, Gaston-E.: *Pythéas Le Massaliote,* Paris, 1936.

Brögger, A. W.: "Opdagelsenes Nye Århundre," *Norsk Geografisk Tidsskrift,* Vol. VI, Oslo, 1936.

Brönlund, Jörgen: "Dagbog i Tidsrummet fra 1ste Maj–19 October, 1907," *Publikationer om Östgrönland,* Vol. I, Köbenhavn, 1934.

Bruun, Daniel: "Old Norse Farms," *Greenland,* Vol. II, Copenhagen and London, 1928.

Bugge, Aage: "Den Grönlandske Skole," *Grönlandske Selskabs Aarsskrift,* 1925–26, Köbenhavn, 1926.

Carlson, William S.: *Greenland Lies North,* New York, 1940.

Chapman, F. Spencer: *Northern Lights: The Official Account of the British Arctic Air Route Expedition 1930–1931,* London, 1932.

Charcot, Jean: *Christophe Colomb vu par un Marin,* Paris, 1928.

La Mer du Groenland, Paris, 1929.

"L'Année Polaire, 1932," *Terre-Air-Mer,* Vol. 57, Paris, May 1932.

Clavering, Douglas Charles: "Journal of a Voyage to Spitzbergen and the East Coast of Greenland, in His Majesty's Ship Griper," *The Edinburgh New Philosophical Journal,* Edinburgh, April–June 1930.

Courtauld, Augustine: (See Chapman, *Northern Lights.*)

Craigie, Sir William: *The Icelandic Sagas,* Cambridge, England, 1913.

Crantz, David: *The History of Greenland,* London, 1767.

Danish Arctic Expeditions, 1605 to 1620 (edited by C. C. A. Gosch), 2 vols., London (Hakluyt Society), 1897.

Davies, John: *The History of the Caribby-Islands,* London, 1666.

Davis, John: (See Markham, A. H.)

Dicuil: *Liber de Mensura Orbis Terrae* (Parthey Edition), Berlin, 1870.

Diplomatarium Islandicum (chiefly in Icelandic), Copenhagen, 1857–76; Reykjavik, 1899–1902, 1900–04, 1903–07, in progress.

Egede, Hans: *A Description of Greenland shewing the Natural History, Situation, Boundaries and Face of the Country,* etc. Translated from the Danish. London, 1745.

Egede, Povl: *Efterretninger om Grönland, uddragne af en Journal holden fra 1721 til 1788,* Kiöbenhavn, n.d.

Ellis, Thomas: *A True report of the third and last voyage into Meta Incognita,* London, 1578. (See also Stefansson: *The Three Voyages of Martin Frobisher*).

Fischer, Joseph: *The Discoveries of the Norsemen in America,* London, 1903.

Flatey Book and Recently Discovered Vatican Manuscripts Concerning America as Early as the Tenth Century, Norroena Society, London, Stockholm, Copenhagen, Berlin, New York, 1906.

Franklin, John: *Narrative of a Second Expedition to the Shores of the Polar Sea in the Years 1825–1826–1827 . . . including an Account of the Progress of a Detachment to the Eastward by John Richardson,* London, 1828.

Frederick II of Hohenstaufen, Holy Roman Emperor: *Reliqua Librorum Friderici II: De arte venandi cum avibus,* edited by J. G. Schreiber, Leipzig, 1788.

Fuglsang-Damgaard, Ad.: "Det Grönlandske Skolevaesen," *Grönlandske Selskabs Aarsskrift,* Köbenhavn, 1937.

Gathorne-Hardy, G. H.: *The Norse Discoverers of America,* Oxford, 1921.

322 BIBLIOGRAPHY

Georgi, J.: *Im Eis Vergraben,* München, 1933.

Giaever, John: "Norges Svalbard-og Ishavs-undersökelsers ekspedisjoner til Öst-Grönland sommeren 1937," *Norsk Geografisk Tidsskrift,* Vol. VII, No. 7, Oslo, 1937.

Graah, W. A.: *Graah's Voyage to Greenland,* translated by G. G. Mc-Dougall, London, 1837.

Greely, A. W.: *A Handbook of Polar Discoveries,* Boston, 1910.

Greenland, 3 vols., Copenhagen and London, 1928–29.

Grönland: I Tohundredeaaret for Hans Egedes Landing. Kommissionen for Ledelsen af de Geologiske og Geografiske Undersögelser i Grönland, edited by G. C. Amdrup, Louis Bobé, Ad. S. Jensen, H. P. Steensby. 2 vols., Köbenhavn, 1921.

Grönlands Historiske Mindesmaerker, 3 vols., Kjöbenhavn, 1838–45.

Grönlandske Selskabs Aarsskrift, Köbenhavn, 1906 to date.

Hall, Charles Francis: *Arctic Researches and Life among the Esquimaux,* New York, 1865.

Hall, James: (See *Danish Arctic Expeditions, 1605 to 1620.*)

Hanbury, D. T.: *Sport and Travel in the Northland of Canada,* London, 1904.

Hayes, J. Gordon: *The Conquest of the North Pole,* London, 1934.

Hencken, H. O'Neill: *The Archaeology of Cornwall and Scilly,* London, n.d. (first published 1932).

Hermannsson, Halldor: "The Problem of Wineland," *Islandica,* Vol. XXV, Ithaca, 1936.

Hobbs, William H.: *Reports of the Greenland Expedition of the University of Michigan, 1926–31,* 2 vols., Ann Arbor, 1931 and 1941.

Holand, Hjalmar R.: *The Kensington Stone,* Ephraim, Wis., 1932.
Westward from Vinland, New York, 1940.

Holm, Gustav F.: *Den Östgrönlandske Expedition, udfört i Aarene 1883–85, Meddelelser om Grönland,* Vol. IX, Kjöbenhavn, 1888.

Holtved, Erik: "Arbejder og Indtryk under to Aars Ophold blandt Polareskimoerne 1935–37," *Grönlandske Selskabs Aarsskrift,* Köbenhavn, 1938.
"Forelöbig Beretning om den Arkaeologiske-Etnografiske Expedition til Thule Distriktet 1935–37," *Geografisk Tidsskrift,* Vol. 41, No. 1, Kjöbenhavn, 1938.

Hornell, James: *British Coracles and Irish Curraghs,* London, 1938.

Hovgaard, William: *The Voyages of the Norsemen to America,* New York, 1914.

Höygaard, Arne: "De hygieniske forhold i Angmagssalik, Östgrönland," *Grönlandske Selskabs Aarsskrift,* Köbenhavn, 1938.

Inglefield, Com. E. A.: *A Summer Search for Sir John Franklin with a peep into the Polar Basin,* London, 1853.

Ingstad, Helge: *East° of the Great Glacier,* New York and London, 1937.

Isachsen, Gunnar and Fridtjov: "Hvor langt mot nord kom de norröne grönlendinger paa sine fangstferder i ubygdene?" *Norsk Geografisk Tidsskrift,* Vol. IV, Oslo, 1933.

Jennov, J. G.: "Isforhold ved den Grönlandske nord-öst kyst," *Naturens Verden,* Vol. 16, Köbenhavn, 1932.

Jonsson, Finnur: *Graenlendinga Saga eda Saga Islendinga a Graenalandi,* Copenhagen, 1899.

"On the Icelandic Colonization of Greenland," *Greenland,* Vol. II, Copenhagen and London, 1928.

Kane, Elisha Kent: *Arctic Explorations,* 2 vols., Philadelphia, 1856.

The U.S. Grinnell Expedition in Search of Sir John Franklin, New York, 1854.

Kent, Rockwell: *N by E,* New York, 1930.

Salamina, New York, 1935.

The King's Mirror (*Konungs Skuggsja*) : (See Larson, L. M.)

Koch, J. P. and Wegener, A.: "Wissenschaftliche Ergebnisse der Dänischen Expedition nach Dronning Louises-Land und quer über das Inlandeis von Nordgrönland 1912–13," *Meddelelser om Grönland,* Vol. 75, Köbenhavn, 1930.

Krabbe, Th. N.: *Greenland, Its Nature, Inhabitants, and History,* translated from the Danish by Annie I. Fausböll, Copenhagen and London, 1930.

Kvaedasfn eptir Nafngreinda íslenzka menn frá midöldum, Reykjavik, 1922–27.

Larson, Laurence Marcellus (Editor): *The King's Mirror,* New York, 1917.

Le Livre du Roy Modus, Chambéry, 1486.

Lindow, Harald: "Trade and Administration of Greenland," *Greenland,* Vol. III, Copenhagen and London, 1929.

Logan, James: *The Scottish Gael: or, Celtic Manners, as Preserved Among the Highlanders,* London, 1831.

Lynge, Kristoffer: "Den Grönlandske Presse og Oplysningsarbejdet," *Grönlandske Selskabs Aarsskrift,* Köbenhavn, 1936.

Markham, Albert Hastings: *The Voyages and Works of John Davis the Navigator,* London (Hakluyt Society), 1880.

Markham, Sir Clements R.: *The Voyages of William Baffin, 1612–1622,* London (Hakluyt Society), 1881.

"Pytheas, the Discoverer of Britain," *Geographical Journal,* London, June, 1893.

McClure, Robert: "Proceedings of Capt. McClure of H. M. Discovery Ship Investigator in search of the Expedition under Sir John Franklin, from August 1850 to April 1853," *Parliamentary Papers,* London, 1854.

Meddelelser om Grönland (chiefly in Danish and English), published by Kommissionen for Ledelsen af de geologiske og geografiske Undersögelser i Grönland, Köbenhavn, 1890 to date.

Mikkelsen, Ejnar: "The Blosseville Coast of East Greenland," *Geographical Journal,* Vol. 81, London, May, 1933.

"Ekspeditionen til Scoresbysund," *Grönlandske Selskabs Aarsskrift,* Köbenhavn, 1924–25.

Med Grönland til Scoresbysund, Köbenhavn, 1925.

De Östgrönlandske Eskimoers Historie, Köbenhavn, 1934.

Tre Aar paa Grönlands Östkyst, Köbenhavn, 1913.

Moss, Edward L.: *Shores of the Polar Sea,* London, 1878.

Mylius-Erichsen, L., and Moltke, Harald: *Grönland,* Köbenhavn and Kristiania, 1906.

Nansen, Fridtjof: *First Crossing of Greenland,* 2 vols., London, 1890.

In Northern Mists, New York, 1911.

Nares, Sir George: *Narrative of a Voyage to the Polar Sea during 1875–6 in H.M. Ships "Alert" and "Discovery,"* London, 1878.

Nathorst, A. G.: *Två Somrar i Norra Ishafvet,* Stockholm, 1900.

Nielsen, Niels: "Evidence of the Extraction of Iron in Greenland by the Norsemen," *Meddelelser om Grönland,* Vol. LXXVI, Part IV, Köbenhavn, 1930.

Norges Svalbard-og Ishavs-undersökelser: various publications on the activities of the Norwegian Svalbard and Polar Sea Researches, Oslo, 1906 to date.

Nörlund, Poul: *De Gamle Nordbobygder,* Köbenhavn, 1935.
"The Finds from Herjolfsnes," *Greenland,* Vol. II, Copenhagen and London, 1928.
Viking Settlers in Greenland and their Descendants During Five Hundred Years, London and Copenhagen, 1936.

Oddson, Gisli: *Annalium in Islandia Farrago and De Mirabilibus Islandia,* edited with an introduction and notes by H. H. Hermannsson, *Islandica,* Vol. X, Ithaca, 1917.

O'Donoghue, Rev. Denis: *Brendaniana: St. Brendan the Voyager in Story and Legend,* Dublin, 1893.

O'Kelly, J. J.: *Ireland: Elements of her Early Story,* Dublin, 1921.

Olearius, A.: *Vermehrte newe Beschreibung der Muscowitischen und Persischen Reisse,* etc., Schleswig, 1661.

Orléans, Duc d': *À travers la Banquise du Spitzberg au Cap Philippe, Mai–Août 1905,* Paris, 1907.
Croisière Océanographique Accomplie à Bord de la Belgica dans la Mer du Grönland, 1905, Bruxelles, 1907.

Ostermann, H.: "The Trade from 1870 to the Present Time," *Greenland,* Vol. III, Copenhagen and London, 1929.

Parry, Sir William Edward: *Journal of a Northwest Passage from the Atlantic to the Pacific performed in the years 1819–20 in HMS Hecla and Griper,* London, 1821.

Peary, Robert E.: *Nearest the Pole,* New York, 1907.
Northward Over the Great Ice, New York, 1904.

Petersen, H.: "The Climate of Greenland," *Greenland,* Vol. I, Copenhagen and London, 1928.

Publikationer om Öst-Grönland, Danmark-Ekspeditionen, 1906–08, Köbenhavn, 1934–39.

Rasmussen, Knud: "Beskrivelse af Thule Distrikt," *Grönland,* Vol. I, Köbenhavn, 1921.
Greenland by the Polar Sea, London, 1921.
Grönland langs Polhavet, Kjöbenhavn, 1919.
Myter og Sagn frà Grönland, 3 vols., Kjöbenhavn, 1921–25.
People of the Polar North, London, 1908.

Reeves, A. M.: *The Finding of Wineland the Good,* London, 1890.

Richardson, Sir John: *Polar Regions,* Edinburgh, 1861. (See also Franklin, *Narrative of a Second Expedition.*)

326 BIBLIOGRAPHY

Rink, Henry: *Danish Greenland,* London, 1877.
　Tales and Traditions of the Eskimo, London, 1875.
[Rochefort, Charles de] : *Histoire Naturelle et morale des Iles Antilles de l'Amérique,* Rotterdam, 1658.
Ross, John: *A Voyage of Discovery,* London, 1819.
Rymill, John: "The Tugtilik (Lake Fjord) Country, East Greenland," *Geographical Journal,* Vol. 83, No. 5, London, May 1934.
Salembier, Canon Louis: "Pierre d'Ailly and the Discovery of America," *U.S. Catholic Historical Society: Historical Records and Studies,* Vol. VII, June 1914, New York, 1914.
Sellman, Edward: *Account of the Third Voyage* [of Martin Frobisher], (first published in Collinson, Richard: *The Three Voyages of Martin Frobisher,* London [Hakluyt Society], 1867; also in Stefansson: *The Three Voyages of Martin Frobisher*).
Schultz-Lorentzen, C. W.: "The Educational System of Greenland," *Greenland,* Vol. III, Copenhagen and London, 1929.
　"Intellectual Culture of the Greenlanders," *Greenland,* Vol. II, Copenhagen and London, 1928.
Stefansson, Vilhjalmur: *My Life with the Eskimo,* New York, 1913.
　The Three Voyages of Martin Frobisher (with the collaboration of Eloise McCaskill), London, 1938.
　Ultima Thule, New York, 1940.
　Unsolved Mysteries of the Arctic, New York, 1939.
Storm, Gustav: *Studier over Vinlandsreiserne, Vinlands Geografi og Ethnografi,* Kjöbenhavn, 1888.
Sundt, Eilert: *Egedes Dagbog i Udtag,* Christiania, 1860.
Sverdrup, H. W.: "Tre av Sommerens Polar-ekspeditioner," *Naturen,* Bergen, 1932.
Sverdrup, Otto: *New Land. Four Years in the Arctic Regions,* London, 1904.
Thomas, Dr. William A.: "Health of a Carnivorous Race," *Journal of the American Medical Association,* Chicago, May 14, 1927.
Thordarson, Sturla: *Landnámabók,* edited by Vald. Ásmundarson, Reykjavik, 1891.
Thorgilsson, Ari: *Íslendíngabók,* edited by Vald. Ásmundarson, Reykjavik, 1891.
Thórhallason, Eigil: *Efterretning om Rudera eller Levninger af de*

Gamle Normaends og Islaenderes Bygninger paa Grönlands Vester-Side, Tilligemed et Anhang om deres Undergang Sammesteds, Kjöbenhavn, 1776.

Thóroddsen, Thorvaldur: *Landfraedissaga Íslands,* Reykjavik, 1892.

Tyson, Capt. George E.: *Arctic Experiences: Containing Capt. George E. Tyson's Wonderful Drift on the Ice-Floe,* New York, 1874.

Watkins, H. G.: "The British Arctic Air Route Expedition," *Geographical Journal,* Vol. 79, London, Aug. 1932.

Wegener, Alfred: *Wissenschaftliche Ergebnisse der Deutschen Grönland Expedition 1929 und 1930–31.* Vols. 1, 3–4, 6, Leipzig, 1933–39.

Wordie, J. M.: "Colonization and Development in East Greenland," *Scottish Geographical Magazine,.* Vol. 44, No. 1, Edinburgh, Jan. 16, 1938.

Ziegler, Jacob: "Schondia," in Richard Eden's *Decades,* London, 1555.

INDEX

Adam of Bremen, 95, 96, 118, 198, 203, 210.
Adamnan, Abbot of Iona, 54.
Administration of Greenland, 275–93.
Akia Island. *See* Hreinsey.
Alaska, 11–12, 13.
Aleutian Islands, 22.
Alexander the Great, 28.
Alexander VI (Rodrigo Borgia), 216–19.
Althing, 87, 88–90. *See also* Parliament.
Amdrup, G. C., 247, 259.
Ameralik Fjord, 238.
American Greenland Commission, 282.
Angmagssalik, 171, 276, 284, 291; Eskimos at, 253.
Angmagssalik District, 66, 68, 276, 281.
Arctander, Aron, 245.
Ari the Wise (Ari Thorgilsson), 64, 81, 116–17, 123.
Arnald, Bishop of Greenland, 144–46, 203.
Arnbjörn, 145–46, 148–49.
Arnold. *See* Arnald.
Aviation, 250, 261, 297, 298, 302, 306, 312; on Inland Ice, 313–15.
Azores, 25.

B

Baffin Bay, 230, 265.
Baffin Island, 18, 73, 78, 79, 192, 266.
Baffin, William, 201, 228; Markham on, 230; voyage to Greenland by, 229–31.
Bardarson. *See* Ivar Bardarson.
Bathhouses, 106.
Beaumont, Louis A., 270.
Bede, The Venerable, on Thule, 55.
Beerenberg Volcano, 53.
Belknap, Ralph L., 301.
Beoc, 45.
Bering Sea, 22.
Bering Strait, first crossed, 10, 11.
Bertelsen, Alfred, 162
Best, George, 192.
Bingham, E. W., 297.
Björn Jonsson, 185.
Björn Jorsalafari (the Pilgrim), 216.
Björn the Rich, 216.
Björneborg, 190.
Black Death. *See* Plague.
Blosseville, Jules de, 257.
Blosseville Coast, 43, 251, 276.
Boats, invention of, 20; Lisiansky on skin, 22; primitive form of, 20–21; skin, 21, 22. *See also* Canoe, Curragh, Umiak.
Bobé, Louis, 200; on Frobisher's contact with Denmark, 224; on settlements in Greenland, 245; on Wallöe's Greenland journey, 242.
Borgia, Rodrigo. *See* Alexander VI.
Brainard, David L., 272.
Bran, voyage of, 45.
Brattahlid, 75, 104, 123, 128, 129, 132, 144.

Brendan. *See* St. Brendan.
Bristol, trade, 208; visited by Columbus, 220.
British Arctic Air Route Expedition, 296.
Brögger, A. W., on antiquity of navigation, 26, 42.
Brönlund, Jörgen, 260–61.
Brun, Eske, 281, 285.
Brunel, Oliver, 225.
Bruun, Andreas, 245.
Burgundy, Duke of, 207.
Bylot, Robert, 201.

C

Cabot, John, 220.
Canoe, antiquity of, 20; outrigger, 21; Algonquin or Peterborough type, 24–25. *See also* boats.
Capes: Alexander, 1; Bismarck, 260; Borlase Warren, 253; Bridgman, 260, 273; Dan, 246; Dyer, 78; Farewell, 1, 17, 54, 222, 246, 273, 275, 295, 304; Hold with Hope, Hudson's, 229, 251; Hope, 278; Lindesnaes, 228; Morris Jesup, 1, 273, 308; Steward, 278; Tobin, 278; Wycoff, 273; York, 265–66.
Cardinal points. *See* Directional words.
Caribou, Eskimos as hunters of, 14.
Caribou, extinction of, in Scoresby Sound, 252; in Greenland, 18; near extermination of, 19; skins exported from Greenland, 112; use of, for food by Greenlanders, 110.
Chapman, F. Spencer, 300.
Charcot, Jean, on accessibility of east coast in winter, 309–10; Greenland voyages and death of, 264; on Jan Mayen Island, 52–54.
Christian I, 199, 202.
Christian IV, 226.
Christianity in Greenland, 90–92, 94–100.
Church in Greenland, 90–92, 94–100, 108, 164–66, 202–6, 210–19, 288–89.
Churches in Greenland, 96–98, 288.
Claudius Clavus, 198–99, 218.
Claussen, Peder, 235.

Clavering, Captain Douglas Charles, 253–57; on Greenland Eskimos, 254–56; narrative of, 253–56.
Clavering Island, 253, 276, 277.
Clavus. *See* Claudius Clavus.
Cleomedes on Pytheas, 37.
Climate, of Alaska, 13; of Greenland, 3, 8, 236–37, 250, 306–8; of Iceland, 7.
Clothes in Greenland, 111.
Cold, 306–8.
Columbus, Christopher, 218, 220.
Cormac's voyage, 45, 54.
Courtauld, Augustine, 250, 296–300; winters alone on Inland Ice, 297–300.
Craigie, William, on Icelandic sagas, 113ff.
Cramer, Parker, 314.
Crantz, David (called Dr. Kranz by Thórhallason), on disappearance of Greenland colony, 171, 172.
Cryolite, 285.
Curraghs, 21, 24, 44ff.; Hornell on, 44–45; Irish deep sea voyages in, 22.

D

Dalager, Lars, attempts to cross Inland Ice, 240.
Danell, David, 196, 233.
Danes in Greenland, 262–69, 265.
Danmarkshavn (Denmark Harbor), 260.
Dannebrog Island, 246.
Davies, John, 197.
Davis, John, finds Eskimoized Norse graves, 195; Greenland called Land of Desolation by, 1, 69; voyage to Greenland, 225–26, 227–28.
Daylight and darkness, at 79°35′ N., 269; Cleomedes on, in Thule, 37; in Iceland, 38, 55; Mela on, in Thule, 27–38, 59.
de Blosseville, Jules. *See* Blosseville.
de Kauffman, Henrik. *See* Kauffman.
de Rochefort. *See* Rochefort.
Dicuil, 55–56; on the Faeroe Islands, 56; on Iceland, 57–59, 60.
Directional words, meanings of, 76–78.

Discovery of Greenland, by Americans, 3; by Europeans, 3; by Greeks, 28 *ff.;* by Icelanders, 61 *ff.;* by Irish, 42 *ff.*

Diseases, 252, 292–93; deficiency, 162, 209, 269, 270, 271, 292.

Domestic animals in Greenland, 106–8.

Dove Bay, 276.

Drift, of the *Hansa,* 257–58; of the *Polaris* party, 268–70.

Dutch in Greenland, 233.

E

East Greenland, accessibility of, in winter, 309–10.

East Greenland Current, 68, 310.

Easter Island, 21.

Eastern Settlement, 78, 86, 93, 101, 225, 245; adoption of Eskimo culture by, 182–83; churches in, 96, 102; colonists of, 102; farms in, 102–3.

Eden, Richard, on Greenland, 200.

Egede, Hans, 180–81, 276; expedition to colonize Greenland, 235–38; seeks lost Greenland colony, 163.

Egede, Povl, life and work in Greenland, 242–44.

Egedesminde, 289.

Eider down, 98, 285.

Eider-duck shelters, 186–90; found by Nares Expedition, 270–71; Isachsen on, 189–90.

Eider ducks, 135.

Einar Sokkason, saga of, 88, 89–90; 143–59; voyages of, 85.

Eiriksson. *See* Erichsen.

Eismitte (Ice Center), Wegener Station at, 263, 300–1.

Elizabeth, Queen, 221, 223, 224.

Ekerold, Hagbard, 296.

Ellesmere Island, 12, 14, 16, 17, 185, 273.

Ellis, Thomas, 193.

Eric of Pomerania, 161.

Erichsen (Eiriksson), Jon, 243.

Erik the Red, Greenland named by, 1, 122; saga of, 78, 122 *ff.;* settles in Iceland, 66; settles in Greenland, 244.

Erik's Island, 122.

Eriksfjord, 122, 123, 128, 287.

Eriksson. *See* Leif Eriksson.

Eskimos, Angmagssalik, 253; Cape York, discovery of, 265–66; Clavering on, 253–56; contact with Norse colony, 164–65, 173–76; culture of, adopted by Norsemen, 179, 180–83, 191, 249; difficulty of learning language of, 242–43; disappearance of, from Scoresby Sound, 252; ethics of, 167–69; food of, 256; as hunters, 13 *ff.;* intermarriage of, with Norsemen, 179, 181–82; Mackenzie River, 11; methods of, adopted by *Polaris* party, 269; migration of, to Greenland, 13; northern East Greenland, 253–56; Polar, 275; prehistoric, in Greenland, 13 *ff.,* 18; present extent of habitation of, 275–79; quarantine protection of, 250; remains of, in northwestern Greenland, 13–14, in Peary Land, 253; seen by Karlsefni's party, 137, 138–39; Thorhallason on, 170–71; throwing sticks of, 82; traveling methods of, 240; Tunes on, 197; use of iron by, 193; in Vinland, 81–82.

Ethnology of the Greenlanders, Graah on, 246–47; Holm on, 247–50.

Eudoxus, 36.

Eugenius III, 211.

Exploration, of east coast of Greenland, 235–64; of north and west coasts, 265–74.

Exports of Greenland, 112, 285.

Eystribygd. *See* Eastern Settlement.

F

Faeringerhavn, 286.

Faeroe Islands, 43, 47, 56–57, 287; Dicuil on, 56.

Falconry, 205–7.

Falcons, 98, 112, 205–7.

Fish, 283, 285–86; export of, 285.

Fishing, 283; restrictions, 285–86.

Fiskenaes (Fiskenaeset), 227, 244.

Flagstoneland. *See* Helluland.

Floki, voyage to Iceland, 62–63.

Fog, 40, 41, 42.
Folsom man, 10, 12, 13.
Food in Greenland, 107, 110, 284.
Forestland. *See* Markland.
Fort Conger, 271, 272.
Fox skins, 283, 285.
Franz Josef Fjord, 259, 276.
Franz Josef Islands, 25, 259, 303.
Frederick II (Holy Roman Emperor), 206, 211.
Frederik II (of Denmark), 224.
Frederik III, 233.
Frederik VI Coast, 276.
Frederiksdal, sheep raising in, 287.
Frederikshaab, 258; established, 238.
Frederikshaab District, 241.
Freydis, 139.
Frieseland, 222.
Frobisher, Martin, 119, 192, 194–95, 198; contact with Danish King, 224; voyage to Greenland, 221–25.
Frobisher Bay ("Strait"), 222, 238.
"Frozen North," Greek conception of, 29–30.
Furdustrandir (Wonder Strands), 134.

G

Gardar, church at, 97, 205, 217–18; Thing at, 87.
Gardar, voyage to Iceland, 61–62.
Gardarsholm, 62.
Georgi, Johannes, 296, 300.
Giaever, John, 310.
Giesecke, Karl Ludwig, 248.
Gisli Oddsson, Bishop, 178.
Glaciation in Greenland, 3; in Alaska and Yukon Basin, 12.
Glacier front identified with Brendan's "column of the sea," 47, 48.
Glaciers, in Melville Bay, 17. *See also* Inland Ice.
Godhavn, 279.
Godthaab, 78, 279, 287, 289, 291, 309; Egede's colony at, 236; seat of the archdeacon, 288.
Godthaab District, 8; explored by Erik the Red, 69; settlement of by Icelanders, 18–19.
Godthaab Fjord, 226.

Graah, Wilhelm (Vilhelm) Augustus, expedition, 242; on population of southeast Greenland, 276.
Grant Land, 272.
Grapes. *See* Wineberries.
Graves, Eskimoized Norse, found by Davis, 195–96.
Greely, Adolphus W., expedition to northwest Greenland, 271–72; on Holm, 250.
Greenland, climate in, *see* Climate; a "closed" country, 283, 285; colonists, diseases of, 162; Eden on, 200; European knowledge of during Middle Ages, 198–219; joins Norway, 91–93; medieval Norse theory about extent of, 232; named by Erik the Red, 1, 69; Norwegian claim to, 232–33, 262–63; Norwegian colonization of, 261–62; Norwegian trade monopoly in, 93–94; insularity of, determined by Peary, 272; position of, 1–2; size of, 1; strategic value of, 294–316; U.S. protectorate, 282; visible from Iceland, 43.
Greenland Administration. *See* Grönlands Styrelse.
Greenland Colony, medieval, adoption of Eskimo culture by, 179, 180–83; contact with Eskimos, 163–65; disappearance of, 160–97; reasons for extinction of, 161; Thorhallason on, 170–76.
Greenland Current, 40, 59, 73, 224; ice in, 311; *Hansa* caught in ice of, 257–58.
Grip, Carsten, 200.
Grönlands Styrelse (Greenland Administration), 279.
Gudrid, 75, 126*ff.*, 133.
Gulf Stream, 40.
Gunnbjörn, voyage of, 65.
Gunnbjörn Skerries, 65, 66, 122; Holm on, 66.

H

Hall, Charles Francis, death of, 267–68; third expedition of, 267.

Hall, James, Greenland called Land of Comfort by, 1, 69; voyages of, 226–28.
Hanbury, David T., on musk oxen, 15.
Hansen, Sören, 249.
Harald the Fair Haired, 64, 115.
Harbors, freezing of, 309.
Hassell, Bert, 314.
Hawking. See Falconry.
Hayes, Isaac I., 267.
Hayes, J. Gordon, on Greenland as an Arctic land, 8.
Health. See Medicine.
Hebrides, 44, 47, 73.
Hegemann, Paul F. A., 257.
Hell, ancient conception of, 51.
Helluland (Flagstoneland), 76, 78, 134.
Hencken, H. O'Neill, on antiquity of navigation, 26.
Henry the Navigator, 201, 207.
Henry VI, 161.
Herjolf, 63.
Herjolfsnes, 73, 97, 124, 162, 192, 202; Nörlund on European character of, 192, 209.
Hermannsson, Halldor, 76.
Hobbs, William H., 314.
Höeg-Hagen, N. P., 260–61.
Höfdi, 97.
Holm, Gustav Frederik, expedition of, 242, 247–50; on Gunnbjörn Skerries, 66; on population of East Greenland, 276; on race blending, 248–49.
Holm Island, 275.
Holsteinsborg District, 6, 314.
Holtved, Erik, on Norse relics, 191, 230.
Hope, Island of, 236.
Hornell, James, on curraghs, 44–45.
Hornstrands, 121.
Hospitals, 291–92.
Hrafnsfjord (Unartoq), 98.
Hreinsey (Akia Island), 111.
Hudson, Henry, voyages of, 229.
Hudson Strait, 79, 223.
Hunters, Eskimo, of northwestern Greenland, 13ff.; prairie, 10–11.
Hunting, 183.
Hvalseyjarfjord (Kakortok), 97.

I

Ice, conditions, 309–11; Greenland, seen by Pytheas, 31, 32; Hansa crushed by, 257; north of Iceland, 38; sea game dependent on, 19; visible from Iceland, 62.
Ice, Inland, attempts to cross, 238–42; aviation on, 313–15; Belknap Station on, 301; Courtauld Station on, 296, 297–300; crossing of, 252, 260; depth of, 300–1; extent of, 6, 12, 16; formation of, 3–7; temperatures on, 307–8; Wegener Station on, 263, 296.
Ice Age. See Glaciation.
Iceberg, resemblance of St. Brendan's "column in the sea" to, 47, 48.
Iceland, 25, 47, 48, 50, 70–72, 287; climate of, 7; colonization of, 63; Dicuil on, 57–59; establishment of republic in, 86; first Norse voyages to, 61ff.; Greenland visible from, 43, 251; joins Norway, 92; population of, 65, 98; sagas, see Sagas; as Thule, 35, 37–38; trees in, 7, 80; voyage to, by Floki, 62; voyage to, by Gardar, 61–62; voyage to, by Naddodd, 62. See also Thule.
Icelanders, discovery of Greenland by, 61ff.; racial derivations of, 71–72; religion of, 72; settlement of Greenland by, 18–19, 85.
Igaliko, stock farming re-established at, 214.
Independence Fjord, 260, 277, 278.
Inglefield, E. A., 266.
Inglefield Land, 190, 230, 266.
Ingolf, 64.
Innocent III, 211.
Innocent VIII, 217, 218.
Ireland, Ptolemy on, 44; Tacitus on, 44.
Irish, as seafaring people, 44; curraghs, see Curraghs; discovery of Greenland by, 42ff.; in Iceland, 61, 63, 64, 70–72.
Iron, in Greenland, smelting of by Icelanders, 111, 194; use of, by primitive Eskimos, 193–94.

Isachsen, Gunnar, on eider-duck shelters, 189–90.
Isidore, 58.
Ivar Bardarson, 111, 163, 170, 182, 199, 228.
Ivigtut, 236; cryolite mines at, 285.

J

Jameson Land, 278.
Jan Mayen Island, 52–54; St. Brendan may have seen, 47–48; Charcot on 52–53; establishment of meteorological station on, 296.
Jennov, J. G., 309.
Jens the Eskimo, 272.
Jochimsen, Matthias, attempts to cross Inland Ice, 239.
John the Bald. See Jon Skalli.
Jon the Greenlander, 92.
Jon Skalli (John the Bald), 172–73.
Jones Sound, 185, 189, 230.
Jonsson. See Björn Jonsson.
Jonsson, Finnur, on churches in Greenland, 96–97; on Eastern Settlement, 102; on population of Greenland colony, 86; on seasonal occupations of Greenlanders, 110.
Joyce, P. W., on Maeldun, 45.
Julianehaab, 78, 244, 289.
Julianehaab District, 8, 246, 286; Erik the Red lands at, 68; settlement of, by Icelanders, 18–19; sheep in, 286.

K

Kagssiarssuk, sheep raising in, 287.
Kakortok, 236. See also Hvalseyjarfjord.
Kane, Elisha Kent, 266.
Kane Basin, 266.
Kappisselikfjord, 171.
Karlsefni. See Thorfinn Karlsefni.
Kauffman, Henrik de, 282.
Keelness. See Kjalarnes.
Kennedy Channel, 266.
Kent, Rockwell, comment on Greenland by, 1.
Ketilsfjord, 97.
King Oscar Fjord, 276.
King Oscar Harbor, 250.

Kings. See under individual names.
Kjalarnes (Keelness), 134.
Koch, J. P., 260.
Koch, Lauge, 261, 274, 302.
Kolbrunarskald, Thormod. See Thormod.
Koldewey, Karl, 257, 259.

L

Labrador, 16, 19, 78, 80, 81, 160, 162, 270.
Labrador Current, 78.
Lambert Land, 233, 260.
Lancaster Sound, 230.
Language spoken in Greenland, 100.
Leif Eriksson (Leif the Lucky), 73, 91, 94, 127ff., 203; discovers Vinland, 74–75; preaches Christianity, 128.
Lemon, P. M. H., 297.
Lindenow expedition, 227.
Lindenow Fjord, 245, 247, 276; vegetation at, 247.
Lindow, Harald, 284.
Lindsay, Martin, 297.
Lisiansky, Urey, on skin boats, 22.
Literature, 290–91.
Liverpool Land, 278.
Lockwood, J. B., 272.
Loewe, Fritz, 296, 300.
Logan, James, on length of St. Columba's boat, 45.

M

Mackenzie River, 11, 16.
MacMillan, Donald B., expedition, 308.
Maeldun, journey of, 45, 46; Joyce on, 45.
Markham, Albert Hastings, 196, 270.
Markham, Clements, on Greek ships, 33; on William Baffin, 230.
Markland, 76, 79ff., 103, 134, 142.
Marshall Bay, 190–91.
Martin IV, 213.
Mary. See Virgin Mary.
Medicine, 291–93.
Meier, Arent, 225.
Mela, Pomponius, on Thule, 37–38.
Melville Bay, 17, 18, 185, 189, 275.
Melville Island, musk oxen in, 15.

Mercator, Gerard (Gerhard), 199.
Meta Incognita, 223.
Michigan, University of, Expedition, 301.
Middle Ages, European knowledge of Greenland during, 198–219.
Migration of man, from Siberia to North America, 10–12; from North American mainland to Greenland, 12, 13ff.
Mikkelsen, Ejnar, 261; establishes colony at Scoresby Sound, 277–78.
Mines, cryolite, 285.
Mirage, 43.
Moss, Edward L., 186, 271.
Musk oxen, 12; in Ellesmere Island, 14, 16; Eskimos as hunters of, 14, 16; in Greenland, 17, 18, 252; habits of, 14–15; Hanbury on, 15; on Melville Island, 15; Sverdrup on, 14–15.
Mylius-Erichsen, Ludvig, 260–61.

N

Naddodd, voyage to Iceland of, 62.
Nanortalik, 236.
Nansen, Fridtjof, on disappearance of Greenland Colony, 163–65; on Norse adoption of Eskimo culture, 179; on Pytheas, 40.
Nares, George, 270–71.
Nares Expedition, 183, 185, 270–71.
Nathorst, A. G., 259.
Navigation, ancient Greek, 21; antiquity of, 20–21, 25–26; Brögger on, 26; Hencken on, 26.
Navy Cliff, 260, 272.
Newfoundland, 81.
Newspapers, 290.
Nicholas II, 211.
Nicholas III, 212–13.
Nicholas V, 95, 214.
Nicolaus Niger. See Claudius Clavus.
Nidaros (Trondheim, Trondhjem), Archbishop of, 95, 211–12.
Nielsen, Niels, on iron smelting by Greenlanders, 194.
Niger. See Claudius Clavus.
Nipisat, 237.
Njalsson. See Sigurd Njalsson.

Nobile, Umberto, 274, 304.
Nordöst Bay, 263.
Nordöstrundingen (Northeast Foreland), 1, 260, 295, 310.
Nörlund, Poul, Brattahlid excavated by, 104, 105; on diseases of Greenland colonists, 162, 209; on European character of Herjolfsnes, 192, 209.
Norman Lockyer Island, eider-duck shelters on, 186, 271.
Norse, cairns, 190; relics, Holtved on, 191, 230.
Norsemen. See Icelanders.
North American mainland, discovery of, by Greenlanders, 73.
Northeast Foreland. See Nördustrundingen.
Norway, 287; Greenland joins, 91–93; Iceland joins, 92.
Norwegian, claim to Greenland, 232–33, 262–63; colonization of Greenland, 261–63; navigation, 42; trade monopoly in Greenland, 93–94, 160, 164.
Nova Scotia, 81.
Nugssuaq Peninsula, 301.

O

Ocean depth north of Greenland, 273.
Occupations in Greenland, 110–11.
Oddsson. See Gisli Oddsson.
O'Donoghue, Reverend Denis, on St. Brendan, 47ff.
Oimekon, 307.
O'Kelly, J. J., on Irish navigation, 44.
Olaf Tryggvason, 74, 90, 127–28, 203, 214.
Oldendow, Knud, 279.
Olearius, Adam, 196.
Olsen, Anders, stock-farm pioneer, 244–45.
Orkney Islands, 71, 195, 287.
Orléans, Duc d', 260.
Össur, 149, 152.
Össur, Archbishop, 144–45.

P

Paars, Claus Enevold, attempts to cross Ice Cap, 238–39.

Pan American Airways, Greenland expedition of, 250, 301, 309, 313.

Papanin, Ivan, expedition of, 273, 303.

Parliament, establishment of first Greenland, 86–87; establishment in Iceland, 86; purpose and function of Greenland, 88ff.

Parry, Edward, 231.

Payer, Julius, 259.

Peary, Robert E., 260; discovers snow-free land at northernmost Greenland, 6; expeditions to northwest Greenland, 272–73; three "farthest norths" of, 273.

Pendulum Island, 253, 258.

Petermann Peak, 259.

Pillars of Hercules, 32.

Pining, Dietrich, 200–1, 202; voyage to Greenland, 208–9, 220.

Pissikfarbik (Pisiksiarvik), 171.

Plague in Greenland, 172–73, 177.

Pliny the Younger, 58.

Polar bears, Eskimo hunters of, 14; used as gifts by Greenlanders, 98, 145, 159, 208.

Polaris. See Tyson.

Polaris Bay, 278.

Popes. *See* under individual names.

Population of Greenland, 85, 98, 275–79.

Pothorst, Hans, Greenland voyage, 200–1, 208–9, 220.

Prehistory of Greenland, 10ff.

Priscian, 58.

Ptolemy, geography, 199; on Ireland, 44.

Pythagoras, 29.

Pytheas, 28ff.; as astronomer, 36; in Britain, 34; Cleomedes on, 37; considered liar, 30, 39; first European to reach Greenland region, 31, 251; Nansen on, 40; ship used by, 32, 33; Strabo on, 38–39; Voyage, 31ff.

R

Ramberg, Kurt Rudolf, 309.

Rasmussen, Knud, 183, 230, 250; on Eskimo migration, 18, 266; on northward penetration of Norsemen, 185.

Reindeer, in Alaska, 12. *See* Caribou.

Rensselaer Harbor, 266.

Republic of Greenland, 85ff., 160.

Resettlement of Greenland, 235–64.

Richardson, John, 11.

Riley, Quintin, 297.

Rink, Henry, 290.

Rochefort, César de, 197.

Rochefort, Charles de, 197.

Rosenvinge Bay, 278.

Ross, John, 230, 231.

Runic stones, 110, 115–16, 184.

Russian. *See* Soviet.

Rymill, John R., 250, 297.

S

Sabine, Edward, 253.

Saemund the Wise, 116, 145.

Saga, of the Blood Brothers, 117; of Einar Sokkason, 88, 89–90, 93, 95, 96, 108, 111, 144–59; of Erik the Red, 78, 79, 117, 120–43.

Sagas, chronicles of the wellborn, 86; discussed by Craigie, 113ff.; narrated at Althing, 89.

Sailing, revival of, to Greenland, 220–34; routes to Greenland in 1000, 73. *See also* Ivar Bardarson for sailing directions.

St. Brendan, description of a "column in the sea" by, 48–49; preparation for voyage of, 44; Salembier on voyages of, 46–47; voyage of, 46ff.

St. Columba, first voyage of, 45.

St. Comgall, 45.

St. Lawrence, Gulf of, 81.

Salembier, Canon Louis, on St. Brendan voyages, 46–47.

Sarqardleq, 227.

Schools in Greenland, 289.

Scolvus, Johannes, 199–200.

Scoresby, William, 251–52.

Scoresby, William, Jr., 251–52.

Scoresby Sound, 251, 252, 263, 277, 281, 302; disappearance of Eskimos from, 252–53; musk oxen in, 252; resettlement of, 277–78.

Scots, voyages of, to Iceland, 42.

Scott, J. M., 297, heads relief party for Courtauld, 299.
Scott Inlet, 257.
Scurvy, 270–71. *See also* Diseases.
Sealand, 61.
Seals, 17, 18; Eskimos as hunters of, 14; at Point Barrow, 15; skins exported from Greenland, 112, 285.
Sellman, Edward, 193.
Settlements in West Greenland, 245.
Seward, William Henry, 294–95.
Shannon Island, 276.
Sheep in Greenland, 204, 286–88.
Shetland Islands, 47, 48, 287.
Ships, Irish and Viking, 43; Markham on Greek, 33; used by Pytheas, 32–33.
Sigurd Njalsson, 146*ff.*
Sigurd the Crusader, 95, 144–45.
Skraelings. *See* Eskimos.
Smith, Elliot, 20.
Smith Sound, 17, 185, 265, 275.
Snow-free areas in Greenland, 6–7, 8, 16.
Snowhouses, 18.
Snowland, 62.
Sokkason. *See* Einar Sokkason.
Sokki Thorisson, 154–59.
Solinus, Julius, on Thule, 58–59.
Sorge, Ernst, 296, 300; measures depth of Inland Ice, 300–1.
South Kangerdluarssuk, 227.
Soviet North Polar Expedition, 297.
Spitsbergen, 25, 229, 232, 251, 261, 302, 303, 304, 310; called "Greenland," 232.
Statenhuk, 245.
Stock farming, 244. *See also* Sheep.
Strabo, 31, 35; on Pytheas, 38–39.
Sturla Thordarson, on colonization of Iceland, 64.
Submarines, 312–13.
Sudur, eleventh-century meaning of, 76–77. *See* Directional words.
Sukkertoppen, 236, 244.
Sundt, Eilert, 180–81.
Suportup-Kangerdlua (fjord), 297, 299.
Svalbard, 232, 251.
Svane, Aksel, 281, 285.

Svein Esthridsson, 203.
Sverdrup, H. U., 312–13.
Sverdrup, Otto, 189; on musk oxen, 14–15.

T

Tacitus on Ireland, 44.
Tasermiutsiaq, 98.
Taserssuaq, Lake, 240.
Thing. *See* Althing and Gardar Thing.
Thjodhild, mother of Leif, 94.
Thomas, William A., on health of carnivorous peoples, 162.
Thorbjörg, 124*ff.*
Thorbjörn, 122, 123*ff.*
Thordarson. *See* Sturla Thordarson.
Thorfinn Karlsefni, 75; voyage of, 75*ff.*, 85, 131*ff.*, 137*ff.*
Thorgilsson. *See* Ari the Wise.
Thorhall, the hunter, 133, 136.
Thorhallason, Eigil, 169*ff.*; on English raids in Greenland, 178; on the plague in Greenland, 177; translation of appendix from his *Rudera*, 170–76.
Thorkel, 124*ff.*
Thormod Kolbrunarskald, 89.
Thoroddsen, Thorvaldur, 61.
Thorolf, 63.
Thorstein, eldest son of Erik the Red, 75, 94, 101, 127, 128, 130–31.
Thule, 34, 37, 43; Britain as, 36; Iceland as, 35, 37; Pomponius Mela on, 37–38; Norway as, 35, 37; Pliny the Younger on, 58; Pytheas' voyage to, 35; Solinus on, 58–59; Venerable Bede on, 55. *See also* Iceland.
Thule District, 275.
Thule Expedition, 277.
Tilander, Gunnar, 206.
Timber, Greenlandic voyages to American mainland for, 103.
Tiningnertok Fjord, 240.
Trade and shipping in Greenland, 93–94, 160–61, 204, 279, 282, 283*ff.*
Tropics, Greek theory of, 29.
Thordarson, Sturla. *See* Sturla.
Tryggvason. *See* Olaf Tryggvason.
Tunes, Nicolas, on appearance of Eskimos south of Upernivik, 197.

Tunugliarfik Fjord, 287.
Tyson, George E., ice drift of, 268–70.

U

Udet, Ernst, 302.
Umiaks, 21, 22ff.; Eskimo care of, 23–24; seaworthiness of, 23–24.
Unartoq. See Hrafnsfjord.
Upernivik, 191; runic stone found at, 110, 184.

V

Vegetation in Greenland, 5–6, 8; in Iceland, 7–8.
Vestribygd. See Western Settlement.
Vigfusson, Gudbrandur, 72.
Vinland, 119, 133, 135–42, 203; characteristics of, 82–83; discovered by Leif Eriksson, 74–75; location of, 76; natives of, 81.
Virgin Mary, importance of, in Greenland Christianity, 99.
Volcanoes in Iceland, 50.
von Gronau, Wolfgang, 302.

W

Walsöe, A. L., 286.
Wandel, C. F., 257.
Washington Irving Island, 186, 271.
Watkins, H. G., expeditions of, 250.
Weather forecasting, 295.
Weather stations, 296, 300, 303ff.
Wegener, Alfred, 263, 296; expedition of, 300–1.
Western Settlement, 78, 86, 101, 170ff., 235, 237; churches in, 97; driftwood in, 104; Eskimoization of, 182; hunting in, 110.
Weyszarch. See Witsarc.
Whales, Eskimos as hunters of, 14; in Greenland, 18, 237; at Point Barrow, 15.
Wilkins, Hubert, 274, 312–13.
Wineberries, 82–83.
Wineland. See Vinland.
Witsarc (Weyszarch) Mountain, 200.
Wolves, 252.
Wonder Strands. See Furdustrandir.
Wrangel Island, 273.

W

Wallöe, Peder Olsen, journeys to Greenland, 241–42.
Walrus, 18, 19; Eskimos as hunters of, 14; skins exported to Europe, 112, 285; tithes paid with products, 98.

Y

York, Cape, Eskimos of, discovered, 265–66.

Z

Ziegler, Jacob, 200.
Zones, Greek doctrine of, 29–30.